OPEN WIDE

HOW HOLLYWOOD BOX OFFICE
BECAME A NATIONAL OBSESSION

Dade Hayes
and
Jonathan Bing

miramax books

HYPERION
NEW YORK

ISBN 1-4013-5985-X

First Edition
10 9 8 7 6 5 4 3 2 1

OPEN WIDE

D.H.
To Stella, with love, for dreams;
and to Margot the Curious

J.B.
To my father, David Bing.
Our trips to the movies are greatly missed.

Authors' Note

This book began as a quest to understand how Hollywood injects blockbuster movies into the cultural jet stream at great cost and sometimes with dazzling results. A generation ago, studio distribution was as slow and cumbersome a business as civil aviation in the early days of flight. Hit movies barnstormed from city to city, blazing a gradual trajectory into the nation's consciousness, hovering in theaters for years at a time. Today, studios compete on a rocket-propelled, billion-dollar battleground influenced by Madison Avenue, Wall Street and Washington.

Opening weekend is the ultimate crucible. The period from Friday to Sunday is when malls fill up and 80 percent of all movie tickets are bought. Box office receipts recorded in those opening hours brand a film as a hit or a flop, instantly influencing the general public, determining a film's revenue potential and library value, and altering the career paths of its principal players. As Tom Hanks put it in an interview while promoting *Cast Away,* "When a movie opens, everybody is throwing up in wastebaskets." Screenwriter John Logan, who wrote *Gladiator,* calls opening weekend "the great, all-consuming behemoth" and compares the phenomenon to Lewis Carroll's "Jabberwocky," with "the jaws that bite, the claws that catch!" We heard variations on that sentiment from countless studio executives, directors and stars. This dread is a weekly ritual for the movie industry, but one that did not exist even a decade ago, before weekend grosses became a mainstream commodity. How did the system reach such an anxious state at such an accelerated pace?

In order to answer that question, we decided to examine a single weekend and document the release campaigns of the films that opened wide on that date, something that has never before been captured in a book. We chose July Fourth weekend 2003, less for its significance as a holiday than for its rare convergence of three movies with considerable budgets and starkly different target audiences: Warner Brothers' *Terminator 3: Rise of the Machines*; Metro-Goldwyn-Mayer's *Legally Blonde 2: Red, White & Blonde*; and DreamWorks' *Sinbad: Legend of the Seven Seas.* We immediately set some limits for our story. We would exclude the movies that flourished quietly at the margins of the blockbusters—films like François Ozon's *Swimming Pool,* which generated more than $10 million in ticket sales after opening on our weekend in nine theaters with no TV advertising. We'd focus only on domestic release campaigns, though foreign box office is a big part of studio profits.

We asked each studio for access to their marketing and

distribution departments, and their responses could be measured in degrees of wariness. MGM, a legendary company seeking a return to its former glory, agreed to open the door. Since the studio had complete control of *Legally Blonde 2*, that invitation was all we needed. Warner Brothers, by contrast, was merely the domestic distributor of *T3*, one major player in the multipartner financing now required to mobilize some of Hollywood's biggest blockbusters. We managed to get a close look at the release campaign by approaching the myriad companies that shaped it: C-2 Pictures, Intermedia, Mostow/Lieberman, and Sony Pictures. Eventually, Warner Brothers also granted us significant access.

DreamWorks was another story. A rigorously private company since its 1994 founding, it does not disclose financial results. Neither does it discuss the goings-on at its manicured animation campus on an industrial Los Angeles cul-de-sac. Executives rarely meet with reporters without a PR specialist present. Perhaps because of that cagey posture, or because of the intense competitiveness of the animation business, our requests for access to the personnel who shaped the *Sinbad* campaign, repeated several times over the course of a year, were denied.

Nevertheless, by attending signal events in the rollout of each film and by conducting extensive interviews with executives, producers and other principal figures, we managed to chronicle the buildup to July Fourth. During the weekend, we tried, in the storied journalism tradition, to follow the money. On opening weekend, it changed hands with dizzying speed. The box office grosses now reach the studios in real time, as each ticket is taken, and the results are spun in the media on Sunday and Monday.

The long holiday period of July 2–6, 2003, did not feature the stratospheric numbers posted when *Harry Potter* or *Spider-Man* opened. Some people asked why we hadn't simply switched midstream to follow *Finding Nemo* or *The Lord of the Rings: The Return of the King,* to capture Hollywood box office at its zenith. But that was never our goal. Rather, it was to depict the complicated crescendo that results in a typical summer weekend at the movies—preferably a bruising one with a clear winner and loser. This book is not intended as a study of triumph, which box office reporting too often is. Rather, it is an attempt to examine a workaday system whose interlocking parts, operating at their customary grinding rhythm, create an American spectacle. S. Charles Lee, who built opulent movie palaces throughout the twentieth century, explained his design philosophy with the adage, "The show starts on the sidewalk." Today's architects of opening weekend start much farther away than that.

Introduction

Inside a low-slung office park along Interstate 8 in the San Diego suburb of Mission Valley, thirty teenage girls are making a movie.

They do not carry cameras or boom microphones. They're not in costume. They don't know the first thing about lighting a scene or dressing a set. They're armed only with their preferences. They know what they like—or at least what they like at this moment in time, on this particular afternoon, March 2, 2003.

That quantifiable conviction is what makes this focus group so utterly essential to *Legally Blonde 2: Red, White & Blonde*. These girls were recruited to help Metro-Goldwyn-Mayer gauge which aspects of the movie work and which ones fall flat. It's the Pepsi Challenge applied to narrative, character development and jokes.

The movie is on an accelerated track. Six months ago, *Legally Blonde 2* did not even have a director or a cast. It had only a star (Reese Witherspoon, earning $15 million to reprise the role of perky, fish-out-of-water sorority queen and corporate lawyer Elle Woods), a release date (July 2) and a concept. As pitched to the studio by producer Marc Platt, the film was an update of sorts of *Mr. Smith Goes to Washington,* pegged to Elle Woods's campaign to reunite her pet Chihuahua, Bruiser, with his mother, a test subject in a cosmetics research facility called V.E.R.S.A.C.E.

The movie was green-lit shortly before Labor Day, and for the next ten months, it was a race to July Fourth weekend 2003. A director, four screenwriters and a cast of actors were mobilized. There would be reshoots, dozens of passes at the trailer and rigorous focus group testing of marketing materials. A rough cut was assembled. Just two weeks after the Mission Valley focus group, a different research audience—more diverse in age, but also mostly female and suburban—would watch the film and weigh in.

Mission Valley, six miles northwest of San Diego, used to be home to dozens of dairy farms. The last one was demolished in 1978, long after I-8 became a quintessentially American roadway on the city fringe, ornamented with motels, fast-food restaurants and the Fashion Valley mall. Many of the girls in the focus group were recruited while shopping. National Research Group, now known as Nielsen NRG, long the dominant conductor of research activities for Hollywood studios, calls these consumer interventions "mall intercepts." Other participants were plucked from the ticket line at a nearby AMC twenty-plex.

Taylor Research, the laboratory where MGM is dissecting the psyche of its target audience, is a forty-six-year-old market research company on the third floor of Mission Grove, an atrium-style complex that resembles a 1970s ski chalet. Its facilities are used to focus-group everything from potato chips to trial juries. Patsy Trice, Taylor's general manager and executive team leader, is a compact, round African American woman with graying hair and soft hands. In her tiny office, a manila folder of records from the focus group lies in the middle of her spotless desk. While she flips through the file, the ceaseless drone of nearby traffic fills the room, commuters scurrying to the office, trucks barreling toward cargo hubs.

"I'll be in the grocery store and see consumer products that we were involved with and I feel pretty good that we were in on the conception stage and helped the evolution of the product," Trice says. "It's the same with *Legally Blonde 2.*"

Ten at a time, the girls are ushered into a windowless, fluorescent-lit room lined on one gray wall with one-way mirrors. They sit in chairs around a horseshoe-shaped table not unlike a classroom. If it weren't for the fruit juice and pretzels outside, the room would be perfectly suited for giving a standardized academic test. On the other side of the mirror hovers a cluster of executives from MGM and NRG. A couple of them stand poised with pen and paper, ready to take notes and jot down impromptu questions for the moderator that flow out of the discussion. A couple of others stand at the window, scrutinizing the girls like detectives eyeing a lineup. Moderator Carrie Gordon, from NRG, begins the conversation, employing a soothing but direct tone.

Pointing to an easel, on which she has written an outline for the hour's activities in magic marker, she asks a series of questions such as "What was the last movie that you saw in a theater?" and "What movies are you looking forward to?" A video camera and microphone records the conversation. Gordon debriefs the group, finding out what movies they have seen. She is careful not to let on initially that *Legally Blonde* is the point of the session, though the girls have all been informed they will be talking about movies. Early on, the girls are told that they are being recorded, but they soon forget. Personalities emerge. Group dynamics take hold.

"I'm going to show you a preview of *Legally Blonde 2*," announces Gordon. "Oh, cool!" one girl cries. "Yeahh!!" say several others. As the trailer plays, the girls keep chattering a bit but shush each other so as not to miss the good parts. When the lights come up, opinions start to fly. "It looks stupid," says one fifteen-year-old. "Can you clarify 'stupid'?" Gordon asks. "It's just a lot of blonde jokes." A twelve-year-old differs. "It looks like it would really crack me up," she says. Some of the girls talk over each other, trying to make a show of their opinions. Aware of the risk of letting a "queen bee" influence the group, Gordon seeks to involve everyone in the discussion. She invites one of the more reticent girls to share an opinion and hits pay dirt. "The lady in the black is really boring," she says, referring to Victoria Rudd, a congresswoman and mentor to Elle Woods played by Sally Field. With that, several in the MGM camp start scribbling behind the glass.

One thing in the trailer doesn't click with any of the Mission Valley girls: the references to inside-the-Beltway politics. This is a serious cause of concern for MGM. The film takes place on Capitol Hill and its story hinges on a bill to ban animal testing drafted by Elle Woods and brought to the floor of the House by an esoteric Congressional procedure called a discharge petition. In between the eye-catching red, white and blue costume changes, technical references to filibusters, fund-raising and House subcommittees are woven like grosgrain ribbon into the fabric of the story. As the shooting script was being finalized three months before the focus group, MGM executives even held a conference call with a production executive's father, who happened to be former chief of staff for Iowa Senator Tom Harkin. The aim was to make sure they knew how to articulate correctly the workings of the federal government. While policy details could be expunged from the marketing campaign and muted in the editing room as the film was tweaked for opening weekend, they could not be removed altogether. What was suddenly, frighteningly clear in Mission Valley was that the heart of the plot of *Legally Blonde 2* could turn out to be its greatest liability.

"One girl asked, 'Why'd she go to Washington?'" MGM marketing chief Peter Adee marveled later. "And I thought, 'Uh-oh.' That's a little scary when you realize that the premise of the movie is not one that the audience will embrace."

The patriotic premise of *Legally Blonde 2* would have ramifications far beyond the final cut of its trailer. It would naturally position the film for release in one of the most ballyhooed slots on the calendar, Independence Day weekend—putting *Legally*

Blonde 2 on a collision course with a big-budget sequel from
Warner Brothers: *Terminator 3*. Starring Arnold Schwarzenegger, the soon-to-be-elected governor of California, *T3*
had months earlier hitched its marketing campaign to the
same release date. In early March, as Adee and the producers
of *Legally Blonde 2* peered through the tinted glass of the
Mission Valley research facility, yet another potential threat
loomed on the horizon: *Sinbad*, a swashbuckling animated
adventure from DreamWorks, the studio behind *Shrek*, a
huge animated smash from the summer of 2001.

The 2003 Independence Day holiday, which, by the studios' calendar, began on Wednesday, July 2, was shaping up
to be an unbridled showdown among rival studio marketers struggling to launch their products into the marketplace in the loudest, flashiest and most enticing fashion.
They would collectively spend hundreds of millions of dollars to distract consumers from their picnics, fireworks, pa-
rades and family vacations. The Fourth had always been
considered one of the premiere release slots for big-budget
popcorn movies. It is the moment in summer when all kids
are finally out of school and audiences as a whole are assumed to be the most available, the most open to being entertained. MGM co-founder Louis B. Mayer claimed he was
born on July 4. The prototype July 4 blockbuster was the
Roland Emmerich UFO invasion thriller, *Independence
Day*, starring Will Smith. Trailers and posters referred to the
film as *ID4;* the release date became the marketing hook. It
grossed $50 million on opening weekend en route to $813
million in worldwide box office. Smith told the press he was

"Mr. July Fourth." *Independence Day* producer Dean Devlin later got married on July 4. Putting this all-American date on a poster was thought to impart the glow of importance, reflecting the holiday's associations with national celebrations and community rituals.

Relative to its competition, *T3* was a formidable adversary. Like *Legally Blonde 2*, it was a familiar commodity, but that's where the comparison ended. *Legally Blonde 2* had a modest budget and few special effects. The first *Legally Blonde* was a sparkly, by-the-numbers comedy that defied expectations. An ode to self-empowerment for teenage girls and campy fun for older audiences, it became a sleeper hit for MGM and helped make Reese Witherspoon a household name. But the Terminator was an international icon. The *Terminator* franchise, starring Arnold Schwarzenegger as an unstoppable killing machine from the future, promised all the elements of a summer-straddling global blockbuster: spectacular action sequences and special effects, video games, a theme park ride and a mini-industry of licensed spin-off products. Twelve years after *Terminator 2*, the Internet was still riddled with *Terminator* fan sites. The marketing campaign for *T3* also had a head start. The first teaser ad had landed in theaters over the weekend of July 4, 2002.

Sinbad was the wild card. It offered vocal performances from Brad Pitt, Catherine Zeta-Jones and Michelle Pfeiffer. The marketing materials hinted at briny, high-spirited adventure, battles between gods and humans, and a slobbering pooch sidekick. Thanks to DreamWorks' deep pockets and uncanny sales moxie, no one would dare write

it off prematurely. The company didn't have vertically inte-
grated cable channels or an Internet service provider to
help cross-promote *Sinbad*. What it did have, to the naked
envy of its rivals, was cash.

One thing was certain: the coming summer would be
one of the most competitive on record. By July Fourth,
every megaplex theater in America would already be a
dense thicket of competing blockbusters held over from
their own opening weekends in May and June: *The Matrix
Reloaded, Bruce Almighty, Hulk, Finding Nemo, Charlie's
Angels: Full Throttle* and *X-2*. These films would cling to
their share of auditoriums in the nation's theaters, leaching
movie-goers away from *Legally Blonde 2, T3* and *Sinbad*.

"This is a fucking war!" Adee had taken to saying. As the
president of marketing at MGM, he had a commanding,
front-lines vantage point of that war—but he wasn't alone.
Behind him stood a battery of anxious filmmakers and
writers, actors and executives, not to mention investors and
consumer products companies that had signed on to ride
the films' coattails. These are some of the collection of characters who have helped make the summer blockbuster system what it is today: a nerve-wracking, opening-weekend
business whose size and scale increase steadily from year to
year. In 1990 movies registered 27 percent of their total
gross in their first week. By 2003 that number had bulged to
41 percent. The average second-week decline was 50 percent. Most of the blockbusters of 2003 were megabudget
spectacles designed, like Schwarzenegger's killer cyborg, to
decimate everything in their path before self-destructing.
These films were shaped by market research at suburban

shopping malls and released in supersized megaplex theaters that had been spawned by a building boom in the 1990s that ripped through the exhibition business, forcing most of the major theater circuits into bankruptcy.

For decades, the hard numbers, the bottom-line profit and loss of individual films, had been a mystery—one that few people cared to solve. Box office data was the exclusive province of a handful of Hollywood sales executives. Hit films played to packed houses for months, not weeks, and their grosses were tallied only in key markets, recorded in pencil jottings and sporadically fed to the sales department in New York or Los Angeles.

Today, box office performance is a cultural obsession, ritually reported by national newspapers every Monday morning, and tracked on Sunday night on the news tickers of CNN, Fox News and E! Box office grosses are information as public as the daily stock tables. They ricochet at the speed of light between theater chains, studio databases and the Web sites and research firms that track their fluctuations from hour to hour, ticket to ticket. They affect the stock of multinational companies and shape the media campaigns of America's top consumer products. They drive studio promotions. Their implications are dissected by advertisers, marketers and cultural anthropologists of all stripes. They are the subject of office pools and are gambling fodder for offshore online casinos. Some studio executives even bet thousands of dollars on these Web sites trying to predict the weekend grosses.

None of Hollywood's weekend maneuvers would matter had American culture not caught the box office bug. Why, we wondered, should anyone whose paycheck does not bear a studio logo care about weekend box office numbers? Shouldn't it be the public's chief concern whether a movie is worth seeing at all? These questions, it turns out, aren't so easily disentangled. Customers are goaded into seeing "the number one comedy in America!" precisely because notions of quality and box office success have merged. The syllogism goes like this: If it makes money, it must be worth seeing. Conversely, if it's worth seeing, it ought to make money. Teenage girls in San Diego may fervently anticipate the release of *Legally Blonde 2*, but true word of mouth— the kind that happens once people have actually seen the movie—is a rare commodity in the first-weekend frenzy. Opening movies is a smash-and-grab business for the studios. They shatter glass, set off alarms and try to escape with the loot before somebody calls the cops. This book is not a jeremiad about the decline of quality in the American cinema. Still, one would have to be living in a cave not to acknowledge some basic realities of Opening-Weekend America. One is that some kinds of movies (star vehicles; those adapted from comic books) lend themselves to this release pattern. Those that don't are often marginalized. What's more, the fixation on box office, not unlike the obsession with election polls or sports team salaries, is a distraction from the substance of the medium itself.

Having spent several years chronicling the film business for *Variety*, we were keenly aware of the proliferation of arcane data that flowed from the nation's thirty-five thousand movie screens to news outlets around the world. And we were aware of how poorly most people understood this data's significance to the studios. The numbers might be reported, but Hollywood's marketing and distribution systems, their real costs and windfalls, are shrouded in secrecy. There is a public Hollywood, a red-carpeted island poking up out of the ocean, and a hidden Hollywood beneath the waves. Many of the people who control the system are so absorbed in the details of their jobs that they never see the system as a whole, and its effects on the culture around them. Most of them don't care. Most are deeply invested in shielding their work from public scrutiny, lest an outsider second-guess their costly decisions and missteps.

There may be no greater illustration of this public-private dichotomy than the fifty-two movie screens at the Ontario Mills mall. The Mills is a cathedral of consumption in Ontario, California, a fast-expanding edge city forty miles from downtown L.A. Two megaplexes, the AMC 30 and Edwards 22, prosper amid 1.7 million square feet of what mall developer Mills Corp. dubs "shoppertainment," encompassing everything from a skate park to outlet stores to a comedy club. The sprawling desert development, at the high-volume interchange of two interstate freeways between Los Angeles and Las Vegas, bills itself as California's number one tourist attraction, ahead of Disneyland. The theaters share a single parking lot so vast that signs offer the perky reminder, "WHERE DID YOU PARK?" Both megaplexes played all three July Fourth movies on many of their screens, meaning showtimes began every twenty minutes. The Mills theaters are fed by the surrounding Inland Empire—a region as populous as Oregon that is adding people, jobs and homes at a faster rate than almost any other in the nation. Rich sources of revenue and high-volume centers of activity, they are nonetheless virtually invisible even to the movie merchants who stand to profit from their new-model infrastructure.

As we embarked on the project, the head of marketing at DreamWorks, Terry Press, sent us a fax on behalf of distribution chief Jim Tharp. "As much as we would love the glory," it read, "neither of us has the guts to allow an outsider to observe our process. If you want a visual representation of what we're afraid will happen, please watch the end of *The Wizard of Oz*."

That cute reference was perhaps more on target than DreamWorks realized. The creator of *Oz*, after all, was L. Frank Baum, a polymath, mostly luckless entrepreneur who moved with his family from Chicago to the fledgling Los Angeles suburb of Hollywood in 1910. There he created his own film studio, the Oz Film Manufacturing Company, on a bucolic stretch of Santa Monica Boulevard, in an effort to leverage his famous children's stories into motion-picture franchises. Baum produced a series of five-reel silent pictures, including *The Patchwork Girl of Oz* and *His Majesty, the Scarecrow of Oz*, before selling his studio to Universal.

The story of box office begins here, with the motion-picture pioneers who migrated to Hollywood in the early twentieth century—the theater impresarios and builders of studios. From the helter-skelter production outfits that surrounded the Oz Manufacturing Company in Hollywood, home to traveling carnivals and menageries of animals, singing cowboys and knife-throwing stuntmen, there emerged a standardized production and distribution system that would turn movies into the dominant form of mass entertainment in America.

Similarly, it would be impossible to grasp the rise of this system without paying attention to the environment in which its films actually generate box office dollars: from the baroque movie palaces that arose in downtown shopping districts like South Broadway in Los Angeles to today's antiseptic but wildly efficient megaplexes, which have exploded in every suburban market, doubling the number of U.S. movie screens over the past decade.

Box office, then, isn't just a story of studios, market research, advertising and movie stars; it is the story of the architectural and retail infrastructure into which the studios plug their product. Movie theaters, from the first picture palace to the latest suburban shopping-mall megaplex, are retail mechanisms, embedded in hubs of retail activity. The show no longer starts on the sidewalk, nor does it end after the house lights come up. It is merchandised in the surrounding restaurants, toy shops and department stores; it is splashed across newspapers, magazines and public transportation. It bankrolls an ever widening spectrum of TV channels, which the studios use, like a thousand hypodermic needles, to inject awareness of their movies into the nation's bloodstream.

Again, the author of *The Wizard of Oz* turns out to be a paradigmatic figure. Baum was an expert on mass merchandising. In 1888 he founded the National Association of Window Trimmers, and from 1897 to 1902, while writing *The Wizard of Oz*, he was editor of *The Show Window*, America's first trade magazine for window dressers. Readers have long discerned in *The Wizard of Oz* a populist allegory for the rural American citizen, imprisoned in an Emerald City of consumer goods and manipulated by a wizard hidden behind the green curtain, a trickster showman and confidence man.

Traveling this unmarked yellow brick road brought us face-to-face with an unfamiliar side of the film industry, one that's rarely glimpsed in the pages of *Vanity Fair* or the *New York Times*. We met the people behind Hollywood's sales culture—those who sell the films into theaters, sell tickets at the box office, and massage the messages the studios want to sell to the public. It's a culture of pollsters and statisticians obsessed with obscure socioeconomic data. It's a culture of distribution executives obsessed with screen counts, rental terms and fucking the competition. And it's a culture of third-generation exhibitors obsessed with movie theater finances: the rising cost of square footage in shopping malls and an operating expense known as the "house nut."

This July Fourth weekend proved an ideal lens through which to glimpse these characters. *Legally Blonde 2, T3* and *Sinbad* are not classics of cinema. They didn't set box office records like *Titanic, Spider-Man* or *E.T.* They didn't redefine the summer blockbuster like *Jurassic Park, Jaws* or *Star Wars*. They will probably not be studied fifty years from now by social historians searching for clues to the cultural forces reshaping American life at the turn of the twenty-first century. But they did cast a clear and revealing light on the phenomenon we sought to understand: the deep intertwining of box office and American life.

In many ways, the studios are still slowly waking up to the realities of their new marketplace. Well into the 1970s Hollywood continued to engineer films meant to open in grand movie palaces in the bustling downtown sections of major cities before "playing off" in suburban multiplexes. A generation later, the process has been reversed. Sprawling theaters in the outlying areas of San Jose, Salt Lake City, Dallas and Phoenix are now the ideal opening-day venues for all but the most marginal films.

Propelling that change is the need to measure each film, to quantify it, to compare and contrast it with the competition. "It used to be that if there was a line in Westwood, all was right with the world," said Jeff Blake, vice chairman of Sony Pictures, recalling the cluster of single-screen movie houses in Los Angeles that used to serve as the industry's barometer of success. Now, the proof of a movie maximizing the system is the lack of any line at all.

Hollywood "can be understood . . . but only dimly and in flashes," F. Scott Fitzgerald famously wrote in his final, unfinished 1941 novel, *The Last Tycoon*. "Not half a dozen men have ever been able to keep the whole equation of pictures in their heads." A half century later, Fitzgerald's half dozen moguls have metamorphosed into a nation of moviegoers poring over a weekly scorecard of hits and misses, entranced by the flashes. Yet the whole equation—where the numbers come from, how they're tabulated and why they matter—has always remained just out of view.

First and Goal

Twenty minutes before kickoff, the Tampa Bay Buccaneers and Oakland Raiders swarmed over the field at San Diego's Qualcomm Stadium, warming up for Super Bowl XXXVII. ABC was broadcasting the game to an estimated 88.6 million people—30 percent of the U.S. population—but had not yet moved from hype to football. A field-level camera panned by the players to focus on a man wearing street clothes and standing on the sidelines. "Look who decided to drop by," ABC reporter Robin Roberts chirped as the camera rolled. "It's the Terminator!"

Next to Roberts stood Arnold Schwarzenegger. Clad in a dark jacket, white, open-necked shirt and oval sunglasses, the actor beamed in the bright sunlight. He leaned back and flashed a smile as wide as the field. The aging action hero did not look his best. He had spent the previous night on a transatlantic flight. Shot from below, he looked tired and unusually pale. Schwarzenegger had as much on the line that day as the athletes on the field. He had come to resurrect a time-worn movie character known as the Terminator. It was his most famous role, and it had made him one of the world's biggest box office attractions. Now, Schwarzenegger hoped, it would also revive his faltering career.

Schwarzenegger wasn't a football fan. But on this Super Bowl Sunday, with millions of potential *T3* ticket buyers watching, he was trying gamely to feign interest. "I tell you, I am a big admirer of both of the teams," he said. "One is kind of the Cinderella story of coming from behind, never having had the chance to be here in the first place. That's an incredible accomplishment, what the Bucs have done. And then there's of course the machines, what I call the living machines, err, you know, the Raiders, who are absolutely fantastic, who have that mentality that they own it, they deserve it and they're probably going to crush everything."

T3 director Jonathan Mostow didn't see the interview live. He spent Super Bowl Sunday at Disneyland with his family. Watching it hours later on his TiVo, he cringed. "He's talking way too much," Mostow thought. "The Terminator is a character of few words, and here he is, blab, blab, blabbing away." Like most of the other key figures involved in *T3*, Mostow is distinctly uninterested in football. The son of an Ivy League mathematician, he grew up in a family populated by classical musicians and academics. Having methodically climbed the Hollywood ladder to direct this, his third studio feature, Mostow usually found himself in an editing room or in front of a computer screen when a big game came on TV. His former producing partner, Hal

Lieberman, said Mostow "walks out of the room as soon as anyone starts talking sports."

Nonetheless, the Super Bowl telecast seemed a natural fit for the franchise. Both were hyper-commodified spectacles of combat and technology that scored their highest ratings with men. Both arrived amid a steadily building drumbeat of hype. On the surface, it all seemed an ideal launching pad for a film that sought not to insinuate itself gradually into the nation's consciousness, but to bulldoze its way in.

Super Bowl Sunday was the only date on the calendar that could justifiably be described as a media holiday. Over the previous six days, journalists, newscasters, talk show hosts, protesters and celebrities of every ilk had converged in San Diego. Before SuperBowl XXXVII, eight of the eleven most watched programs in U.S. television history had been Super Bowls. The Super Bowl XXXVII telecast would prove to be the highest-rated TV event of the previous five years. It was also an orgy of consumption. Some 40 million pounds of avocados—nearly half of them harvested from local orchards in San Diego County—would be made into guacamole served at game-day parties from coast to coast. Americans would eat more than 14,500 pounds of chips. Beer and wine sales nationwide would spike 34 percent from the previous weekend.

Along with their snacks and beer, viewers would be asked to swallow a flood of consumer plugs and product promotions. For advertisers—especially movie advertisers—football's season finale is the ultimate pitch session, a full-contact game within the game. Madison Avenue is enamored not only of the broad reach of the Super Bowl—a rarity in today's splintered TV landscape—but also of the eagerness with which viewers chew over the commercials. The standard rate for Super Bowl ads in 2003 was $2.1 million for thirty seconds.

Warner Brothers had secured three and a half minutes of airtime, most of it for free. Months before the kickoff in San Diego (an easy trip from Schwarzenegger's Los Angeles home), the studio had staked out three prominent "shots" during the telecast. Schwarzenegger's interview on the field with Robin Roberts was part of the pregame show. A few minutes later, he would be featured as the Terminator in an introductory sequence produced by the National Football League that would be, in marketing parlance, "cobranding" for both game and movie. In the second quarter, he would watch from the sidelines as Warner Brothers' first thirty-second *T3* TV spot hit the air.

For the sixty-eight thousand fans at Qualcomm Stadium, the football game was a letdown; the Buccaneers clobbered the Raiders, 48–21. But for the TV audience at home, the real drama was in the ancillary events and filler: the pregame countdown, halftime spectacle and ads that transformed the game's sixty minutes of playing time into a day-long weenie roast around a virtual campfire. What Schwarzenegger couldn't know on game day was that the event would prove to be almost as unmitigated a disaster for *T3* as it was for the Raiders. The Terminator went 0-for-3.

First, Schwarzenegger fumbled the sideline interview. He

struggled to explain the idea behind the sequence that was shot to introduce the Super Bowl, but the right words eluded him. "The Terminator is arriving back from the year 2029," Schwarzenegger offered, "to warn the people there are Terminators amongst them. And I'm talking obviously about the great football players, the incredible athletes, that are smashing together, that have no fear, that are, err, relentless." When ABC cut from Schwarzenegger to pregame show anchor Chris "Boomer" Berman, creator of the baseball-highlight catchphrase "back, back, back!" he mused, "If Boomer met the Terminator, would we go 'back, back, back'?"

Again, Mostow winced. "I'll be back" was the Terminator's signature line of dialogue. It was a line straight out of a 1970s vigilante movie like *Dirty Harry* or *Billy Jack,* whose unhinged protagonists were a template for the Terminator—tight-lipped, disaffected Everymen who fought the system with fists and bullets. Schwarzenegger had just seventeen lines of dialogue in the original *Terminator,* but none resonated quite as profoundly as "I'll be back," a retort to a fussbudget police receptionist who tells the Terminator to take a seat and wait his turn. Leaning forward in his leather bomber jacket and huge wraparound sunglasses, the Terminator glowers at the receptionist, drones "I'll be back" in his heavy, Austrian accent, and turns on his heels. Seconds later, he drives a car through the front door and crushes the receptionist, then steps from the driver's seat, guns blazing, and mows down every police officer in the building.

The line "I'll be back" would prove remarkably malleable.

It would recur as a self-referential joke in subsequent Schwarzenegger movies, like *Twins, Running Man, The Last Action Hero* and *T2*. Mostow would tweak it for *T3* to add some sizzle to the showdown between Schwarzenegger and his nemesis, a female Terminator called the T-X. "She'll be back," the Terminator says, after pushing the T-X into an elevator shaft. Schwarzenegger would use the line as a campaign slogan when he ran for political office, much as Ronald Reagan had once aped Dirty Harry's famous catchphrase, "Make my day." But it wasn't supposed to be fodder for network anchor chitchat. Having thrilled to *The Terminator* shortly after arriving in Los Angeles in the early 1980s as an aspiring filmmaker, Mostow considered "I'll be back" to be a totem of the franchise whose integrity needed to be guarded. Unable to pry himself away from the editing room, Mostow had declined to direct the spot. It was a decision he would regret.

The one minute forty second segment was not cheaply produced. It featured rudimentary versions of the computer graphics used in *T3*. But it hijacked the Terminator, transforming him into a shameless NFL shill. Sitting on a police motorcycle in the trademark Terminator getup of black leather jacket and sunglasses, Schwarzenegger announces: "I'm back." The concept is that Tampa Bay defensive tackle Warren Sapp and Oakland quarterback Rich Gannon are machines created by Cyberdine Systems, the fictitious corporation that created the Terminator. Schwarzenegger calls Sapp "one mean machine" and quips, "It's *Hasta la vista*, baby." A voice-over booms, "These machines came online and moved deliberately, methodically toward their programmed objective." The actor goes on: "They cannot be bargained with. They will not surrender. They will not stop. Trust me." Then, with the Super Bowl trophy tucked under one arm, Schwarzenegger goes for the big finish. "Now," he intones, removing his sunglasses to reveal a flesh-and-metal-ringed hole where his left eye should be, "are you ready for some football?"

The audience might have been ready, but the Terminator clearly wasn't. His over-cooked comments had thus far done nothing to dispel the stigma that clung to *T3*—that it was a retread of past action movies, the selling-out of a popular franchise, an empty star vehicle for an aging actor. "With the third *Terminator,* there were dollar signs on everything," said James Cameron, director of the first two installments, before a retrospective 2004 screening of *Terminator 2.* "The original sense of guerilla filmmaking was gone. By the third one, it was all about business and it just wasn't interesting."

The task at hand, however, was making the film *look* interesting.

"We badly needed to do something to say, 'We're here' in a big way," Mostow recalled a few months later. "When I saw it, I said it smacks of cheesiness. The whole reason you want to see this movie is to see Arnold back as this character, and they're giving it away for free. It was a tradeoff of that and the awareness, and the fact that Arnold and this character are so important that it warrants occupying this bully pulpit—that in American culture, the Super Bowl is as big as it gets."

Dawn Taubin, the head of domestic marketing at Warner

Brothers, wasn't watching at home as Schwarzenegger muddled through the pregame telecast. She was sitting in the stands in San Diego, equipped with a miniature radio that played the audio track of the ABC telecast, and tuning in every time a Warners commercial came on the air. The thirty-second TV spot for *T3* didn't air until halftime. By then, the Raiders were already facing a deficit they would never make up. The ad began as the screen went to black. The Warner Brothers, Intermedia and C-2 logos flashed. Fade in on a postapocalyptic scene of twisted metal, a steel skull with a gleaming red eyeball in the foreground. Title cards announce, "On July 2nd, the machines will rise." There's a quick computer-animated battle sequence featuring an army of marauding robots. Then comes the shot of what appears to be the female Terminator, played by Kristanna Loken, in a sleek red leather jumpsuit. She runs through a forest, jumps from a hillside and lands on the roof of a speeding hearse like a surfer shredding a giant wave. It didn't look scary. Loken's jerky movements made her seem suspended by wires. Then the Terminator appears, carrying a shotgun and trudging toward the camera. He doesn't speak. The only spoken words are a generic, Mr. MovieFone-style voice-over: "*Terminator 3: Rise of the Machines*. This film is not yet rated."

That uninspiring, $2.1 million plot of Super Bowl real estate was the first strike in a six-month TV advertising campaign that would slowly gain steam in the months to come. The studio would buy a thirty-second spot during the NCAA basketball tournament in March, and in the season finales in

May of *Survivor, Fear Factor, The West Wing, Friends, Will & Grace, 24* and *That 70s Show.* By opening weekend, Warner Brothers had produced dozens of distinctly different TV spots, each tilted to reach a different demographic. Visual content and messages were relentlessly honed.

"You have a harder-edged male action spot for *Fear Factor* as opposed to a bigger, broader general spot for *Friends,*" explained Taubin. "When you are buying like this, over a very long time, as opposed to a three-week buy, I believe you need creativity that's not going to burn out." Not one of Taubin's media buys, however, would reach as wide an audience as the Super Bowl spot.

Viewers get more sophisticated every year when it comes to Super Bowl ads, rating and debating them with nearly the same analytical zeal they bring to the game itself. Still, they are largely unaware of the game's function within the movie world. Since the late 1980s, when film ads became common during the game, the Super Bowl has provided an initial point of impact for the enormously expensive enterprise of launching a movie into the marketplace. Years of revenue from theaters, DVDs, theme parks and soundtracks, are influenced by these thirty seconds. It is opening weekend in miniature, a moment when the craftsmanship of the movies is completely displaced by the effectiveness of a TV commercial. Nine movie ads appeared during Super Bowl XXXVII, nearly as many plugs as there were for beer.

For marketing executives at the studios, the Super Bowl advertising derby is a pricey variation of the office Super

Bowl pool. Many of them are friends and watch the game together. Terry Curtin, the head of marketing for Revolution Studios, who has also worked for Disney and Universal, watched Super Bowl XXXVII at the home of Paul Apel, CEO of New Wave Entertainment, a trailer house that created ad campaigns for all the major studios. Curtin had anted up on behalf of Revolution Studios for an ad touting the high-concept Adam Sandler and Jack Nicholson comedy, *Anger Management*. It went on to become one of Hollywood's biggest hits of 2003.

Universal Pictures wasn't so lucky. The Super Bowl brought fans the first extended glimpse of the Hulk, the computer-animated creature from Ang Lee's adaptation of the beloved comic book. They didn't like it. Some took to the Internet and complained that the Hulk looked more like Shrek or Gumby. Universal head of marketing Adam Fogelson maintains to this day that the negative reaction was a canard spread by a few disgruntled fans. But it was a blow to the studio. "We were fighting the word of mouth and bad publicity from the get-go," he said. "The Super Bowl ad provided a platform from which people could start firing the gun."

The first Super Bowl ads in 1967 cost $42,000 for thirty seconds. Unsurprisingly, the products advertised were aimed at men: Tareyton cigarettes, Haggar acrylic and rayon slacks, Schaefer beer. Movie studios took a while to get in the game, since TV advertising did not become a fixture of studio marketing campaigns until the late 1970s. By the early 1980s, the Super Bowl had become a showcase for cutting-edge ads serving every demographic. In 1984 a sixty-second segment for Apple's Macintosh computers directed by Ridley Scott would set the bar for all Super Bowl spots to come. The ad featured a blonde female runner flinging a hammer through a giant TV screen representing IBM's "Big Brother." As Bernice Kanner notes in her book, *The Super Bowl of Advertising*, Scott hired two hundred extras and built a seven-story set on a London soundstage. The spot never aired again on television, but is still considered one of history's most effective TV ads. The late 1990s brought a resurgence of high-tech ads, but many didn't register. Computer.com, Kforce.com and Epidemic.com were among the Internet firms that bet their company's venture capital in vain.

Most people experience Super Bowl ads in group settings. By Kanner's estimate, Super Bowl parties consist of roughly seventeen people, a larger gathering than even the typical New Year's Eve party. In that environment, TV commercials play more like short versions of the trailers attached to movies in theaters. Living rooms behave like movie theaters. Ad agencies and clients surf the Web for instant reaction. *USA Today,* the *New York Times* and the *Wall Street Journal* are among the traditional outlets that review all of the major ads. Other analyses have sprouted on the Internet. TiVo issues a ranking of ads watched multiple times by its subscribers.

But the Super Bowl is also an old-fashioned broadcast event. Everyone watches it. From an advertiser's standpoint, it carries an air of nostalgia, a throwback to an era before demographic consciousness, when the majority of the country could be counted on to sit in front of their television sets to watch a single network show. All this makes the Super Bowl a Roman Coliseum for advertisers. A Super Bowl ad that strikes the synapses with the right concussive burst of pyrotechnics—like *Independence Day*'s trademark 1996 shot of a space ship vaporizing the White House—gives a sharp boost to the widespread consumer desire both to see the film in theaters and to be among the first to see it, on opening weekend, before the novelty begins to fade.

The 2003 telecast offered the first glimpse of the summer competition. Along with *T3* and *Hulk* were spots for *Bad Boys II, Bruce Almighty, Charlie's Angels: Full Throttle* and a smattering of winter and spring films, like *Daredevil, The Recruit* and *Old School*. These movie spots bumped up against high-concept ads for Pepsi Twist (a horrified Ozzy Osbourne sees his kids transformed into the Osmonds) and Anheuser-Busch (a zebra referees a game played by Clydesdale horses). But most of them paled next to Warners' virtuoso thirty-second spots for *The Matrix Reloaded* and *The Matrix Revolutions,* two films that were quickly emerging as the ones to beat in 2003. *The Matrix* became a sleeper hit after opening in March 1999. Since then, its mystique had only grown: It became a harbinger of a new kind of blockbuster—brainy, stylish and wildly inventive, freely bending the rules of time and space in the service of a high-octane storyline that seemed new and original. Its directors, brothers Andy and Larry Wachowski, were anti-social Hollywood outsiders, and details of the production of two *Matrix* sequels, shot in one continuous stretch over 180 days the previous year, were veiled in secrecy. But the Super Bowl *Matrix* ads appeared to deliver on the high expectations. They had startling special effects, kaleidoscopic martial arts battles and a sleek elegance befitting a Prada spread in a glossy magazine, and they brought party conversations around the country to an awestruck halt.

For Taubin and for the producers of *T3*, those expectations would become a major headache. Warners was releasing *T3* and the two *Matrix* sequels. The two franchises were predicated on the same basic concept: a cosmic battle to save the human race from malevolent machines. But if *T3* looked like a cynical retread of a '90s action movie, *The Matrix* appeared to be the face of the future. *The Matrix Reloaded* would be released one month before *T3*, and as the anticipation continued to build, it would steal the thunder from *T3*, leading to recriminating charges by its filmmakers that Warners was picking favorites.

"*The Matrix* could have put out my bar mitzvah video and people would have gone, 'Oh my god!'" Mostow later grumbled.

So how did *T3* fare?

USA Today's Ad Meter poll, which uses a focus group of 108 volunteers in McLean, Virginia, to rate the Super Bowl ads with hand-held meters, ranked *T3* number forty-two out of fifty-five ads. That placed it sixth among the game's nine movie ads. The highest-scoring spots were for comedies: Universal's *Bruce Almighty* and Revolution's *Anger*

Management. The Matrix Reloaded finished No. 26, the third-highest movie.

Warners' internal market research showed a significant bump in the general public's awareness of *T3* after the Super Bowl. "We were happy with the increase," Taubin later said. "That's why you advertise on the Super Bowl. When you're looking at an early summer date, you have a long way to go. It's meant to be an early pop." But six months before opening weekend, it was still tough to see how *T3* would rate against the summer competition.

A reviewer for Flak, one of the many Web sites evaluating the game's effect on movies, offered this recap: "Ahnuld is back. Scenes of things exploding, robots running amok, a new hot female cyborg to battle our hero. No plot is evident . . . but did I mention things explode? Loudly? With his recent box office record, advancing age and possible plans to run for governor of California, he needs this film. Even if we don't."

Some fans in online chatrooms rallied to the Terminator's defense. "Sure, it was cheesy but in a funny/intentional way. I loved that, it rocked!" wrote one viewer, Cimmerian King, on the Web site TheArnoldFans.com. Other, less partisan sites were dominated by negative opinions. The bottom line: Few people had gotten excited by their first taste of *T3*.

On the first episode of his ABC talk show *Jimmy Kimmel Live*, the host ridiculed Schwarzenegger. Warren Sapp, the Buccaneers' defensive hero, had been helicopter after the game to Kimmel's Hollywood Boulevard set as a publicity stunt. Before interviewing Sapp, Kimmel replayed Schwarzenegger's rambling pregame comments.

"That might be the gayest thing I've ever heard," Kimmel said. "He still talks like Colonel Klink."

Legally Bland

The show had already started by the time Reese Wither-spoon and Ryan Philippe slipped unnoticed through a side door of a packed suburban megaplex. On this low-pro-file weeknight mission, they had driven forty-eight miles from the west side of Los Angeles to the Edwards Aliso Viejo Stadium 20, a mall-based theater complex in a planned community of forty thousand in the heart of Orange County. The manager whisked them into a place where the audience would never spot them: the projection booth. The cloak-and-dagger measure suggested this was not merely a night out at the movies for stars trying to dodge autograph hounds. It was the second test screening of *Legally Blonde 2*. The date was April 15. In about ten weeks, the film would be sent to 3,350 theaters across the country. At that point, however, even Witherspoon did not know for sure if there was actually going to be a movie to ship.

Going incognito was not an easy feat for this couple.

Since appearing together in *Cruel Intentions* in 1999, the two blondes had become Hollywood's preeminent twenty-something power pair. They had piled up acting credits while crafting an image of domestic bliss. Tabloid and glossy star magazine reporters dig through their garbage. Witherspoon at this moment was on the steeper upward trajectory. She was no longer the working actress known for her white-trash vamp in *Freeway* or her determined student-council candidate in *Election*. She was a leading actress coming off two major hits, *Legally Blonde* and an even bigger success, *Sweet Home Alabama*. Philippe had experimented more, moving from teenage fare like *White Squall* and *I Know What You Did Last Summer* to Robert Altman's *Gosford Park* and indie hit *Igby Goes Down*.

As Witherspoon and Philippe gazed through the darkness of the auditorium, they surveyed the audience, comprised almost entirely of regular moviegoers recruited locally by NRG, the same company that had run the teen-girl focus groups in Mission Valley. For those viewers, the screening was a simple diversionary visit to the local mall. Scattered among them, however, sat about a dozen spectators with considerably more at stake: the principal figures involved in *Legally Blonde 2*. MGM's president was here. So were executives from the production, marketing, publicity and distribution departments, plus the film's producer, director and screenwriter. They sat in camps—suits on one side, "creatives" on the other. Several months' work and almost $100 million was at stake with *Legally Blonde 2*. The point of the screening was not only to see if the film held together, but to get a sense of how it would open. Chris McGurk, the vice-chairman of MGM, is not known for understatement. He professed to be confident heading into the showdown against *Terminator 3*. C-2 Pictures, the production company run by *T3*'s flamboyant, go-for-broke producers, Andy Vajna and Mario Kassar, resides in a graffiti-covered warehouse a block from the office park that housed MGM until the summer of 2003. "I just saw Andy and Mario a couple of days ago," McGurk said, gesturing in the direction of C-2's headquarters, "I told them this is the headline I want: 'Elle Shocks the Terminator.' It could happen." Most of the others involved with the film were not as sanguine. They were all too aware of the marketing challenges that lay ahead.

Driving south from Los Angeles, the star, producers, director, writer and studio executives may have been heading to the same theater, but they had widely divergent agendas. Chatting with each other by cell phone, they contemplated everything from Witherspoon's upcoming *Vogue* photo shoot to which theater circuits would play the movie and the effect of it all on MGM's stock price.

"Generally these screenings start with an impending sense of dread," observed marketing president Peter Adee. "And usually it's the old adage—a movie is never as good as the dailies or as bad as the first cut. But there is always a sense of doom. You build it up psychologically so there's relief afterward. Then there is a lot of discussion of what to do, where it worked and didn't work."

Director Charles Herman-Wurmfeld had his own

qualms. It had been clear before the start of shooting that the opening scenes of the screenplay weren't right. MGM, as is common, had hired a few screenwriters to do "polishes," including Don Roos, a well-known polisher whose fee was roughly $100,000 per week. He worked for eight weeks, detaching from the production at the time shooting began in November. He took a stab at rewriting the opening scenes, but his version was ultimately scrapped. A reading of the script in late September, when cast members, executives, filmmakers and writers gathered to hear the words spoken out loud demonstrated that the problem areas went beyond the beginning. There was a sense around that table, Roos said, that the script needed major surgery. "It all fell apart in the last sixty pages," he said. "Elle wasn't being Elle. My eyes were very big because I knew we had a lot of work to do." Because MGM had promised shareholders and exhibitors a *Legally Blonde* sequel on July 2, filming had to begin whether or not the script flaws had been fixed. Decisions to put business before film craft were made almost daily in Hollywood, especially in the sequel business. Warner Brothers famously fast-tracked *Lethal Weapon IV* without a script at all, writing it as it was filmed; Universal began shooting *American Pie 2* despite serious questions about one major character played by Chris Penn. After negative reaction to him by test audiences, the character was entirely eliminated from the final cut.

Fixing the opening to the film was not Herman-Wurm-feld's only concern. This trip to Aliso Viejo was the first time he was going to screen his movie for the star—a nerve-wracking experience for any director. He traveled to the theater in a 1984 Volvo that was so beat-up that when he approached studio gates for meetings, he liked to joke, "They always asked me, 'Pickup or delivery?'" When he and producer Marc Platt had begun production in early November, they'd shared a strong hunch about the weakness of the first couple of scenes. The first test screening a few days ago had confirmed their suspicions. The scenes showed Witherspoon's Elle Woods character meeting Sally Field's Rep. Victoria Rudd at a press conference announcing a victory in a legal case Elle has litigated concerning beauty products. Rudd urges Elle to consider a career change, telling her, "Washington could use more blondes."

Showing this compromised early version of his film to the Orange County crowd was a "terrifying experience," said Herman-Wurmfeld, whose biggest credit as a director of feature films was the low-budget indie hit *Kissing Jessica Stein*. He had gotten this assignment from Platt after *Legally Blonde* director Robert Luketic opted out, wanting to avoid a sequel rut so early in his own nascent career. "Driving into mall country," Herman-Wurmfeld said, "I realized I had left the safety of the city. I was convinced I was the only gay Jew in the whole complex. Someone was going to come after me and they would start pointing: 'It's him! It's him! It's the gay Jewish artist!'" The thirty-seven-year-old director's preternaturally blue eyes and broad, toothy smile stand out from his shaved head. Raised in Manhattan, he attended Oberlin College, where he immersed himself in the theater, a calling he would follow in Vermont until coming to Hollywood with just a bicycle and a banjo in 1997. Issues of personal comfort aside, he was wary of how Orange County feedback could affect his film. "With all due respect to audiences of all shapes, colors and sizes, we found the most conservative audience to watch this movie. I had never really been forced to examine the needs and desires of the Mission Viejo audience."

Herman-Wurmfeld and his assistant found seats "away from the suits," he remembered, "not because I don't love and adore them, but because I wanted to really hear what was being said around me. I sort of wore my sweatshirt hood up. You can sort of blend in anywhere. I fancied that somehow I could pass as one of the kids. So I would sit just off on my own and listen to people laugh and groan or not respond or whatever."

The Edwards screening was a production test, as opposed to a marketing test. Unlike the session at Taylor Research, which focused only on the film's trailer, the outcome of the screening would not specifically be applied to television ads or event planning. It was largely to provide feedback to Herman-Wurmfeld, Platt and everyone else rushing to get the film from rough form to polished, theater-ready shape in just three months.

Given the movie's accelerated path, whatever feedback they got would be valuable. But time was not on their side. Herman-Wurmfeld described the schedule as "optimistic at best, destructive at worst." Adee considered it "a pressure-cooker of extraordinary levels. You have to look at the numbers and have an opinion about why they are what they are

instantaneously. It is *now*. There is no, 'Let's analyze this.'"
Added publicity chief Eric Kops: "There was never a lull.
With other movies, production ends and there's a lull while
you open other movies. But this movie was never on the
back burner."

Elle Woods's presence on the screen at the Edwards Aliso
Viejo Stadium 20 was made possible by the go-go market for
sequels created by hits such as *The Mummy Returns* and
Austin Powers in Goldmember. In another era, the film might
never have been made. A generation earlier, it was an ac-
cepted rule of box office that a sequel would take in only half
the proceeds of its predecessor. This sequel had seemed a
seductive idea as soon as the first *Legally Blonde,* a far more
modest and organic undertaking, became a runaway summer hit in 2001. Robert Luketic's original wasn't exactly a
milestone in the art of filmmaking, but Witherspoon gave
the character of Elle Woods a contagious wit and charm.
Like Mike Myers playing Austin Powers, she looked to be
having a blast and she invited the audience to play along
with the film's conceit. Elle's pink-and-blonde radiance
stood out in a summer of glowering, male-dominated
blockbusters like *Minority Report* and *Planet of the Apes*.

Platt summed up the original *Legally Blonde* story as "a
fish out of water, a person who doesn't belong in the environment she's in and then comes to be part of the environment." For its target audience, he added, "being a pretty girl
who gets to wear great clothes, and yet still be smart and demand that others respect her for her intelligence, is a wish

fulfillment. It is something they aspire to." As soon as he'd read Amanda Brown's novel in unfinished manuscript form, he'd been smitten by the character. Elle is a Bel Air–raised sorority sister and Hawaiian Tropic girl whose raisons d'être are spa treatments and shopping sprees. She is dating a hunky fraternity boy and wants nothing more than to become Mrs. Warner Huntington III. When he rejects her for being a ditzy blonde, she is initially crushed. But she soon decides—initially to win Warner back, but then as a realization of her hidden potential—to get into Harvard Law School. The upbeat second half of the movie sees Elle become an accomplished Harvard student, make over her stodgy classmates and land a sensitive new beau played by Luke Wilson. Writing in the *Village Voice,* Jessica Winter sized up the film as "one of your racier Be Yourself after-school specials crossed with *Who Moved My Cheese?* for *Cosmo* girls."

Watching Elle self-actualize in a rough-cut screening of the first movie, MGM publicist Eric Kops had felt the intoxicating rush of possibility. Kops had risen through the ranks at MGM by weathering ups and downs with aplomb. Fueled by Diet Cokes and Marlboro Lights, he worked tirelessly but not humorlessly, and his gossipy-yet-earnest demeanor endeared him to colleagues and journalists alike. Not many executive vice presidents would celebrate their birthday as Kops did in 2003—by vacationing in Hawaii with his assistant and other coworkers. In a wall case in his office hangs an autographed, 8-by-10 glossy photo of Joey Lawrence. Massaging his forehead, he punctuates rueful war stories about the industry with a reedy, stuttering laugh. With gelled, dark-brown hair, black-framed glasses and prominent chin, the 6-foot-2 Kops looks a bit like pop singer Morrissey. That may not be entirely coincidental—as a student at UC San Diego, he worked part-time as what he calls a "baby publicist" by promoting concerts, including one by Morrissey. "My friend and I were next to the stage and at one point Morrissey lay down and hung his head off the stage," Kops recalls. "And I was like, 'Do we have to act professional or can we just rush the stage?'"

While working for several years promoting independent films for publicity firm MPRM, he thrived by championing underdogs and finding novel ways to imprint them on the marketplace. At MGM, where he had spent the bulk of his career, Kops was not always handed a ball he could run with. Sure, he worked on the company's mainstay James Bond films and the occasional sleeper hit. But he also suffered through plenty of catastrophes. The studio's forays into big-budget terrain yielded flops like *Rollerball* and *Windtalkers*. Then there was *Molly,* the Elisabeth Shue affliction drama that had the dubious distinction of premiering on major airlines *before* limping in and out of theaters with a $17,396 gross. Or *Supernova,* a sci-fi mess that burned through three directors before landing in theaters with the telling tagline, "In the farthest reaches of space, something has gone terribly wrong."

Legally Blonde represented a rare opportunity for both Kops and MGM. For decades the studio had been a second-tier company despite its sterling heritage and star-studded library of films. Part of the issue was size. MGM was too lean to compete with larger studios like Warners or Sony. Merger talks with Sony, DreamWorks and Vivendi Universal in recent years had never borne fruit (though in the spring of 2004 they began to heat up again). Elle Woods, nevertheless, had all the makings of a home-grown heroine. Since taking control of the company in 1999, Chris McGurk and Alex Yemenidjian had made cost-conscious franchise-building a large part of their goal in turning things around. James Bond was already a marquee brand, but the company had to spend lavishly to make and market the films and then share profits with Albert R. "Cubby" Broccoli, longtime producer of the franchise, and his partners. McGurk, who had direct oversight of studio operations, was eager to establish a range of easily duplicable properties whose DVD sales alone could justify their modest costs. As *Legally Blonde* came together, executives were also developing *Agent Cody Banks* and *Barbershop,* films that management intended to sequelize. "We're very focused on creating film franchises that have a very different set of economics than the 'originals' business," explained McGurk. "A film like *Legally Blonde* makes us feel a lot more comfortable."

Kops sensed a chance to make a real impact with *Legally Blonde,* which he would promote with a combination of grass-roots ingenuity and major-studio flash. The movie's fizzy pop sensibility inspired him so powerfully that he threw himself completely into the task of persuading colleagues about his promotional strategies. "In meetings, I'm Norma Rae," he said. In trying to get audiences on board, he would key on a particular sequence: After Elle has been dumped, she decides to pull herself up by her own heel straps. A montage shows Elle buying a computer and raising her hand in class. A template for young female empowerment was born. Kops, drawing on his years in the independent publicity realm, knew that the more the marketing and publicity teams tried to channel Elle's energy, the more effective they would be.

For one thing, Kops recognized the potent marketing combination of self-empowerment and beauty products. Working with sponsors like Vidal Sassoon, he raised awareness of the movie by devising a central gimmick: National Blonde Day, held July 9, 2001. There were free makeovers and salon days nationwide. A series of mailings went out from the Blonde Legal Defense Club, whose stated calling, according to a "spokeswoman" named Fern Magnin, was to "stop the widespread belief that blondes are dumb and incapable." *Cosmopolitan,* which Elle lauds as "the Bible" in the film, held a contest to turn ten women into "Blonde Bombshells." Entrants had to write a three-hundred-word essay explaining "why blondes are just as brilliant as brunettes."

Not seeing the MGM Lion logo or any explicit connection to the movie on National Blonde Day material, journalists across the country, and even some from overseas, assumed the holiday was real. Several legitimate newspapers ran articles announcing it. Kops recalled, "We were getting calls from people saying, 'Do you know about this? Are you going to hook up with the people putting on this holiday?'"

Released on July 13, 2001, *Legally Blonde,* which cost a

mere $20 million to make, stunned box office prognostica-
tors by grossing $20.4 million in its opening weekend and
going on to collect $96.5 million in North America alone.
Its appeal was partly a function of the environment in
which it played: suburban, mall-based megaplexes, hundreds of places that looked just like the Edwards Aliso Viejo
Stadium 20. The movie, festooned with shimmering pastel-
colored nail polish, shoes, clothes and beauty products,
served as a bridge between the mall shops and the theater. It
was a study in wish fulfillment; however empowering its
you-can-do-it message may have been, it also went down
smooth. It gave the audience as much pleasure as a trip
through a mall where they could afford all of the nicest
things. Amanda Brown, author of the *Legally Blonde* book,
has confessed to choosing Stanford Law School over Harvard Law because Stanford had a better mall.

A blowup of the front page of the July 16 issue of *Daily
Variety*—whose lead headline was GOLDILOCKS ROCKS
B.O.—stood for two years in Kops's office. "I would show
that to Reese and say [of the sequel], 'That's what we're all
shooting for,'" he said. The core audience wanted to view
the film again and again—it would go on to sell 3.5 million
copies in DVD. In part because of his work on *Legally
Blonde,* Kops was promoted to head of publicity at MGM.

In the immediate afterglow of the original film's success,
the seeds for a sequel were sewn. Work also began on a TV
sitcom pilot. Though it never grew into a network show, its
director, Charles Herman-Wurmfeld, would remain in the
Legally Blonde fold. Marc Platt had two thoughts about

where to take Elle Woods in a sequel: London, where she could turn the Royal Family pink, or Washington, where she could give the government a makeover. Washington seemed like a better canvas.

At age forty-seven, Platt is renowned as a producer of films for teenage girls. He is the father of five children, including two daughters, and he excels at devising what he calls "character environments": settings where audiences want to spend ninety minutes and people with whom they want to be friends. Though no one in the film business would want to admit it, it's the same operating principle that governs TV sitcoms. Though *Legally Blonde* remains his high-water mark, his résumé also includes rocker-girl romp *Josie and the Pussycats* and *Flashdance*-y hip-hop melodrama *Honey*. Even *Wicked*, his Broadway musical twist on *The Wizard of Oz*, turns on the catty rivalry between Glinda the Good and the Wicked Witch echoing scheming snob Selma Blair's rift with Reese Witherspoon in *Legally Blonde*.

Platt's modest offices are in a plain-looking bungalow on the Universal lot, where he served for two years as head of production and now has a production deal. Under the deal, he must bring any project to Universal first and only after they pass can he set it up at another studio. Universal turned down the first *Legally Blonde* and, in Hollywood's daily game of musical chairs, it soon found a buyer in MGM. In Platt's bungalow at Universal, a lounge set up for conversation and video viewing is dominated by a large framed poster of *The Wizard of Oz*, a blown-up publicity still from the 1939 MGM classic. It was a gift from the studio after the first *Legally*

Blonde. It shows Dorothy, the Scarecrow, the Lion, the Tin Man and the Wizard of Oz, arms on each other's shoulders, marching past a giant hardcover copy of the novel. Along one wall is a shelf of scripts bound with brown and green leather. On a wide coffee table that occupies most of the square footage of the room are production stills from his movies. In one, Platt camps it up with the cast of *Honey*. He's wearing a coat with a fur hood, wraparound sunglasses, and a necklace with a large silver crucifix. The room is a hodge-podge of comfortable, mismatched furniture and sports memorabilia. Platt's Baltimore roots and love of baseball are revealed by a Louisville Slugger baseball bat signed by Cal Ripken, a copy of *Sports Illustrated*'s first issue from 1954, and a plastic-sealed copy of the *Baltimore Sun* from the day after Ripken ended his streak of 2,632 consecutive games played. Only the producer's gray hair and stately four-door Jaguar parked out front hint at his being middle-aged. Dressed in a long-sleeved T-shirt, faded jeans, white Nike sneakers and white athletic socks, he comes across as collegiate and clean-cut. His restless energy makes his hands perpetually gesticulate, and he props his feet on the coffee table to tip his chair to and fro.

Movie people recently began to recognize that teen girls travel in packs, have more discretionary income than ever, and can sometimes persuade their entire family to see a particular movie. Hugely profitable hits such as *Bring It On, Save the Last Dance, Mean Girls* and *Freaky Friday* attest to their clout. This potent market segment is elusive but can sometimes be reached through effective use of cable TV channels and Web sites aimed directly at them. "The Internet has made it a culture of immediacy, of 'I can get it now and I can get it instantly,'" said Platt. "A good producer of any product understands that. When I was a kid, I'd come home and spend my evenings on the telephone. My kids come home and they're on the Internet." After a pause, he added: "Kids are very used to saying, 'Hey I'm buying this online' and it shows up at your house in two days. Look at the music business, and how the building of stars doesn't happen anymore. Somebody's hot for six months, then you're on to the next. It's in the culture. It's like ADD."

One advantage Platt has in getting this audience's attention is that he knows the machinery and politics of studio operations. After beginning his career as an entertainment lawyer and then running business affairs for talent agency ICM, he successively became head of production for three studios, Orion, TriStar and Universal.

In setting up *Legally Blonde 2,* Platt knew he had to act fast or possibly lose Reese Witherspoon. By the spring of 2002, she was eyeing several scripts from the privileged perch of a newly minted star who could turn any project into a "go picture." He went to Eve Ahlert and Dennis Drake, the screenwriting team behind the Renee Zellweger romantic comedy, *Down With Love.* They wrote an early draft, in which Elle Woods fought for passage of an environmental bill. Platt then turned to Kate Kondell, a Stanford graduate who had earned a good living rewriting scripts but hadn't yet gotten a screen credit. She worked at balancing the specifics of the script's political milieu with the carefree abandon and mischievous materialism of Elle Woods. From the beginning, finding the ideal quotient of politics in the plot was a struggle. One MGM executive familiar with the production said that political terms like "filibuster" were assiduously excised from each draft of the script, as was a scene of Republicans squaring off against Democrats on the softball field. One key plot element developed in those early drafts stuck: Elle Woods would go to Washington to combat animal testing. Working for Rep. Rudd, she would champion a piece of legislation called Bruiser's Bill, named for her Chihuahua. And Bruiser would get a campy subplot, coming out as a gay dog. Bruiser, who goes through several costume changes, would get a new wardrobe, including a black leather fetish outfit.

Washington was a backdrop that entranced the people making *Legally Blonde 2,* although nary a frame of principal photography was shot in the nation's capital. (Utah's statehouse stood in for the U.S. Capitol.) Herman-Wurmfeld has an activist bent. He is prone to ranting about the evils of SUVs and the excesses of corporate America. Doug Liman, the director of *Swingers* and executive producer of *The O.C.,* the Fox drama set in the suburbs surrounding Aliso Viejo, has known Herman-Wurmfeld since high school. The two collaborated on a documentary of Vermont governor Howard Dean that was used during Dean's run for the Democratic presidential nomination. Herman-Wurmfeld feels a special fidelity to Dean because since 1970 his family has owned a 150-year-old farmhouse on one hundred acres in Goshen, Vermont. The director spent two years in his early twenties teaching drama at a Vermont high school.

It is not surprising then that the director summed up the film this way in an interview included on the *Legally Blonde 2* DVD: "This is about the little girl taking on the system. Martin Luther King said the day we stop speaking up for things that matter is the day we start to die a little. The essence of this story is a little how-to manual of grass-roots political activity. For anyone who ever wanted to get involved but thought, 'What do I know?' For those people there is a very strong thread that goes through the film that says, 'You know what? You can do it. Go out there and make your voice heard.'" Witherspoon agreed: "The film should have addressed the feeling people have had lately about being disconnected from the government and not having a voice."

While polishing the script, Don Roos sensed that the story was not on the same crowd-pleasing ground as the original *Legally Blonde*. "That was a problem we just couldn't solve," he said of the Washington setting. "Because it was happening there, you had to explain to that audience, and to me, frankly, because I don't know a thing about legislation, how the whole game works. Then you can see how she succeeds or not. That's quite a job for a summer movie—to try to show the audience, 'Here are the steps she has to achieve, now let's watch her achieve them.' It's not an easy game to explain. It's not the same as in the first version, where she has to get good grades in school and she has to solve a courtroom case. We all know about courtroom cases. We all know if somebody's a liar or not. It's all very accessible."

By July Fourth 2002, Platt believed the script was in good enough shape to formally present to Witherspoon. "I said to Kate, 'There are probably three movies [on Witherspoon's list] before *Legally Blonde 2,* so let's really work as hard as we can to get a script because something might fall out. So Kate and I spent every day of the summer sitting in this office pounding out a script and met with Reese a couple of times along the way. We finally got a draft we were fairly satisfied with the third week of August. As circumstances would have it, during that period, with all Reese's other projects, the scripts came in apparently to her disappointment. I found myself on Labor Day getting a call from Reese saying, 'I want to do it. I'm in.'"

Platt spoke with MGM vice-chairman Chris McGurk, with whom he had already discussed the patriotic, "red, white and blonde" marketing concept. They agreed that the subtitle was a good branding touch, and selected a release date to suit it: July 2, 2003. Ten months away.

Not long after Labor Day, word spread that MGM had paid Witherspoon $15 million for the sequel and granted her an executive producer credit. Jennifer Simpson, who ran Witherspoon's production company, Type A Films, was given the title of coproducer. In the end, these credits were little more than carrots used to close the deal. Witherspoon and Simpson made notes on the script, but once production started Witherspoon focused mostly on acting, though Don Roos noted her frequent invocation of what she called "Elle logic" to fine-tune pages of the script in the crucial weeks leading up to the shoot. More than her sure handle on the character, Witherspoon's schedule accelerated the whole enterprise. Soon after coming aboard, she was signed to appear in *Vanity Fair*, an adaptation of the William Makepeace Thackeray novel which would begin shooting in London in the spring of 2003. Her window of availability was narrow.

"I remember the blitz of publicity about how Reese was making $15 million and that a sequel was happening, all through September and October and November," Kops said. "She was the '$15 million girl' in a million stories and I remember it feeling just like I had to start running." Using marketing materials that drew heavily on MGM's *Legally Blonde* campaign, Disney released Witherspoon's *Sweet Home Alabama* on September 27—not typically a season when blockbusters are launched. It opened to a September record of $35.6 million and grossed $127.2 million to become Witherspoon's biggest hit. It would bring in another $204 million from DVD sales. "Everyone thought that $15 million was a lot of money [to pay her for *Legally Blonde 2*]," Adee said. "And then *Sweet Home Alabama* opens and it was a validation that she was the real deal and America's sweetheart from a movie standpoint. So the expectations and the event quality of it were pushing themselves up and we just had to manage it as best we could. The audience was telling us, 'This is our thing.'"

Unfortunately, few members of the audience at the Edwards Aliso Viejo Stadium 20 felt like *Legally Blonde 2* was their thing. They didn't fully embrace a sequel that threw so much new information at them right from the beginning.

Plus, the movie was judged only intermittently funny, not the best feedback for a comedy. "The original beginning started kind of abruptly," Kops said. "In the first movie, there was that girl on the bike who was riding around and sort of brought you into that world. In this one it was boom! She's a lawyer and you're in the story."

After the lights came up, NRG, the market research firm paid by MGM to moderate the screening, distributed questionnaire cards on which audience members scribbled answers. Some of the questions were standard and others customized to *Legally Blonde 2*. Assessing feedback from cards is often a benighted process. Billy Wilder used to make comic reference to one memorable card that came back after a screening of *Ninotchka*. It read: "I laughed so hard I peed in my girlfriend's hand."

NRG evaluates the cards, which studios review in conjunction with results from focus-group sessions that immediately follow almost every test screening of a movie. A total score is assigned to each screening, based on how people rated the film on the following scale: excellent, very good, good, fair and poor. The other important consideration is how many people would "definitely" recommend the movie to a friend (as opposed to "probably," "probably not" or "definitely not"). Commonly, when people in Hollywood described test screening, they refer only to the percentage of the audience that checked the "top two boxes" to rate the film either very good or excellent. A score of 80 percent or higher is considered a strong test result. Even more consequential are the recommend rate and the answers to other questions about adjectives used to describe the film and to list favorite or least favorite scenes.

After the cards were tallied but before the focus group ended, an ad-hoc meeting was held inside the theater. "We had these cluster-near-a-broom-closet meetings," Herman-Wurmfeld recalled, "with Chris McGurk and Marc Platt and Reese's manager and myself and [studio production chief] Michael Nathanson. We're gathered at the back end of a dark hall of a movie theater, seeing the report, the quick thumbnail sketch of how the movie played." Witherspoon called the testing process "the strangest part of making a film. When you're making it, you're in a bubble and then you go see it with an audience and you think, 'Wow, that's not funny at all' and people are on the floor. And then there are things that I see that I think are hysterical, but it was probably because I was there and it was funny on that day. I was really surprised by the huge response the dog got. I thought it was wry and it was witty. But I didn't realize it was going to be roaring laughter."

The scores were mediocre, falling well short of 80 percent. They were especially weak among viewers who had not seen the first movie. Few people loathed *Legally Blonde 2*, but few loved it. There were rough patches throughout. Elle's friend Paulette and Bruiser both got high marks. Sally Field and Bob Newhart, playing Sid Post, the doorman of Elle's Watergate-like apartment building, did not test well.

Herman-Wurmfeld felt uneasy because the numbers being thrown at him seemed "pseudoscientific at best." He complained that his cut was criticized for not appealing enough to boys, who seemed likely to resist the film's pink-colored charms no matter what. Jennifer Coolidge, who plays Elle Woods's friend Paulette, felt the tests could not help but flatten out the comedy in *Legally Blonde 2*. "When it's testing in front of audiences, if you put your hand in your butt it gets a laugh," she said. "So there are various ways to cheat it so you're not really being funny. You can't be subtle sometimes. I was doing a scene in a movie recently and what I was doing was so not funny but they kept telling me, 'But it's testing well, so keep doing it.' And it really is like the monkey smelling its butt. It's that basic. That's what's scary. It can test well but it can be humiliating that some of those moments end up in a film."

With two screenings under its belt, MGM knew it had numerous refinements to make. Sitting on a prime summer release date, how narrowly targeted could the film afford to be? Herman-Wurmfeld suspected that the test would only give MGM more reason to soften the political empowerment message in an effort to reach Middle America. As the director saw it, the film's path to opening weekend would emulate the race to the middle that happens in a presidential election year. "The movie is sort of progressive in its worldview," he said, "so if you design a progressive movie to suit the conservative audience, then you probably can do more of pleasing everybody. I understood the impulse."

Pleasing anybody, let alone everybody, would entail reshooting the initial scenes and arriving at the optimal level of political content, a process Herman-Wurmfeld likened to "balancing peas on a scale." The plot pivoted on an obscure Congressional procedure. And no matter how much of a political animal the director might be, he also got the gig by directing the *Legally Blonde* TV pilot, which followed his work on a *Facts of Life* reunion movie. He talked about suffusing the film with pink light so that it would look "like rock candy." How felicitously could politics be blended with rock candy without the movie alienating its teen fan base? "When you make a sequel, do you try to be all things to all people again? Reese and I decided no," Platt said. "We had to be true to the core audience the initial one was made for, so we consciously made a movie that was again for that younger age group that we hoped would cross over but if not, that's what it was going to be."

Get Me Sinbad

Some studio moguls have God complexes; Jeffrey Katzenberg identified with Moses. One of the first animated films he put into development at DreamWorks SKG, the studio he cofounded in 1994 with his friends Steven Spielberg and David Geffen, was *The Prince of Egypt*, the Old Testament story of Moses freeing the slaves from the Pharaoh. When the film was released in 1998, Katzenberg was embroiled in a nasty legal battle with his former boss, Disney CEO Michael Eisner. Katzenberg had served as Disney's animation czar under Eisner before being expelled from the Magic Kingdom, and he was determined to transform DreamWorks into a rival animation superpower.

Katzenberg approached *The Prince of Egypt* with evangelical zeal. He imagined sequels about Noah and Job, books of scripture decorated with DreamWorks cartoons, and computer games depicting each of the ten plagues. The film was screened for dozens of religious leaders around the world, in-

cluding seventy-five cardinals, bishops and archbishops at
the Vatican. "We are going to own the Bible!" he shouted at
one meeting in the Bel-Air headquarters of DreamWorks Interactive, pounding the table, relishing the role of the prophet
liberating the animation industry from years of dominance
by Disney. "That day was his Howard Dean speech," recalls a
former executive who was there. "Spittle was flying and he
was just raving. He had to show Disney where to stick it. People gossiped about it for weeks. We couldn't believe he was
willing to hawk the Bible to bring money in."

Such venal impulses in the early years of DreamWorks
were masked by the utopian aura that surrounded the company. No executive had a title. Employees ate elaborately
catered free breakfasts and lunches. The fanciful studio logo
depicted a boy sitting on a crescent moon, dangling a fish-
ing rod. Launched with $2.7 billion in investment capital,
DreamWorks arrived in the year of *Pulp Fiction* and Kurt
Cobain, amid the reverberations of alternative cinema and
alternative rock. It was conceived as the alternative studio,
in the artist-friendly spirit of the original United Artists,
founded in 1919 by Mary Pickford, Douglas Fairbanks,
Charlie Chaplin and D. W. Griffith.

Spielberg, when not busy directing and producing films,
would drop in at the company's five offices, stretching from
Bel-Air to the San Fernando Valley. The auteur behind *Close
Encounters, E.T.* and *Jurassic Park* would attempt to pump up
the troops by explaining how Hollywood storytelling magic
could blend with computer technology in a bureaucracy-
free setting where ideas would reign. There would be

movies, yes, but also Web sites, CD-ROMs and video games. Microsoft invested in DreamWorks Interactive. Sega and Universal poured money into GameWorks, a chain of hyperstimulating video-game parlors billed as "Steven Spielberg's three-ring circus."

Some observers doubted that the three-ring circus at DreamWorks corporate headquarters would last. Katzenberg's chief interest was animation; Spielberg was focused on making his own films; Geffen was drifting away from the film business, frequently shuttling between the Clinton White House and Hollywood. But if any of the three understood what it took to run a film studio, it was Katzenberg, who had skipped college to work for Paramount Pictures, rising through the executive ranks in meteoric fashion before following Eisner to Disney, where he became chairman of the studio in 1984 at age thirty-four. The job of supervising DreamWorks' film operations would fall on Katzenberg, along with the burden of proving that feature animation could be its greatest asset.

In mid-1999, just as *Prince of Egypt* was winding up its run in U.S. theaters after collecting a respectable $101 million, Katzenberg green-lit another mythical animated yarn. It was an old-fashioned, hand-drawn project called *Sinbad: Legend of the Seven Seas*, a version of a tale as timeless as the fables he had spun into animated blockbusters when he was chairman of Walt Disney Studios in the early 1990s. Those films, chief among them *Aladdin, The Lion King, The Little Mermaid* and *Beauty and the Beast*, revived that studio's once tattered animation division.

The story of Sinbad the sailor comes from *The Arabian Nights,* a book that has served for decades as a spicy trove of inspiration for Hollywood films. The silent era is awash in *Arabian Nights*–inspired exotica—tales of Bedouin bandits, harem girls and magic carpet rides, the most famous being Douglas Fairbanks's *The Thief of Bagdad* and Rudolf Valentino's *The Sheik.* Special effects pioneer Ray Harryhausen took up Sinbad's story three times—in *The Seventh Voyage of Sinbad, Golden Voyage of Sinbad* and *Sinbad and the Eye of the Tiger.* Douglas Fairbanks, Jr., wielded his scimitar in *Sinbad the Sailor;* Sebastian Cabot, Gene Kelly, Shemp Howard and Lou Ferrigno had each done turns as Sinbad. And Tim Matheson played Sinbad, Jr., in a 1965 TV series of the same name.

The idea was a throwback for DreamWorks, but one with a pedigree. Like *Prince of Egypt, Sinbad* was a vehicle for the studio to capture some of the glory of the first films ever called blockbusters. Multimillion-dollar ancient epics like *Quo Vadis?, Ben-Hur, Samson and Delilah, David and Bathsheba, The Ten Commandments, The Robe* and *Spartacus* helped usher America into a new era of spectacular big-screen entertainment in the 1950s. They were some of the most lavish productions of their day. They engendered a consciousness of production scale and budget and, therefore, a degree of interest in the financial consequences of their release—all key elements in the opening-weekend culture of today.

Hollywood called these films colossals, and almost everything about them was big. They were sagas packed with detail, featuring casts of thousands and sweeping sets. They were shot in supersaturated color in new wide-screen formats: Cinerama, Todd AO, CinemaScope, VistaVision, Panavision, Ultra Panavision, Super Panavision 70, SuperTechnirama 70. And they were long. *Quo Vadis?*, *The Ten Commandments* and *Ben-Hur* ran for three hours or more—not including the intermission and orchestral scores that often preceded and followed the show. Back in the 1950s, soaring production costs weren't a liability; they were a sales handle. In 1951, MGM and Loews published a full-color, multipage *Variety* insert trumpeting the $7 million budget of the Roman epic *Quo Vadis?* "So costly a production is indeed unheard of in the history of this industry," the ad proclaimed. It called *Quo Vadis?* "the Greatest Motion Picture of All Time." The Academy of Motion Picture Arts and Sciences agreed, showering *Quo Vadis?* with eight Oscar nominations in 1952, including one for best picture. Like *Ben-Hur* and *The Ten Commandments, Quo Vadis?* was an industry perennial; it was produced twice as a silent feature, in 1912 and 1924. Its scenes of gladiatorial combat, marching centurions, slave girls in shackles and burning temples gave rise to a profusion of publicity materials decorated with rococo scenes of Roman life, and the film proved ripe for exploitation by a society enamored of wide-screen exotica. There were *Quo Vadis?* window displays at Woolworth's and Kresge's department stores. The overstuffed press book for exhibitors was lined with licensing prospects like *Quo Vadis?* shirts, sweaters, hats, wallpaper, chocolates and haircuts. "There is positively no limit to the merchandising opportunity with this picture," the book declared. "It's truly a phenomenal space-getter!"

Before this era, the term blockbuster wasn't used to describe a hit movie. A blockbuster was an aerial bomb capable of destroying a city block. Blockbusting was real-estate parlance for inducing home owners to sell their property by exploiting racial fears that minorities would move into the neighborhood. *Variety,* never shy about new slang, appropriated the word for its 1951 review of *Quo Vadis?* declaring the film "a box office blockbuster."

But in one critical sense, *Quo Vadis?* and the other colossals were small events. They didn't open wide. They didn't play the whole country instantaneously but were rolled out slowly to first-run theaters in hubs like Los Angeles, New York, Kansas City and Chicago that charged the highest admissions. Many began life as roadshows—showcase features meant to resemble a stage performance, running for short stints in movie palaces with reserved seating, printed programs and stiff ticket prices—slowly generating interest from the national press as they rotated away from first-run houses to second- and third-run neighborhood theaters in the outer suburbs.

Katzenberg's *Sinbad* wouldn't have that luxury. It would be precision-designed, like any summer event film, for mass exploitation in a single wide release. It was a pattern Dream-Works had used before with the live-action sword-and-sandal adventure, *Gladiator*, the Russell Crowe saga that opened in early May 2000 and grossed $458 million worldwide on the way to an Oscar for best picture. Katzenberg hired *Gladi-ator* screenwriter John Logan to write the *Sinbad* script. Never mind that in *The Arabian Nights,* Sinbad is a sailor from Baghdad who sets sail from the port of Basra—a less than romantic geographic nexus following the U.S. invasion of Iraq in March 2003. The story would be a hodgepodge of mythologies. Like Hercules, or Jason in his quest for the Golden Fleece, the new Sinbad would battle a phalanx of fantastical monsters, woo a feisty maiden named Marina, and captain a wooden ship across the high seas. His quarry would be something called the Book of Peace, and his nemesis would be Eris, goddess of chaos, an ethereal seductress invented wholesale by DreamWorks.

"As a studious writer, I said, 'OK, I'm going to do Sinbad. I have to read the Sinbad stories!' assuming, naïvely, 'Well, there's going to be a Sinbad story—like there's a *Beowulf* or there's a *King Lear,*'" Logan recalled. "So I was like, 'Get me this Sinbad, will ya?' The DreamWorks people get me ten volumes and are like, 'Here's the *Arabian Nights* Sinbad, here's the Persian Sinbad, here's the Greek Sinbad and here's the Roman version of Sinbad, but he's not called Sinbad.' It was astounding because Sinbad is one of those Homeric figures like Ulysses that people have told stories or myths about—the 'wandering seafarer' through the ages. So, the process of developing the story was weeding through that material and trying to get to the essence of what makes that guy in that story interesting."

The film would blend such timeworn storytelling with slangy repartee and earthy humor—the same combination of old and new that had proved to be a highly saleable formula for many of the animated yarns Katzenberg oversaw at Disney. "There are three classic stories: Tarzan, Aladdin and Sinbad," Katzenberg says on the film's DVD. "And Sinbad had never been tackled in animation."

Sinbad had, in fact, been the subject of an animated feature film in 2000, produced on a smaller scale: Trimark's computer-animated *Sinbad: Beyond the Veil of Mists*, with a budget reported to be $20 million. The director was Joe Alves, who had directed *Jaws 3-D* and had worked as Spielberg's production designer on *Jaws*. It was one of the first cartoons to use motion-capture technology to record the minutiae of facial expressions and bodily movements. It, too, had a gallery of monsters, and featured the voice of a proven box office draw, Brendan Fraser. But *Sinbad: Beyond the Veil of Mists* never got a theatrical release. It went straight to video.

DreamWorks tackled the story with gusto, assembling an all-star cast of voices, with Brad Pitt in the principal role (replacing Russell Crowe, who was tied up shooting *Master & Commander*), and Catherine Zeta-Jones, Dennis Haysbert and Joseph Fiennes. Chosen as codirectors were Tim Johnson, who co-directed *Antz*, and Patrick Gilmore, tapped by Katzenberg for his work creating video games for DreamWorks Interactive. The pair set to work on the film, overseeing a team of animators that DreamWorks estimated at 550 but Johnson in interviews put at 750. The painstaking, hand-drawn animation process ran up a production budget of at least $60 million. But more than three years into the project, on November 29, 2002, the studio realized it might be sailing into a disastrous headwind. That's when the Walt Disney Co. opened *Treasure Planet*.

The animated update of Robert Louis Stevenson's classic novel incongruously transported its characters to outer space. Shortly after its release, *Treasure Planet* joined the ranks of Hollywood's most disastrous flops. It opened feebly in the middle of the high-stakes holiday season—a time frame in which Disney cartoons have traditionally excelled. The film took in a meager $12.1 million on opening weekend and grossed a total of $38.1 million over eleven weeks before disappearing from movie theaters—a staggering shortfall for a film with combined production and marketing costs close to $200 million.

Instead of concealing his losses, Disney chairman Michael Eisner subjected the studio's animation division to a public flogging. The studio announced a $74 million pretax writeoff on *Treasure Planet*, and on January 28, in a letter to shareholders, Eisner blamed a sharp drop in first-quarter income on the movie's performance. Disney animation division head Thomas Schumacher stepped down and the studio slashed hundreds of animation jobs.

That upheaval prompted an outburst of bad press for Disney, reviving allegations that the heyday of Disney animation was over, that the studio's homegrown, traditionally animated films were losing an internal battle against the cutting-edge, computer-crafted films from Pixar Animation Studios in Emeryville, California, the company responsible for Disney-distributed groundbreaking hits like *Monsters, Inc.* and *Toy Story*.

Katzenberg could appreciate the drama as well as anybody at Disney. For years, he had been Eisner's protégé at Disney and a student and champion of the studio's rich history in animation. At a 2003 tribute to veteran Disney animators Frank Thomas and Ollie Johnston, Katzenberg said that he reread their book, *The Illusion of Life: Disney Animation*, every year during his family's vacation in Hawaii. Katzenberg called it "the Bible." "No two people have taught me more about making animated movies," he said of the authors. The aura of the Magic Kingdom began to fade, however, when it became clear that Katzenberg was not in line to succeed Eisner as CEO. Katzenberg had rejuvenated its moribund animation division, which throughout the 1970s and 1980s had been churning out forgettable animated features like *The Great Mouse Detective, The Fox and The Hound,* and *The Black Cauldron.* He felt he deserved the promotion. Upon examining the numbers more closely, he also concluded that he'd been cheated out of bonuses during his tenure. In 1994 he filed a $300 million breach of contract suit against Eisner and Disney. The trial dragged on for years and captivated Hollywood. Its most riveting testimony came from Eisner, who was asked on the stand if he had said of Katzenberg, "I hate the little midget." Eisner ducked the question but lost the battle. The case was eventually settled for a reported $270 million.

The animation divisions of Disney and DreamWorks were bound to be competitive, but the circumstances of

Katzenberg's exit turned a professional rivalry into a grudge match. Two months before *Prince of Egypt* was released, the companies waged war, going head to head with rival, computer-animated insect comedies. DreamWorks subsidiary Pacific Data Images (then an independent supplier to the studio) had created an animated film called *Antz,* while Disney partner Pixar countered with *A Bug's Life.* Katzenberg was accused of stealing the pitch for *A Bug's Life,* a charge he denied. The press feasted on the allegation which DreamWorks vigorously denied. Though they were released a month apart, *A Bug's Life* squished *Antz* at the box office, $163 million to $91 million. The next animation outing for DreamWorks was even worse. On March 31, 2000, just five days after *American Beauty* (a project shepherded by Spielberg) won Oscars for best picture, best director and best actor, Katzenberg's animation crusade hit a low point. The big-budget hand-drawn adventure *The Road to El Dorado* fizzled at the box office, opening to $13 million and grossing just $51 million. The failure made for "a tough six or nine months," Katzenberg said. "I was sweating."

The perspiration abated in May 2001. With Disney animation headed for a disappointing summer thanks to the clunker *Atlantis: The Lost Empire,* DreamWorks released a pet project of Katzenberg's, *Shrek,* a film that flung invective at his former employers while rewriting the rules of feature animation. The creators of *Shrek* had grafted the jolly green ogre from a William Steig picture book onto a knowing satire of the last fifty years of Disney animation. The film pits Shrek against a fairy-tale despot, Lord Farquaad, who resembled a diminutive Eisner with a Prince Valiant haircut, and who has cruelly banished various Disney characters—the Three Little Pigs, the Seven Dwarfs, Pinocchio and Tinkerbell—from his ultrasanitized magic kingdom.

Shrek opened May 18, a radical move at a time when Disney held its splashiest animated features until June, when most kids were thought to be available because they were finally out of school. It opened to $42 million and became an instant classic, ultimately recording $480 million in theaters worldwide and selling 35 million DVDs. The film was rated PG, not G, which was then the custom for animated films. It featured television ads with live-action clips of its high-caliber cast: Mike Myers, Eddie Murphy and Cameron Diaz. *Shrek*'s enduring appeal was its cool factor, which extended from its cheeky digs at Disney and smart MTV-inflected soundtrack to the irreverent marketing campaign, which included things like green Baskin Robbins ice cream, green Shrek ketchup, Shrek Beauty Mud Mask Cream and signs in Wal-Mart promoting "Savings All Ogre the Store." Crucially for DreamWorks, *Shrek* was sequel material; exploratory work on *Shrek 2* became a major production upon the first film's release. Despite its successes, the company had not to that point come up with a renewable film franchise. It didn't have a library of comic book characters or horror movies to resurrect. One *Shrek* wasn't enough; it needed *Shrek 2*. To secure the cast, DreamWorks agreed to pay each of the three stars $10 million, an unheard-of sum for a couple days' recording-studio work done in street clothes.

With *Sinbad,* such coolness would be hard to come by. *Sinbad* was an old-fashioned boys' adventure. But as one DreamWorks insider notes, "Animation is defined by mothers and girls. The reason why boys went to see *Shrek* is that it was funny." It wouldn't be a stretch for Brad Pitt to play a lovable rogue, or in the words of *Sinbad* screenwriter John Logan, "the kind of guy you want to go on a road trip with." But this was a sanitized, *cartoon* version of the movie star— a chiseled seaman with billowing pants, a headband, sash and pointy boots.

At DreamWorks, losing left a lasting sting. As a "mini-major," DreamWorks could not rely on a hit sitcom, overseas cable channels or magazines to pick up the slack if its movies faltered. Along with MGM, it was one of Hollywood's last pure-play film entities. After a decade of building up fifty features in its library, the value of the company was about what it was when it started: roughly $3 billion. New credit lines and financing had been arranged. The company was undeniably a going concern. It was just that its founders— Jeffrey Katzenberg, Steven Spielberg and David Geffen— hadn't made a profit yet, nor had original investors like Microsoft cofounder Paul Allen. Many in Hollywood and on Wall Street assumed that a merger was the endgame for DreamWorks. But for now, it remained the ultimate boutique.

One thing was clear: DreamWorks marketing chief Terry Press was already beginning to feel the heat as July 2 approached. The producers of most films at DreamWorks work hard to get Press on their side. Katzenberg didn't have to. He was her boss. In January, *USA Today* reported

"DreamWorks' next blend of hand-drawn and digital techniques, *Sinbad: Legend of the Seven Seas* may feel uncomfortably similar to the pirate-populated *Treasure Planet*, though Katzenberg says, 'Our film is galaxies away from *Treasure Planet.*' Katzenberg isn't throwing in the pencil on traditional animation yet. . . . 'It's disingenuous to blame the technique for any failure. It's bad stories not told well. It's like saying a novelist had a bad book because it was typed on a laptop instead of written longhand.'"

Earlier in January, before the *USA Today* article, the first test screening of *Sinbad* was held at the Megaplex 17 at Jordan Commons. The suburban Salt Lake City location, often used to test-screen family films, was built by Mormon mogul Larry H. Miller, who owns car dealerships and the NBA's Utah Jazz. The theater attracts a large, all-ages crowd, which helped it set records for the highest opening-weekend gross for each of the first two *Harry Potter* films. *Sinbad,* according to those who were there, didn't cast the same spell. The story line left everyone cold. The movie's themes of loyalty between old friends and the romantic chemistry between Sinbad and Marina eluded younger audiences, especially the boys who would rather have watched Shrek pass gas. As changes were made, the film would be tested again and again to maddeningly indifferent feedback. One insider confesses: "I never learned a thing from any of the cards. No one ripped into it." There was a ray of hope, however. There was one character that test audiences perpetually wanted more of: Sinbad's slobbering canine sidekick, Spike.

Spike wasn't originally in the movie, noted producer

Mireille Soria. "He was added about halfway through. He started out as an Akita but he was too perky-looking."

DreamWorks wasn't the first studio to discover that animal antics sell. MGM would make Elle Woods's Chihuahua a fixture in the *Legally Blonde 2* marketing campaign; a trailer often attached to *Legally Blonde 2* in theaters was for *Good Boy*, an MGM comedy about a talking dog from outer space. Films like *Cats & Dogs, Snow Dogs* and *Kangaroo Jack* have benefited from the timeless appeal of anthropomorphized beasts. Why couldn't *Sinbad* do the same, with the right sales pitch?

Spike didn't speak but he was about to become the star of *Sinbad*. "Jeffrey Katzenberg decided Spike could be a good matchmaker," codirector Johnson recalled. "A lot of the shots of Spike were late additions." Entirely new scenes were ordered from the creative team. Sound technicians brought in a range of pooches to provide the snorts, growls and licks that would be Spike's nonverbal dialogue. The mantra of DreamWorks animation became, "We need more dog."

Birth of a Blockbuster

On the morning of August 3, 2002, director Jonathan Mostow met Arnold Schwarzenegger at Burbank Airport to fly to San Diego on a private Warner Brothers jet. The filming of *Terminator 3* had begun quietly three months earlier with footage shot by a small unit on location in the streets of L.A. By August 3, Mostow was in the home stretch of the one-hundred-day shoot, overseeing an army of actors, stuntmen, set builders, lighting and sound technicians. Filming spilled across several soundstages at L.A. Center Studios, a production facility spanning twenty industrial acres along the Harbor Freeway in downtown L.A. When Mostow arrived at the airport, he was famished. He had been shooting until midnight the previous night, and had skipped dinner and breakfast, hoping he might be able to grab a snack on the plane. "Studio jets usually have these fabulous buffet spreads," he recalled later. "There was fucking nothing on this thing."

The director and star were on a clandestine mission. They were traveling to the giant comic-book trade show Comic-Con, a mecca for blockbuster movie fans. Mostow's appearance at the convention was announced in advance, but Schwarzenegger was a surprise guest, a gambit certain to whip the Comic-Con crowd into a frenzy. Opening weekend was still eleven months off, but the *T3* marketing campaign was gathering momentum. Over July Fourth weekend, Warner Brothers had fired its first signal flare, branding its release date with a fifteen-second *T3* trailer. This teaser trailer, shipped to thousands of theaters with prints of *Men in Black II* and *Mr. Deeds*, was just a logo—a metallic, three-dimensional *T* and a *3*, with a date, July 2. *T3* was at this juncture the only film with a claim to the date. It appeared to have an unobstructed path to opening weekend.

Warners was focusing its early marketing firepower on wowing the hardcore *Terminator* fans: the sci-fi fanatics who collected *Terminator* action figures, comic books and trading cards, committed lines of dialogue to memory, and filled Internet chat rooms with speculation about the latest production stills and trailers. In May 2002, the first media interviews were held on the L.A. Center Studios set. Few major news outlets were invited. But Web correspondents for fan sites like Darkhorizons.com and Chud.com were there in force. The same Webzines also made the annual pilgrimage to Comic-Con, and they covered the event the way the mainstream media covered the Super Bowl. Within days, details of the convention and analyses of the trailers and footage screened by the studios, would be trumpeted across the Web. To these fans, Mostow was an untested commodity. Even an endorsement from the Terminator himself might not dispel the suspicion that Mostow couldn't fill the shoes of James Cameron, director of the first two *Terminators*.

Mostow and Schwarzenegger arrived late in San Diego, and a car was waiting on the tarmac to ferry them to a rear door of the hulking steel-and-glass Convention Center, perched like a postmodern cruise ship on the rim of the San Diego harbor. Darting through a subterranean hallway, the pair ascended a flight of steps and arrived at a forty-five hundred–seat ballroom on the second floor. It was packed with people. "There'd been no chance for anything," Mostow said. "Not to go to the bathroom, not to get a cup of water." Mostow had never faced so large an audience. He had never before shared the stage with Arnold Schwarzenegger. And he was so hungry that his hands were shaking. Mostow introduced himself, then told the crowd, "I brought my favorite robot, Mr. Arnold Schwarzenegger. It was like I'd announced, 'It's Moses.'"

For a moment, any doubts about *T3* vanished from the room. The crowd erupted into wild applause. "It goes without saying," a blogger named Berge Garabedian, presiding spirit of the fan site Joblo's Movie Emporium, later wrote, "that I would have gotten up on stage and given Mr. Mostow a hand job if Arnie had asked at that point." Schwarzenegger plied the crowd like a televangelist. "We know you're the biggest and best fans we have," he said. "Give Jonathan Mostow a big hand. He's fantastic!" The two screened footage from the film and fielded questions. The first question was for Mostow—a knee-buckling curveball: "You aren't the original director of the *Terminator* movies. Are you going to ruin this like they ruined *Batman*?"

It wasn't the first time Mostow would grapple with that question, and it would continue to haunt him until opening weekend. Eleven years earlier, *Terminator 2: Judgment Day* had rampaged through theaters around the globe, taking in $517 million in worldwide box office. It won four Oscars, was named best movie of the year by MTV, and entered the pantheon as one of the most beloved science fiction thrillers in a generation. In 1994 Universal Studios unveiled a *Terminator 3-D* ride in three of its theme parks. To the fans at Comic-Con, the franchise belonged to them, to Schwarzenegger and to James Cameron, who invented the character and directed the first two *Terminators*. It didn't belong to Mostow.

The character of the Terminator was last glimpsed melting slowly in a cauldron of liquid steel in 1992 in the penultimate moments of *T2*. A few years later, the franchise, too, appeared lost forever. The key personnel from the first two *Terminators* had dispersed. Some had severed ties for good; three of the producers had gone bankrupt. Cameron had virtually dropped off the map in 1998 after winning an Oscar for *Titanic*, the highest-grossing film of all time. Cameron's ex-wife, Gale Anne Hurd, who produced the first two *Terminators*, was an executive producer of *T3* but she was busy producing *Hulk* for Universal. Hurd wasn't on speaking terms with most of the *T3* producers and hadn't set foot on the set. Schwarzenegger's *T2* costar, Edward Furlong, was gone, replaced by a little known actor named Nick Stahl, who was just twenty-two years old when he began shooting the film. The copyright history was long and contentious. The *Terminator* was like some cursed artifact that brought untold riches and untold frustration to anyone who fell under its spell, and it now belonged to a shadowy network of international financiers. There were thirteen producers on *T3*. Most had nothing to do with the two previous *Terminators*. Who were these interlopers, and what claim could they stake to one of the great sci-fi sagas of all time?

The story of the Terminator begins in 1980, when Schwarzenegger was still a bodybuilder and struggling actor, and when Hurd first met Cameron at New World Pictures, exploitation movie king Roger Corman's low-budget film studio. Cameron was a college dropout who began working for Corman as a model builder and production designer in 1980. Hurd, who graduated Phi Beta Kappa from Stanford, was hired as Corman's assistant in 1978, and soon took over his publicity and marketing department, where she designed campaigns for movies like *The Brood* and *Rock 'n' Roll High School*. Marketing held a special place at New World. Corman's advertising materials were like circus sideshow promotions ("They're Here . . . Hungry For Flesh!" barked the posters for New World's 1978 *Jaws* knockoff, *Piranha*), and they were often created well in advance of principal photography. The major studios would eventually follow Corman's example, developing films out of marketing concepts. By the time *T3* began production, Warner Brothers had already outlined its marketing plans, down to the timing of the trailers.

Cameron and Hurd's first collaboration was 1980's *Battle Beyond the Stars,* a campy, $2 million sci-fi romp described by Corman as "*The Seven Samurai* in outer space." Two years later, Corman hired Cameron to direct *Piranha II: The Spawning.* Cameron was kicked off the film, but later said that he dreamed up the idea for *The Terminator* while he was in Rome, suffering from a bad case of the flu, hanging around the *Piranha II* postproduction office in the hopes he might be rehired.

A paranoid thriller about a robot assassin from the future, *The Terminator* might have been right at home on the shelf at New World. According to Corman, Cameron later said all he did on *The Terminator* was "take everything we did on *Battle* and just do it bigger." *The Terminator* had a bigger budget, roughly $6.5 million. But it had other virtues—a gutsy female protagonist, real emotional resonance, and a clever conceit perfectly suited to a new era of special-effects-driven blockbuster sequels: In the future, machines and computers would run amok, igniting a nuclear holocaust and eradicating the human race—all except for a small band of resistance fighters led by a man named John Connor. Most of the action in *The Terminator* would take place in the present day, before John Connor was born. A single killing machine would be sent from the future to terminate his mother; a single man would be sent from the future to protect her. A star-crossed romance would bloom between the man from the future and his protégé. Cameron sold his concept and all underlying rights to Hurd for a dollar, on the condition that he would direct it.

Several studios passed on the project. Hurd finally set the project up at Hemdale Films and Orion, both independent entities, which commissioned Cameron to shoot *The Terminator* on a B-movie budget. He improvised wildly to pick up shots wherever he could. Some scenes called for animatronic robots built by the prop artist Stan Winston; others were created using tinfoil and spray paint. Most of *The Terminator* was filmed in unfashionable sections of downtown Los Angeles, a gritty world far removed from the trappings of the movie industry. Linda Hamilton played Sarah Connor, a waitress who is chased by the Terminator through the slums and industrial outskirts of the city. The producers considered casting O. J. Simpson as the Terminator, but Cameron settled on Schwarzenegger. With his shaved eyebrows, bodybuilder's physique and emotionless gaze, the actor was an unstoppable monster, a human bulldozer.

Released in late October, *The Terminator* was a critical and box office smash. It generated $39 million in ticket sales and became a popular rental item in the burgeoning home-video market. *The Terminator* put Schwarzenegger on the road to international superstardom; the eponymous cyborg would become his signature role. It also put Cameron's career on the fast track, leading to screenwriting assignments for *Rambo: First Blood Part II* and *Aliens,* which he also directed. But as their careers vaulted to new heights, the Terminator was mired in legal problems. Hemdale and Orion went bankrupt. Fifty percent of the franchise still belonged to Hurd, but she divorced Cameron after five years of marriage in 1989.

Enter Mario Kassar, a Beirut-born producer, and co-founder with Andy Vajna of Carolco Films, the company behind *Rambo* and the Schwarzenegger vehicle *Total Recall.* Kassar was eighteen years old when he began his career in the film business as an international sales agent. He recalls thumbing his way around Europe as a teenager and falling asleep on the beach of the Hotel Martinez, the grandiose edifice on the Cannes waterfront that would later be a base of operations for him. "I always had this fantasy about Cannes," he recalls. "I had nothing in my pocket. Just a backpack. I was looking at the hotel and thought, 'What a great hotel. Maybe one day I can sleep in it.' And of course, the French cops came and woke me up and threw me off the beach."

Kassar and Vajna met on the beach at Cannes in the mid-1970s and formed Carolco Pictures in 1976. Vajna was a Hungarian entrepreneur who came to Hollywood from Hong Kong, where in the 1960s he ran a wig manufacturing business, mass-producing hair pieces for Revlon and Pierre Cardin, and a jeans company selling prefaded jeans. Vajna sold the jeans business and bought two movie theaters in Hong Kong, then opened a foreign sales outfit called Panasian Films and produced his first film, *Opium Trail.*

The first Vajna and Kassar coproduction was *First Blood,* the 1982 Rambo prequel starring Sylvester Stallone. It was an auspicious start, and it formed the cornerstone of a library of franchises that two decades later would be some of the most valuable in Hollywood. The duo produced *Rambo* and *Basic Instinct.* Carolco acquired stakes in *SpiderMan* and *X-Men* from Marvel Comics. They began plotting *Basic In-*

stinct 2. The Cannes Film Festival became a second home. In the 1980s, Kassar cut a dashing figure on the French Riviera. He rented one-hundred-foot yachts and in 1990 threw one of the most lavish parties in the history of the festival. He chartered a 737 and flew more than fifty of his friends from Hollywood—including Schwarzenegger, James Cameron, Adrian Lyne and Renny Harlin—to the airport in Nice. A phalanx of black Mercedes waited on the tarmac to whisk them to the soiree at the ultra-swank Hotel du Cap. The Gypsy Kings performed and a fireworks display lit up the sky with the names of talent from forthcoming Carolco films.

Vajna left Carolco in 1989, cashing out shares worth close to $100 million, to form his own production company, Cinergi. But Kassar kept investing in new projects, and in 1990 he saw a window of opportunity in the Hemdale bankruptcy. He paid $5 million for the 50 percent share of *Terminator* sequel rights that belonged to Hemdale; Hurd, who still owned half the franchise, sold him the rights to *T2* for another $5 million, while preserving her own stake in subsequent sequels. Kassar lured Schwarzenegger and Cameron back and put *Terminator 2: Judgment Day* into production at a new studio, Columbia/Tristar. Schwarzenegger didn't receive any upfront cash. In lieu of a salary, the producers bought him the ultimate status symbol, a $12 million Gulfstream III jet.

Kassar and Vajna were showmen who understood that Hollywood was built on such flamboyant acts of munificence. In some respects, these were men in the tradition of Hollywood's first immigrant pioneers, garmentiers with

European accents who earned their fortunes from vaude-ville houses, music halls and nickelodeons, and plowed their profits into the fledgling dream factory. But Vajna and Kassar weren't empire builders. They were shrewd op-portunists. They tried but failed to build an empire in Carolco Pictures. The company would ultimately declare bankruptcy in 1996 following a long IRS audit.

Hollywood insiders had long suspected that Carolco played by its own rules. When a senior Carolco executive, Jose Menendez, and his wife were shot at close range at their Beverly Hills home in 1989, it was widely suspected to be a mob hit (Menendez's two sons, Lyle and Erik, were later convicted of the murders and are serving life sentences). Carolco also funneled millions of dollars through offshore tax havens before the IRS clamped down. Today, Carolco is remembered as much for its hits as for its lavish spending on talent and com-pany overhead, chartered planes and hundred-foot yachts, and for its deft manipulation of international tax loopholes.

When *T2* was released on July 2, 1991, few imagined that Carolco would soon be bankrupt. With a budget north of $100 million, it was the most expensive film ever. But it was also one of the biggest hits of the year, and the digital crafts-manship by George Lucas's effects company, Industrial Light and Magic, was so revolutionary it created a new genre of special effects: morphing. Cameron had given his old concept a new twist. *T2* was set in 1994, ten years after the first installment. This time Schwarzenegger played a good Terminator, sent back in time to protect John Connor from a malevolent, more advanced model—a shape-shifting Terminator made out of liquid metal. The protean Terminator did things nobody had seen before onscreen, morphing seamlessly from a shiny metal object to a fully clothed human being, emerging fluidly from the checkerboard tiles of a hospital floor. The marketing campaign carefully concealed whether Schwarzenegger's character was good or evil. Opening weekend brought a furious outburst of merchandise and media hoopla. There was a *T2* novelization, toys, comic-book spin-offs, leather jackets and other apparel. There was a Terminator convention at the Los Angeles Stouffer Concourse Hotel. A Guns 'N' Roses song on the soundtrack shot to the top of the charts.

But for Kassar, the celebration didn't last. After *T2*, Carolco turned out a series of costly flops: *Cutthroat Island, Universal Soldier, Chaplin* and *Showgirls*. The IRS, which had already begun investigating Carolco in the early 1990s, tightened the screws. In 1996, a federal grand jury indicted Carolco's former president, Peter Hoffman, for tax evasion. Hoffman was never convicted, but in 1998, pled guilty to a misdemeanor charge of filing a false tax return. Carolco filed for bankruptcy in 1996 and its assets, including its 50 percent stake in the *Terminator* sequel rights (the other half still belonged to Hurd), were put on the block. In 2002, Kassar agreed to pay the IRS $45 million to settle tax disputes dating back to 1998.

Today, in the conference room of Kassar's office, there are photographs of the producer in headier times, dancing gaily at a party twenty years ago and standing at the Hotel du Cap, his hands raised triumphantly, flanked by Arnold Schwarzenegger and Sylvester Stallone. But the Carolco debacle has clearly taken its toll. "The last years of Carolco were really hard on me," Kassar said. "It was like a dark tunnel. I used to smoke and drink, I didn't give a shit about anything. I was excessive, enjoying life. Then I said, fuck it, I have to get my head in place. I became a health freak, started jogging and lost weight."

As Carolco cratered, Schwarzenegger's career also began to deteriorate. He collaborated with Cameron in 1994 on another big hit, *True Lies,* then appeared in a succession of action vehicles with shrinking box office returns: $233 million (*Eraser*), $209 million (*End of Days*), $116 million (*The Sixth Day*), $83 million (*Collateral Damage*). He said on several occasions that he would return to his trademark role as the Terminator only if James Cameron would direct him. "Even if *Terminator 3* is the best script ever, no! I'm only interested if James Cameron directs it and if Linda Hamilton is in it," he declared at one film junket. But as other projects floundered, *T3* gradually became more attractive.

Though Cameron now says he was never interested in directing *Terminator 3,* his intentions weren't so clear in the fall of 1997. When Carolco's *T3* rights were put up for auction, Cameron was dubbing the soundtrack of *Titanic* at George Lucas's SkyWalker Ranch in Marin County, California. The delays and cost overruns of *Titanic* had already generated a fierce media firestorm, locking Cameron in a tense standoff with Twentieth Century Fox, which had an exclusive contract with Cameron including an option on his next film. *Variety* began publishing a regular update about the film on its front page, the Titanic Watch, with a drawing of a sinking ship. The two *Terminator* films were arguably Cameron's crowning achievements. The Terminator was his creation, but he didn't own it and he couldn't control it.

Into the breach came Kassar and Vajna. After Carolco capsized the pair quietly began planning to bring the Terminator back to life. The two vacationed together in Cannes and decided to open a new production company, a Carolco sequel which they called C-2. The first order of business would be to rescue from the Carolco bankruptcy the copyright to Kassar's greatest triumph. "I lost *Spider-Man* and *X-Men*, I lost *Total Recall* and *Rambo*," Kassar said. "These were all my titles, that I developed. Now there's only fifty percent left of something I'm not going to lose no matter what. It's called *Terminator*."

The *Terminator* auction occurred on October 15, 1997, at U.S. bankruptcy court in downtown Los Angeles. Gale Anne Hurd was in the courtroom. She still owned 50 percent of the franchise, and she hoped to prevent Vajna and Kassar from obtaining the other half. Hurd still hoped to partner with Cameron to develop a new *Terminator* through his production deal at Fox, but she knew Cameron wouldn't work for another producer. "Jim had committed to *T3*," Hurd said. "But he wasn't going to work for someone else. He didn't have to." Another suitor was Bob Weinstein, co-chairman of Miramax, who had quietly raided the Carolco library, buying the sequel rights to *Rambo* and *Total Recall*. Weinstein bid $8 million for the *Terminator* rights. C-2 matched the bid and won the auction. With C-2 in possession of half the copyright, Hurd could have held onto her share and blocked the movie forever; instead, she sold it to them for $7 million in return for an executive producer credit on *T3*.

But what exactly had C-2 purchased?

C-2 had no commitment from Cameron or Schwarzenegger. There was no script. Vajna and Kassar had tried but failed to secure an early financing and distribution deal from the studios. "They thought we were idiots for buying the rights," Vajna said. Immediately after the bankruptcy auction, Vajna and Kassar called Cameron. "We said, 'We're coming with a silver plate to you, we'd love you to be involved,'" Kassar recalls saying. According to Vajna, Cameron curtly rejected the notion. "You stole my baby," he told them. Mostow is fond of saying that the Terminator's leather jacket and sunglasses made the character the most recognizable screen icon ever. That was probably true in the early 1990s, when the Terminator was parodied in movies like *Hot Shots! Part Deux*, *Wayne's World* and Schwarzenegger's own ill-fated blockbuster spoof, *The Last Action Hero*. By the late 1990s, however, the *Terminator* brand was getting rusty, and so was Schwarzenegger.

Still, Vajna and Kassar forged ahead. They began developing scripts for *T3* and *T4*. With typical swagger, they told *Daily Variety* they hoped to produce the two films in one fell swoop, in the vein of *The Lord of the Rings* trilogy, which was shot over several months of continuous filming. And Vajna and Kassar began to sell territories overseas, recouping most of their original $15 million investment from the Tokyo studio Toho-Towa, in exchange for distribution rights in Japan.

In 2000 C-2 signed a first-look deal with Intermedia, an international sales and film financing company founded by two British expatriates, Guy East and Nigel Sinclair. Intermedia had recently merged with Pacifica Film Development, a production and financing company run by a German producer named Moritz Borman. The merger was a complex shell game that gave Intermedia access to German tax fund money and brought the company under the control of a new Munich-based holding company. Listed on Germany's booming Neuer Markt stock exchange, Intermedia was transformed, virtually overnight, into a financial powerhouse with a market capitalization of one billion U.S. dollars, and it was anxious to parlay those funds into box office hits.

Some of Intermedia's films eked out a profit; many didn't. The company would eventually lose tens of millions financing the doomed Russian submarine action film, *K-19: The Widowmaker*. Intermedia wasn't certain it wanted to produce *T3* when it signed its cofinancing deal with C-2. Borman didn't remember much about the first two *Terminator*s and had to rent them from a video store before making a commitment. The company commissioned a consumer survey to determine whether the general public would pay to see a *Terminator* film without its pricey superstar, Arnold Schwarzenegger. The response was overwhelmingly negative. The first C-2 and Intermedia coproduction was to be *Basic Instinct 2*. But that film fell apart, stepping up the pressure on Intermedia to generate another instant blockbuster. "We had announced that *Basic Instinct 2* was our big movie," Sinclair said. "It leaked in Germany and the share price had gone up because of it. We were very exposed on this project." To make matters worse, the Neuer Markt collapsed, and the international film and television market that had once been Intermedia's lifeblood began to dry up. The partners consolidated operations. East and Sinclair left to become independent producers, leaving Borman in charge of a company with fewer than one hundred employees in L.A. and Munich.

Intermedia nevertheless gave Vajna and Kassar new leverage. Vajna and Kassar distrusted studio executives and were distrusted by them. "We don't work well in a studio environment," Vajna said at the Cannes Film Festival eight weeks before *T3* was released. "Studios are great distributors. But they're like elephants. They're slow to move and slow to react." C-2 had brought the film to the brink of production without studio money, through sheer willpower and an up-front, personal gamble of $15 million. The studios refused to take the same up-front risk on *T3*. Therein lay the film's greatest financial potential for its producers. If they, not the studios, controlled the financing of the film, they could dictate how much they got paid, what territories they controlled, what ancillary revenue they retained. They would keep the merchandise rights, a lucrative sideline usually controlled by the studio's consumer products division, inking deals with more than thirty licensees in the United States alone; they would retain a big share of the TV spin-off and home video rights; and they would own the rights to all subsequent sequels.

C-2 and Intermedia perceived that the time was right for an independently financed production of such scale. In 2000, the year in which C-2 and Intermedia signed their co-production deal, Hollywood's appetite for sequels was steadily growing. The call for presold titles, in the forms of franchises and remakes, was echoing from the studio ranks to the corporate offices of their globe-straddling parent companies. These companies—Disney, Sony, AOL Time Warner, Vivendi Universal and News Corp.—drew only a small percentage of their profits from the box office performance of movies, but relied on film entertainment to supply a stream of product for their international subsidiaries. These corporations feared the volatility of the movie business, and they began to see the ancillary revenues of sequels and franchises as panacea for the industry's problems. They wanted content for their home video arms, TV channels, consumer products divisions, theme parks and video games. It was a system that thrived on the sort of formula thrillers that Carolco churned out in its heyday and that two decades earlier were the mainstays of Roger Corman's low-budget film factory. But it produced them on a huge scale, with movie stars and state-of-the-art digital effects, and launched them into the market with tens of millions of marketing dollars.

But even as the studios thirsted for sequels, they found them increasingly hard to pay for. Vivendi Universal was

$19 billion in debt, following an acquisitions spree by its big-dreaming CEO Jean-Marie Messier. Network TV advertising was in a slump, as was attendance at theme parks like Disneyland and Universal Studios. After the dot-com bubble burst, AOL Time Warner began bleeding red ink. Its film slate was committed to other expensive blockbusters, like *Harry Potter* and the *Matrix* sequels. Studios like Warner Brothers, Universal and Disney were determined to build their release schedules around a handful of big-budget sequels, but they were under sharp pressure to share the risk with outside financiers.

C-2 and Intermedia capitalized on this weakness. They developed a *T3* script by a writer named Tedi Sarafian. The script had an intriguing gimmick: the Terminator would return from the future as John Connor's protector to battle a new, souped-up Terminator. The new Terminator would be a female Terminator called the T-X. The producers dangled the script in front of Arnold, offering him $30 million—the biggest upfront salary ever paid to an actor—to return to the franchise. He took the offer. Intermedia and C-2 flirted with a handful of directors—among them Ridley Scott and Ang Lee—before reaching a deal with Mostow, whose two previous films were genre thrillers *Breakdown* and *U-571*. *T3* was a great opportunity for Mostow, but it came with enormous risk. "It was like being asked to direct *E.T. 2*," Sinclair said. Mostow was undaunted. He hired two friends from Harvard, John Brancato and Michael Ferris, to rewrite Tedi Sarafian's script, and eight months later, in November 2001,

Intermedia and C-2 auctioned the Schwarzenegger/Mostow package to studios.

The auction was a typical feat of showmanship for a pair of industry mavericks who liked to see their company logo spelled out in fireworks at a party on the French Riviera and who once bought a Gulfstream III for their leading man. "They wanted to make sure the occasion was dressed up to feel very special," one of *T3*'s producers said. "Although it was all very respectful, it was like one of those jewelry shops where you have to make an appointment and the door is locked and there's a guy with a gun who lets you in, and by definition you know you're not going to spend less than twenty-five thousand dollars there." In this case, the men with the guns were Ken Ziffrin and Skip Brittenham, two of Hollywood's most formidable attorneys, who engineered the auction. C-2 and Intermedia's terms were faxed to every studio, but the script remained under wraps. Vajna's office booked suites at the Four Seasons in Beverly Hills and two other hotels. Only a handful of executives were invited to each location to read the script. The suitors included Jeffrey Katzenberg at DreamWorks, Jonathan Dolgen and Sherry Lansing at Paramount, Rick Finkelstein at Universal, Amy Pascal at Sony, Bob Weinstein at Dimension and Alan Horn and Lorenzo di Bonaventura at Warner Brothers.

Several studios bid on *T3*. Warners offered $50 million against 50 percent of the gross for domestic theatrical and home-video rights. As part of the studio's pitch, Warner's president of domestic marketing, Dawn Taubin, outlined her strategy for the film. A *T3* trailer would be attached to *The Matrix Reloaded,* which was scheduled to open in May of the same year. Warners promised the film would be released on July Fourth weekend, a date which had been a bonanza for *T2.*

Warners' contribution to the production budget would later go up to $55 million. Sony would take international rights for $75 million. These funds would go into a pot to cover production expenses. But C-2 and Intermedia weren't just interested in the size of the advance. They were also attracted to the possibility that Warners could harness its TV and cable empire, and its online sibling, AOL, to transmit the franchise directly into the circulatory system of the nation. Working months in advance of opening weekend, Taubin would marshal enormous resources to shape those campaigns. Overseeing a staff of more than a hundred people, Taubin engineered the widest possible interest in Warners' lead titles, stamping advance word of their release into every nook and cranny of the culture.

Taubin engineered these campaigns from an office building in Burbank. Armed with sheaves of market research, she met with the filmmakers and actors, and decided where to aim the studio's marketing resources. But she didn't go to Comic-Con, and she wouldn't see firsthand the resistance Mostow faced from the fans who thought it was audacious for him to step into Jim Cameron's shoes.

For Mostow, the pressure to succeed was enormous and it came from all sides. "You come to a party where everybody involved in it is reinventing themselves," Sinclair said.

"Intermedia desperately needs the movie. Andy and Mario desperately need the movie. This was a critical opportunity for Arnold. And here is the guy who has become the solution to all of their problems. On him rests everything." But the pressure from the fans was perhaps most daunting. Asked at Comic-Con if he was going to ruin the franchise, Mostow was defensive—and who could blame him? "I said, 'Next July, why don't you pay eight bucks and you tell me,'" Mostow recalled. There was an awkward silence. "I'll answer that serious question with a serious answer," he went on. "I'm making the movie that, as a fan of the franchise, I'd like to see as the third installment." The fans at Comic-Con cheered, but they still weren't entirely convinced.

Casino Royale

MGM had cloned Elle Woods. Two Elle look-alikes wore Jackie O–style pink Chanel suits with three-quarter sleeves, pink pillbox hat and pink high-heel pumps—the same costume Reese Witherspoon wore on the poster for *Legally Blonde 2*. The simulation, occurring in the capital of simulation, Las Vegas, was choreographed to entice movie theater proprietors at the annual convention for exhibitors and studios known as ShoWest. The Elles were picked from photos e-mailed to MGM from a few local modeling agencies that service the thriving Vegas convention scene. A rival studio executive said, "It's just like casting a film. You've got all their headshots in the computer and you talk about how each one is going to make your movie look."

MGM had rented space for this promotion at ShoWest's two-hour publicity bazaar called the Exhibitor Relations Schmooze-a-Rama at the Paris Las Vegas hotel. As hun-

dreds of conventioneers milled about, chewing stale sand-
wiches from a sprawling buffet, the ersatz Elles loitered at a
Legally Blonde 2 kiosk hung with curtains in different
shades of pink and draped with white-and-gold bunting.
They took turns fussing like flight attendants over conven-
tion-goers who snapped their pictures with disposable
cameras supplied by MGM. The studio gave away *Legally
Blonde 2* tote bags and nail polish made by hip beauty-
product purveyor OPI, and raffled off a trip for two to the
L.A. premiere.

All around the Paris Ballroom, studios had erected
shrines to their coming attractions. There was a wedding
cake and a faux bride and groom for *American Wedding*; a
tiki-themed beach display for a horror comedy called *Club
Dread*; and kegs of beer for the prurient comedy *Boat Trip*.
"It's a real beer crowd," Artisan distribution chief Steve
Rothenberg enthused. DreamWorks had devised a kitschy
infomercial set to promote *Envy*, a Ben Stiller–Jack Black
comedy directed by Barry Levinson. In tones of yellow-
green and electric blue, the display centered on the product
that Black's character invents in the film, a solution called
Vapoorizer that makes dog waste disappear. The previous
year, the DreamWorks kiosk had featured a life-sized horse
statue for the company's animated film *Spirit*. In 2003 the
only evidence of *Sinbad* was a coffee mug given out in a
goodie bag that also contained trinkets like an *Anger Management* teddy bear and a *Pirates of the Caribbean* T-shirt.
The goodie bag also held the only sign of *T3* at ShoWest: a
baseball cap embroidered with the *T3* logo. The film's pro-

ducers, long suspicious of Warner Brothers marketing loyalties, would not have been pleased to see the studio's elaborate booth for *The Matrix Reloaded,* where the film's seductive Super Bowl commercial played on plasma screens mounted on silver poles.

Other films suffered from too much hype. There was no way to tell at ShoWest, but *Club Dread* and *Envy* were troubled productions, and both sat on the shelf for another year before being released. The booths of the Schmooze-a-Rama offer a faint echo of the showmanship days when studios and theaters would have to work hand in hand in order to make a movie a hit. But they're also a visible manifestation of the sharply increased power of studio marketing departments in a day when the balance of power has shifted dramatically toward the studios—not surprising given the hundreds of millions of dollars they pour into the production and marketing of their major summer films. Exhibitors have become little more than the keepers of infrastructure and capacity, controlling little beyond seating, ticket prices and concessions. They are a key component in the scale and immediacy of opening weekend, but they no longer engineer the hits.

The deepening rift between the studios and the movie theaters is carefully papered over at ShoWest. To promote their product, studios host rubber-chicken banquets centered on screenings of trailer reels, or sometimes entire films, surround sound thundering from ten-foot speaker towers. Movie stars are flown to Vegas to spend a few minutes onstage at the convention, thanking exhibitors for supporting their movies, reminding the assembled masses that they're on the same team. But beneath the staged camaraderie and the ballrooms of hype, the relationship between the studios and exhibitors is fraught with tension.

Film distribution is an arcane, Hatfield-McCoy enterprise whose idiosyncratic rules and horse trading are not particularly easy for outsiders to comprehend. Studios control the product, but they often suspect that exhibitors are short-changing them. In the drive-in era, Universal used to hire helicopters to fly over theaters and count the cars to ensure exhibitors reported sales properly. Today, studios hire data-tracking firms like TNS Media Intelligence. Its clipboard-toting employees loiter in lobbies and in the back row of theaters to gauge reaction to trailers, to make sure the right trailers play with the right features, and to keep tabs on whether theater managers are letting patrons sneak into shows they haven't paid to see.

Films are rented to theaters for a sliding percentage of the box office gross. The longer a film plays in theaters, the higher percentage of the gross the house gets to keep, minus a figure called the "house nut," which covers operating expenses such as utility bills and staff wages. But studios and movie theaters negotiate new terms for every title. It's an arrangement that creates profound distrust on both sides. Studios have an incentive to open wide, then ditch a title after a couple of weeks, while theaters are looking for a flat trajectory—a film with legs like *My Big Fat Greek Wedding*, which premiered at ShoWest before opening on a handful of screens in April and playing for almost a year, ending with a domestic gross of $241 million.

ShoWest did not acquire its name until several years after its inception. The first ShoWest took place in San Diego in February 1975, the year of *Jaws*, when the western branch of the National Association of Theater Owners decided to hold a joint meeting with the National Association of Concessionaires. The studios didn't pay much mind and attendance totaled only about two hundred. Major topics of discussion were rising popcorn and soda prices and the relative profitability of ten-ounce cups versus twenty-four-ounce cups. Few records of the event exist. Universal took out a full-page ad in *Variety* timed to run during the convention touting the success of the Peter Benchley novel and promising the film would be released "June 20—everywhere" amid "the biggest national TV spot campaign in industry history!"

At the time, there were sixteen thousand movie screens in the United States. Show-a-Rama, another industry gathering in March whose programs overlapped with ShoWest's, was held in Kansas City from 1958 to 1983. By 2003, there were thirty-five thousand screens, and more than ten thousand people in attendance at ShoWest. In those transformative years since 1975, the business of its attendees—the booking of films into theaters—had evolved from a highly personalized transaction to the impersonal agenda item of a handful of multinational media conglomerates. These conglomerates control 90 percent of box office revenues and a handful of theater chains own 90 percent of the top-grossing U.S. screens.

Disconnected though it is from the single-screen movie palace days, the exhibition culture is still a cauldron of grudges and longstanding antagonism. Many circuits have been run by the same families for three generations. Many distribution executives have worked on both sides of the distribution-exhibition fence, a reality that informs the atmosphere any time they get together. In booming, cured-beef baritones, they announce who's just fucked them on film rental terms and precisely whom they have fucked in return. For years, studios and theaters were fiercely protective of box office data. Marcie Polier, who founded Centralized Grosses, a box office tracking service that became Nielsen EDI, remembers working as a twenty-three-year-old "gross girl" in the L.A. headquarters of Mann Theatres in the mid-1970s. "In that world, nobody speaks," says Polier. "They yell." The Mann office, she says, "was like the floor of the New York Stock Exchange. You would get the number on the phone, then write it up in pencil, total the figures on an adding machine, type them up and Xerox them. People would be yelling, 'Don't give them the grosses!' And then people on the other end of the line are telling their girls, 'You get that fuckin' gross!' Girls would end up in tears."

The fragmented, regional nature of the theater business has for years fostered a good ol' boy culture that persists today. The golf course, which is also where deals are sometimes done and films booked, is a frat-boy forum where carousing is often encouraged. In 2001 Regal Cinemas hosted a golf outing at a public course in Las Vegas that featured kegs of beer and strippers, according to two participants. Each December, exhibitors and distributors gather for a ritual turkey and deer hunt.

David Tuckerman, head of distribution for New Line Cinema, does not hunt or play golf, and he rolls his eyes when talk turns to the trade conventions. Still, he is usually there. Standing in the lobby of the World Center Marriott for a recent edition of ShowEast, the counterpart to ShoWest held every October in Orlando, Florida, wearing a black polo shirt to match his dark-tinted, rectangular-framed sunglasses, he mused, "This is all just a big dance. Everyone complains about it but everybody has to be here. The people you do business with have to see you moving."

Tuckerman's parents and grandparents showed pictures at their New Jersey–based theater circuit that began in the 1920s. It was eventually sold to Music Makers Theatres, which in turn was sold to Loews, the national New York–based chain where Tuckerman spent several years before coming to New Line. Tuckerman is a direct link to the bare-knuckled culture of the old theater circuits. A native of Perth Amboy, New Jersey, he resembles Jerry Garcia, had Jerry Garcia gone into sales instead of music. He wears a pinky ring, and his shaggy, mostly gray beard frames a square, resolute face. Tuckerman's new 7-series BMW has a vanity plate that reads "Tuck." The koi swimming in his Hollywood Hills pond are all named after New Line colleagues.

Having worked both sides of film booking, Tuckerman knows when he has to go to the mat. One such occasion came in 2001, when New Line had gone from being a "review terms" distributor to being "firm terms." That basically meant that they would join several studios in the practice of agreeing with theaters up front on how the gross would be divided, as opposed to settling after the film had completed its run, as some companies still do. Believing that New Line was not as robust as its rivals in terms of product pipeline, Regal Cinemas balked at the firm terms proposed for *Rush Hour 2.* Tuckerman could not make an exception and Regal, not having seen the film, held its ground. The film opened to $67.4 million—without showing on a single one of Regal's 4,067 screens at the time. Not only had the exhibitor sorely underestimated the drawing power of that Chris Tucker–Jackie Chan sequel, but it also had no inkling of the New Line juggernaut coming four months later: *The Lord of the Rings: Fellowship of the Ring.* As that film's December release approached, Regal knew it could not afford to miss out again. It assented to New Line's firm terms.

By his desk at New Line's Beverly Hills headquarters, next to a Golem statue and sundry *Lord of the Rings* figurines, Tuckerman keeps a waist-high wheel that looks like a miniature version of the Wheel of Fortune, inscribed with months, dates and dollar grosses. Tuckerman uses it to razz anxious filmmakers who want to know how distribution arrives at a proper date. "This one producer came in and asked and we said, 'Well, we usually cut the head off a chicken and let it run around and wherever it drops, we just read the entrails.' She ran right out of here."

Tuckerman also keeps a wall-sized magnetic board in his office, with small magnets representing every film being released over the next six months. Often, several magnets are clustered on the same dates, some of them targeting the exact same audience. Tuckerman's job is to know where to make New Line's magnets stick.

For movie marketers, ShoWest isn't a sales event; it's an elaborate dress rehearsal for the summer, staged in the heart of America's blinking, neon bastion of hype. A few weeks before ShoWest 2003, one high-ranking Universal executive dismissed the event as "a total wank." But the studio was there in force, a battery of executives arriving on the Universal jet to screen a product reel, attend a lunch for *Hulk* sponsored by Pepsi Cola, and to support their star producer, Brian Grazer, who was presented with the ShoWest lifetime achievement award. The same Universal executive who dismissed the whole exercise eagerly asked journalists on the last day of ShoWest, "So, what did you think of our *Hulk* trailer?"

In 1999 Fox screened a trailer for the summer's most anticipated film, *Star Wars, Episode I—The Phantom Menace*, using digital projectors—a novelty at the time. Footage of *The Lord of the Rings* was first shown here, during a lunch of burgers and fries. The final creative effort of Stanley Kubrick's life was cutting a thirty-second ShoWest teaser trailer for *Eyes Wide Shut*. *Godzilla*'s outsized marketing campaign roared to life in Las Vegas with a trailer screening punctuated by a room-shaking sound system and loud explosions. In the 1990s studios took to jetting their biggest stars to the convention for grand banquets that cost upward of $1 million. And the stars, realizing that growing media coverage of ShoWest along with the attention of theater owners could make a difference at the box office, were glad to comply. One of the awards displayed in Arnold Schwarzenegger's Santa Monica office is a plastic trophy from 1993 naming him ShoWest International Star of the Decade. "Studios value the kind of instant feedback on upcoming product that only showing it to thousands of people who have a major stake in a film's success or failure can provide," film critic Kenneth Turan has observed.

Every studio sends a contingent to ShoWest, but the majority of conventioneers come from the lower echelons of the exhibition business—mom-and-pop circuits like Coming Attractions from Ashland, Oregon, whose film rentals comprise less than one percent of the box office. So although ShoWest is in many respects a media event, it is one skewed to the sensibilities of small-time exhibitors—a resolutely PG group whose taste tends toward family features and schmaltz. Not all films screened fit that description. In 1996 Universal Pictures brought a rough cut of *Casino* to ShoEast. As director Martin Scorsese looked on, scores of viewers streamed out of the theater in disgust after enduring scenes destined for the cutting-room floor. One lingering shot showed a head in a vise, being squeezed until its eyeballs popped out. The *Hollywood Reporter* ran a front-page story on the negative reaction of exhibitors, and Universal protested by withholding films from ShowEast for two years.

ShoWest brings these radically different film industry cultures together for four uneasy days of business meetings, technology demonstrations, cocktail parties and panel discussions, all squeezed into a $760 million, eighty-five-thousand-square-foot resort-casino, a model of the French capital with an ersatz Louvre and Opera House, and a fifty-story replica of the Eiffel Tower. It's hard to imagine a more fitting environment. Paris Las Vegas is a pulsating, glassed-in playground with a bewildering array of retail and recreational activities, all of it an exaggeration of the megamalls and "destination centers" where movies open wide. Beyond the tintinnabulation of its nearly two thousand slot machines there's a cobblestone-paved shopping district with Parisian street signs, cafés, brasseries and a French bakery. Inside the guest rooms, a television channel is devoted to an endless, *Entertainment Tonight*–sponsored reel of movie trailers and smash-cut star profiles. Paris Las Vegas is open twenty-four hours a day, seven days a week, and the house line, 888-BON-JOUR, never stops ringing.

The myriad casino distractions had considerably less pull on conventioneers on the night of March 4, when *Finding Nemo* received its first industry screening. The film was the first summer release created by Pixar Animation Studios and distributed by the Walt Disney Company. The relationship had already produced billions of dollars in revenue from two *Toy Story* films, *A Bug's Life* and *Monsters, Inc.* At the mouth of the Théatre Des Arts, snarling mischievously from behind a velvet rope, was a life-size, blue fiberglass replica of Bruce, a shark who stars in the film as the leader of a twelve-step recovery program for undersea predators. His name was an inside reference to the mechanical shark Steven Spielberg used in *Jaws,* named after his attorney, Bruce Ramer. In the coming months, the fiberglass shark—known to the trade as a theater standee, reproduced and shipped at a cost of nearly $10,000 apiece—would appear in hundreds of multiplex lobbies around the country, heralding the arrival of the film on May 30. *Finding Nemo* would become the biggest hit of the summer, grossing $330 million in North American theaters. That tally eclipsed the $313 million recorded by Disney's *The Lion King,* Jeffrey Katzenberg's magnum opus and previously the top-grossing animated film of all time. Bruce's benevolent scowl would be plastered across billboards, buses and McDonald's Happy Meals. Bruce would be licensed to manufacturers of plush dolls and inflatable pool toys. Random House would publish a *Finding Nemo* picture book with Bruce on the cover, his pointy nose rising from the ocean floor, mouth agape—a sly tribute to the famous jacket for *Jaws,* the best-seller that has sold twenty million copies since it was first published in 1974.

Spielberg wouldn't be tickled by *Nemo*'s splashy debut. DreamWorks was preparing its own big-budget computer-animated undersea saga, *Shark Tale,* for release in the fall of 2004. *Finding Nemo* threatened to steal its thunder. Dream-

Works marketing chief Terry Press, a former Disney marketing executive who had come to DreamWorks with Katzenberg, sat discreetly in the back of the theater on a surreptitious fact-finding mission. ShoWest, like the Super Bowl, affords studio marketers a rare chance to assess whether or not the competition has the goods. Normally, they are so focused on their own campaigns that they don't catch rival films until they reach DVD.

With her pixie-ish haircut and boxy pin-stripe suits, Press resembles one of the pre-Code screen heroines she might have written about in the program notes she compiled as a film programmer in the 1980s for the Los Angeles County Museum of Art. Her brassy style is well suited to an autonomous company like DreamWorks and vice versa. Since jumping into the void with Katzenberg in 1995, she has been DreamWorks' chief spokesperson. Unlike most of her peers, however, her purview encompassed a remarkable array of company activities. In some respects, she functioned as DreamWorks' fourth principal. She accompanied the three founders to everything from videogame development meetings to visits to the Clinton White House. She set release dates and even acquired material for production. Recently, seated at a benefit luncheon next to Vicki Iovine, author of the "Girlfriends' Guide" books, she pitched Iovine on the idea of a movie based on the popular series. Admirers and detractors alike tend to agree with Katzenberg, who once said Press possesses "an unerring instinct for how to put movies into the world."

Long before hitting her stride at DreamWorks with live-action movies like *American Beauty, Saving Private Ryan* and *Gladiator,* Press made her reputation on animation while at Disney. One of her achievements was helping secure a best-picture Oscar nomination for *Beauty and the Beast,* the first such honor for an animated film. Watching Disney pump *Nemo* at ShoWest with a brand of razzle-dazzle she knew all too well, Press could not have helped but roll her eyes. The screening began with an effusive display of corporate cheerleading. The curtains parted to reveal a live orchestra and a line of leggy chorines in crimson sequins and feathery headgear billed as the Fabulous Disney Dancers. Out came mustachioed nightclub crooner Robert Goulet, dressed in a tuxedo with a crimson bow-tie. Goulet belted out "You've Got a Friend in Me," Randy Newman's song from *Toy Story,* another Pixar hit. He formed a kick line with the Disney Dancers, and a loud cannon shot resounded from the stage. The audience flinched, a shower of multi-colored fish-shaped confetti descended from the ceiling, and Disney's motion picture chairman, Dick Cook, Press's former boss at Disney, sauntered onstage, locking arms with two dancers. Pixar financier Steve Jobs and founder John Lasseter then took turns schmoozing the assembled exhibitors. Jobs, dressed in faded blue jeans and New Balance sneakers, told the audience Pixar planned to increase its pace of production, creating a new film every year. Lasseter, a portly man who wore a dark, baggy suit over a banana yellow Hawaiian shirt, talked about the "fine art of eating snack food." His favorite theater concession, he said, was root beer sucked through a stalk of red-vine licorice.

When Disney screened *Finding Nemo* in Las Vegas, the studio was in the midst of renegotiating its distribution deal with Pixar. Disney was eager to demonstrate to Pixar that it could squeeze the greatest profits from its rental deals with exhibitors. The *Finding Nemo* stage show sent a powerful message to the audience: it suggested that the Pixar-Disney partnership was strong, with more hits on the horizon. As 2004 began, those future hits appeared to be headed to another studio after Pixar and Disney broke off negotiations to extend their deal. But with no way to predict that back in March 2003, small theater owners who wanted more Pixar movies from Disney would have to capitulate to tough terms on *Finding Nemo*—a rental agreement guaranteeing them just 40 percent of the gross, compared to an industry average of 45 percent, despite the fact that *Finding Nemo* had legs. "They took it in the shorts," said New Line's David Tuckerman.

Cook's career was built on this kind of brinksmanship. He'd been at Disney for decades (as a teenager, he sold Monorail tickets at Disneyland), and the majority of that career was spent in distribution. Cook understood the changing culture of exhibition. When promoter-producers of an earlier era, like Joseph E. Levine, William Castle or Mike Todd, wanted to get theater circuits' attention and motivate the media, they threw lavish dinners and staged stunts in the lobbies of movie theaters. Studios in the megaplex era flew to Las Vegas.

Engineering a hit involves a considerable measure of secrecy, and an event like ShoWest, with its profusion of industry panels, is littered with traps for marketing executives who resent being asked to disclose their methods. Those participating in *Variety*'s March 5 ShoWest panel on the state of film promotion were all practiced in the art and science of opening weekend, but the harsh spotlight made them feel like little more than performing bears. Panelists on the stage at the Théâtre des Arts, the same spot occupied by Disney Dancers and fish-shaped confetti the night before, included DreamWorks' Terry Press and Warner Brothers' Dawn Taubin. MGM marketing chief, Peter Adee was enjoying being a spectator after having been a panelist the year before. "You always say something silly and get quoted saying it," he told us with a dismissive wave of the hand.

What seemed an innocuous discussion was in fact a high-stakes contest, bearing a sharp resemblance to the World Series of Poker played across town at Binion's Horseshoe. Marketing executives know the strength of their own hand, often long before the media or the industry at large has a clue, but they don't quite know exactly how good anyone else's cards are. The game can be nerve-wracking, especially when it comes to summer movies. Playing it in front of an audience is dicier yet. Everyone is trapped in the same casino, and everyone is obligated to ante up.

Press had no choice but to bluff. She had witnessed test screenings of *Sinbad* and knew that she did not have *Shrek, Gladiator, Saving Private Ryan* or another one of the high-caliber event films she had expertly guided into megaplexes in previous summers. Instead of merely going quietly, she created distractions. She asked moderator Charlie Koones, publisher of *Variety*, if the panel was on the record. He confirmed that it was. From that point, she seemed ready to find any excuse to leave the stage. She charmed the crowd—though not her fellow panelists—with her vampish, Bette Davis–like badinage. She complained that the Golden Globe Awards had grown too powerful. Asked by Koones if anything kept her up at night, she cited the rising cost of *Variety*'s ads during awards season. At one point, when Koones good-naturedly asked why she was fidgeting, she announced that she was late for her plane back to Los Angeles.

Press was not abashed about needling her competitors in a public forum. When Dawn Taubin detailed the complexities of marketing *The Matrix Reloaded*, a film that many predicted would own the summer, Press leapt at the bait. It is tricky, Taubin explained, to account for merchandising partners, sky-high expectations and the inherent challenge of releasing two installments of a megabudget franchise within six months (*The Matrix Revolutions* was due out in November).

"If I had a *Matrix* I would sleep like a baby," Press interjected. "I wouldn't be up past nine-thirty any night." The audience laughed. Taubin maintained a genial front, but the comment had clearly taken her off guard. Koones tried to get things back on track. "Well you have a big animated picture coming this summer," he prompted Press.

There was a pause.

"Yeah, we have an animated movie," Press said. "It's really, really unique and really, really, really delightful."

Koones asked Press if she was concerned about the cluttered summer marketplace.

She replied, "No, because it's family product and people are always desperate to find something to take their kids to see. I'm more worried about selling a combination 2-D/3-D movie than I am about when we're going to release it."

The conversation moved to another topic.

As the mother of five-year-old twins and a veteran of the animation business, Press understood the constant demand for family entertainment. She also knew the function of ShoWest. This was her third consecutive appearance there to promote an animated film. The first two seemed far more bankable and played to her strength. In 2001 she screened *Shrek* to favorable notice and orchestrated a gutsy promotion in which hotel maids entered the rooms of those out attending the screening and left a Shrek cookie next to the bathroom sink. In 2002 she accompanied Katzenberg and pop star Bryan Adams to Vegas to promote *Spirit*. Adams and composer Hans Zimmer performed their music from *Spirit* as clips of the film played in the fashionable Palms casino nightspot Ghostbar, whose vertigo-inducing balcony looks out on the street fifty-five floors below. That year Press had been comfortable with the cards she was dealt: a hand-drawn story of a wild horse on the nineteenth-century prairie with measurably strong appeal to girls and their mothers.

By contrast, sitting in the spotlight and fielding direct questions about the fortunes of *Sinbad* seemed nightmarish. There was still plenty of time for her to, in Katzenberg's phrase, put *Sinbad* into the world. But she was still struggling to figure it out. Explaining that process in public was anathema, sending Press into another unhappy reenactment of *The Wizard of Oz*. The public was tugging at the curtain, but she was desperate to keep the great and powerful wizard hidden from view.

Marketing executives may complain about feeling marooned at ShoWest, but that sentiment applies to just about any visitor from Hollywood. The evening of March 5 brought a screening of Revolution Studios' Adam Sandler–Jack Nicholson comedy *Anger Management*, and an after-party with throbbing dance music and an open bar. But the high-rollers backing the movie betrayed a strong desire to be anywhere else but at their own party. "I could go back to my normal life anytime," confessed Jeff Blake, the Sony Pictures vice chairman overseeing *Anger Management*, mopping sweat from his brow.

Several executives decamped to the bar and restaurant at Mandalay Bay. Taubin was there. Terry Curtin, a former Warner colleague of Taubin's who is now head of marketing and distribution for Revolution, arrived by limo with Geoff Ammer, her former Disney colleague who now heads marketing for Sony Pictures. En route, they relived some of the freewheeling 1990s days of million-dollar publicity events like the *Armageddon* premiere at Cape Canaveral that featured a performance by Aerosmith. Joe Roth, who founded Revolution, played roulette at the Paris casino with a retinue of Revolution executives including his partner, Tom Sherak, who served lengthy stints at both General Cinemas and Twentieth Century Fox. Tom's son, William Sherak, a producer with a deal at Revolution, was with his dad. Steve Elzer, head publicist for Sony Pictures, wore a wildly colored shirt with a Vegas theme of cards, dice and roulettes. Sandler, the star of the show, was hiding out at Charlie Palmer Steak at the Four Seasons. Nursing a serious cold, Sandler did an un-Vegas thing and turned in before midnight.

Other stars' appearances at ShoWest lasted no longer than a dose of NyQuil. They popped in to show support for the films they made and the studios that backed them. And some came to collect awards. Amid the deluge of awards in the early part of the year, ShoWest's involve the least intrigue. They are arranged long in advance, strictly on the basis of which star has a movie to plug, either an Oscar contender or an upcoming release. The free hit of publicity is well worth the trip. In 2003 Catherine Zeta-Jones collected the Supporting Actress of the Year trophy. Christopher Walken was named Supporting Actor of the Year. The banter ranges from the sarcastic to the sincere. Presenting Sandler with the Male Star of the Year prize, Kevin Nealon pointed out that Sandler had made "a lot of unwatchable crap." Diane Lane was crowned Female Star of the Year. "This is the first time I've won anything in Vegas," she quipped before choking up in her acceptance speech.

In the free-spending boom times of the 1990s, far bigger stars showed up in far bigger numbers. In 1996 Tom Hanks, Meg Ryan, Warren Beatty, Sigourney Weaver, Winona Ryder, Sandra Bullock, Morgan Freeman and Keanu Reeves all materialized at the same luncheon hosted by Twentieth Century Fox. When a nine-minute segment of *Independence Day* was screened that day, the film's writer and producer, Dean Devlin, wanted to hear the reaction of the exhibitors. So he abandoned the green room and crawled under a table toward a side of the room that would afford a good vantage point. Lifting up the tablecloth, he felt a tap on his shoulder. It was George Lucas. "Nice effects," he told Devlin.

Schwarzenegger also joined the festivities in 1996. In a profile of the star for *Cigar Aficionado*, reporter David Shaw of the *Los Angeles Times* described a whirlwind trip to and from ShoWest on the star's Gulfstream III, the same one he had received as compensation for acting in *Terminator 2*. Busy filming *Eraser* for Warner Brothers, Schwarzenegger left the set to stump for *Jingle All the Way*, a holiday release from Fox. He had his moment onstage and paused for a few photo ops. After the lunch concluded with an indoor fireworks display and the four thousand guests started to disperse, Schwarzenegger made the trip from stage to limo in a minute and sixteen seconds. The jet took off promptly, bound for Los Angeles. Schwarzenegger was back on the L.A. set of *Eraser* just three hours after he had left.

For exhibitors and studio executives without a jet ticket out of town, one annual ShoWest ritual not to be overlooked was the state of the industry address by Jack Valenti, the president of the Motion Picture Association of America, who was eighty-three at the time of ShoWest. On March 4, Valenti arrived at the convention to deliver his annual "state of the industry" address. He would hand down the official tally of box office revenue collected in the previous year and tell the assembled theater owners what a bargain movies are when compared with other forms of popular entertainment. None of this information was unknown to anyone in the crowd, but the media would report it as news since Valenti had made an annual custom of delivering it.

Dressed like an undertaker in a dark suit and black tie, the diminutive lobbyist offered a stark contrast to the Vegas frivolity. Valenti was appointed to head the MPAA in 1966 after stepping down as an aide to President Johnson. In 2003 he was nearing retirement, and he appeared fixated on the goal of almost single-handedly elevating the discourse of his profession. A few months earlier, Valenti had published a column in *Variety* urging people in Hollywood to set aside their scripts over the Christmas holiday to read books by the men whom he deemed the greatest writers of English prose—Lord Macaulay, Edward Gibbon, Winston Churchill, William Prescott, Francis Parkman and H. G. Wells. The title of Valenti's ShoWest address would have been more suitable for a seminar paper presented at a literary conference on the Transcendentalists: "Emerson's Doctrine: The Very Good, the Not-so-Good, the Brooding Menace, and the Wonder and the Beauty of Human Behavior."

Standing onstage next to John Fithian, the phlegmatic head of the National Association of Theater Owners, Valenti reported that the average cost of making and marketing a studio movie approached $90 million in 2002, a 14 percent surge from the prior year and the biggest jump since 1997. Production budgets were sharply rising, he said. The average negative cost of a film produced by one of the seven studios that belonged to the MPAA was $58.8 million in 2002. In 2001 it had been $47.7 million. Ten years earlier, it had been $38.1 million. Valenti described marketing costs as "that lumbering grizzly prowling the outer edges of the movie forest." (In 2003, the grizzly pounced, as marketing costs rocketed 28 percent.)

Since Valenti's statistics came from the studios, there was no way of independently verifying them. What was beyond dispute was the total box office tally, which passed $9 billion for the first time in 2002, as the number of ticket sales increased 10 percent, the best improvement since 1957. Valenti offered three reasons for the admissions boom: "a good many of the movies," he opined, "were first-class stories, compellingly told, with superior acting, writing and directing"; and ticket prices, he said, were fair and reasonable. But Valenti reserved his highest praise for "the state-of-the-art theaters with flawless digital sound, dazzling luminance on the screen." Valenti applauded exhibitors for the "hospitable way you allow customers to sit in Olympian comfort in stadium seats which have allowed me never again to have to stretch my neck as I bob and weave to see the screen."

Valenti was right. The theatrical experience was changing rapidly, and there was no better gauge of these changes than the trade show floor, one of ShoWest's most bizarre spectacles-within-the-spectacle. Held in the bowels of Bally's, the bargain-rate hotel connected to Paris by a shopping corridor, the trade show is a venue for vendors proffering everything from theater seats to projection systems to cleaning services. Most people come for the concession samples, filling goodie bags with gummy worms and nacho cheese cups. Here can be found a selection of high-concept snacks that haven't yet gained favor with the big theater circuits. One treat that drew a crowd was the Burger Pipe, which was made to taste like a hamburger though it was shaped like a hot dog—a perfectly space-efficient meat tube for theaters accustomed to heating dogs on rotating metallic cylinders. In case that sounds a little too heavy, don't worry. A Chicken Pipe was also available.

Elsewhere, vendors touted *Hulk* Sour Gummis and pina-colada-flavored *Hulk* cotton candy, sweet 'n' sour popcorn, sun-dried tomato cream cheese and a flash-frozen ice cream treat called Dippin' Dots. Arrayed across the rest of the fluorescent-lit expanse was a dizzying array of movie theater marginalia and fast-food novelties. There were perhaps a dozen manufacturers hawking the newest and latest seats, and dozens more selling projectors, marquees and automated ticket-takers. There were competing solutions to make theatre floors less sticky. And there was a garish, calliope-like contraption made for lobby entertainment by the Ragtime Company. Encased in an upright oak-paneled cabinet, the machine stood about six feet tall, four feet wide and two feet deep. It resembled a dining room buffet stuffed with musical instruments instead of fine china. Behind its glass window were robotic arms that systematically plucked a guitar, banjo and bass, blending those sounds with a flute, bells, accordion and piano to simulate a ragtime band. Cymbals and snare drums kept a computer-guided tempo. It was an elaborate variation on the player-piano—a throwback to a honky-tonk era before multiplex theaters, when movie houses weren't homogenized recreation centers with interchangeable lobbies.

Ken Caulkins, a wild-eyed man from Ceres, California,

has owned the Ragtime Company for thirty-one years. He quickly mentioned that Peter Jackson owns several of the machines, pointing to a photo of the *Lord of the Rings* maestro in his brochure as evidence.

At almost $40,000 a pop, Caulkins needed only to move one unit to call his trip to ShoWest a success. Offering a demonstration, he touched a computer screen to select one of the more than twenty thousand songs stored on the machine's hard drive. Out came the theme to *The Price is Right*.

A neighboring proprietor approached with a grimace. "Excuse me, would it be too much to ask you to turn that down?" Caulkins refused. He defiantly punched in another code to activate a new track: Britney Spears's "Oops, I Did It Again."

"This is really for creative people, like Peter Jackson," he said, casting a sidelong glance at the retreating interloper. "All creative people like it. Anyone who doesn't is a stick in the mud."

In the distance, the slot machines ceaselessly chimed.

Frankenstein Lives

E lle Woods may not be known to pick fights, but this time she took dead aim at the Terminator. In a close-up shot, she playfully taunted: "I'll be back!" Instead of a sawed-off shotgun or laser cannon, her weapons were a chic handbag and heels.

That pink wink at *Terminator 3* was to be the centerpiece of a television commercial for *Legally Blonde 2* that would air in the waning days of the $40 million television assault leading up to the movie's opening. The television campaign was assembled in the spring of 2003 in the stylish Hollywood warren known as Aspect Ratio, one of the top trailer houses in a hotly competitive cottage industry. The TV spots were just one of several stages of the film's marketing campaign crafted at Aspect. Producer Marc Platt and director Charles Herman-Wurmfeld had met with MGM executives here back in October 2002 to hammer out a thirty-second teaser trailer to go with MGM's latest James Bond adventure, *Die*

Another Day. Then members of the MGM marketing team reconvened in the spring to assemble a full-length trailer.

The packagers of Elle Woods still had two months to perfect their pitch before the big weekend, but already they were getting useful feedback. A profile was emerging from the test screening data. They were starting to get a sense of what the movie was and what it was not. "This is the national anthem for teenage girls!" Peter Adee often exulted as work progressed. Now, MGM finally had quantitative evidence to prove Adee's assessment. "The younger girls loved it," Adee said of the Taylor Research focus group. "As you got older, it became more of a 'Hmmm. What else you got?' That made us really hone the trailer a lot. That helped us to take out all the politics and focus even more on Reese. I'm talking about the facets of her personality that you responded to the first time. All the Washington inside jokes— 'phhht.'" Packaging a sequel was a balancing act, Adee said. "They wanted to relive the first movie. You can't do that with a sequel. You want to be reminiscent of the first movie but you have to be new and improved."

Having determined at the production test in Aliso Viejo that the beginning of the film was unworkable, MGM had commissioned a reshoot. The principal flaw with the beginning, according to the focus group after the screening, was that it made the film's overall pacing "average," which is death for a light comedy like *Legally Blonde 2.* Two scenes would be substituted for the Sally Field opening. In the first, Paulette the hairdresser and Elle's friends Serena and Margo would flip through a scrapbook that would recap some elements of the first movie and set up the plot of the second. A successive scene would be a surprise party thrown for Elle by her friends.

Knowing he was about to lose his star for any advance publicity and marketing efforts once filming on *Vanity Fair* began in London on May 23, Adee asked Witherspoon to deliver the "I'll be back" line expressly for the TV ad in the course of the reshoots. It was something MGM wanted to have in its back pocket for later in the campaign, something to enliven the blue-and-pink cavalcade should it start feeling tired.

The TV ad campaign would not start in earnest until June. A more immediate and consequential hurdle was creating a trailer that would speak directly to the film's core audience. As crucial as television ads have become, a well-executed trailer arguably has greater impact. The Internet abounds with trailer sites like JoBlo.com, Coming Soon.net and Yahoo! Movies, places where a trailer is not only available for downloading in perpetuity but where enthusiasts can deliver their opinions of it in chatrooms and stoke advance buzz—pro and con. In theaters, trailers are two and a half minutes of unfettered access to a captive audience, a far cry from ads confronting the passivity, fickleness and daunting scale of television audiences. Trailers cannot be preempted by war in Iraq. When Adee was at Universal, he saw trailers put the studio on a remarkable hot streak as one blockbuster lit the fuse for the next. "You can get enormous penetration and talk to your audience all summer long," he said. Trailers have come full circle since their origins at the end of films (thus the name "trailer"), a practice believed to have started with the 1913 serial *The Adventures of Kathlyn.* Each installment ended with a title card bearing an enticement such as "See Next Week's Episode: The Pit of Death!" Pioneering editor of the modern trailer Jack Atlas has said, "They were supposed to get people bored enough to leave the theater to make room for someone else."

Strategically, trailers and features are more deeply interrelated than many moviegoers realize. "Attachments" are an integral part of the marketing and distribution process. A studio will generally attach a trailer of one of its own upcoming features to one of its current features, meaning the lab will physically attach the trailer when the feature print is struck. That does not guarantee that every theater will play it—plenty of exhibitors cut off the attachment in favor of their own mix of trailers—but it does make it onto the screen 90 percent of the time, according to studio surveys. It also occupies the most desirable real estate in the trailer reel—the last thing run before the feature.

There is also a method of providing trailers called "in the can," which means a separate trailer reel, about the size of a hockey puck, is included along with the feature reels. An exhibitor then has the option of playing the trailer or not—usually, that decision stems from the quality of his relationship with the distributor. A third and even more unusual tactic is known as "chasing the print," in which a random, stray trailer is shipped directly to the theater in the faint hope that it will make its way on screen.

Since the mid-1990s, when cofinancing deals between studios became widespread, more and more trailers have been going in the can, but they get played only about 60 percent of the time. The jockeying for position on the trailer reel attached to a major title can begin up to a year in advance. As the opening-weekend contest has come to a boil, especially in the summer, studios and filmmakers have taken extreme measures to secure placement. Sony publicly admitted to paying theaters to play certain trailers, a practice that many say is widespread. Phil Anschutz produces movies as well as presiding over Regal Entertainment Group, the nation's largest theater chain. For months in advance of the April 18, 2003, opening of his movie *Holes,* Regal encouraged its theater managers to give the film's trailer ample screen time, say several employees of Regal-owned Edwards Theatres. The move certainly did not hurt—the modestly budgeted film opened to $16.3 million and grossed $67.4 million in the U.S.

George Lucas and Steve Jobs, acting CEO of Pixar, flouted the conventions of the trailer business in 2001. Without consulting the studios distributing their films, they reached a deal whereby a 60-second trailer for *Star Wars, Episode II—Attack of the Clones* would be attached to Disney's release of Pixar's *Monsters, Inc.* Fox, the long-time distributor of Lucas's *Star Wars* films, had a Farrelly Bros. comedy, *Shallow Hal,* opening a week after *Monsters.* Fox execs privately groused that they could have benefited from having the *Star Wars* trailer debut in front of *Shallow Hal,* which had a lackluster opening gross of $22.5 million.

The studio remembered the watershed moment in modern trailers that occurred with *Star Wars, Episode I—The Phantom Menace,* whose teaser trailer screened for the first time before Universal's *Meet Joe Black,* the notorious Brad Pitt turkey. *Joe Black*'s $15 million opening weekend would have been even more feeble had *Star Wars* fans not bought tickets and crowded into theaters to watch the trailer, only to walk out en masse once that minute of film was over.

MGM targeted Warner Brothers' April 4 teen-girl release *What a Girl Wants,* according to Adee, for the debut of the *Legally Blonde 2* trailer. It would also attach the trailer to two of MGM's spring titles: *Bulletproof Monk,* opening April 16, and *It Runs in the Family,* opening April 28. The former, a male-oriented martial-arts action movie, and the latter, an adult drama starring three generations of Douglases (Kirk, Michael and Cameron) and Kirk Douglas's ex-wife, Diana Douglas, were far from ideal platforms for the makeover capers of Elle Woods. Except for the cost of making the trailer, however, it would be free advertising, but Adee would not be playing the game of power dominoes he did in 2001 when Universal's summer began with *The Mummy Returns,* which begat *The Fast and the Furious,* which begat *Jurassic Park III,* and so on. He would have to sell Elle Woods on the front of a martial-arts shoot-'em-up and a geriatric drama.

To help studios cope with the pressure-filled process of cutting an effective trailer on a deadline, an array of trailer houses blossomed in the late 1970s and early 1980s. Many were founded by ex-studio admen. Aspect Ratio, the linchpin of a cluster of entertainment advertising companies owned by Aspect Holdings, marked its twenty-fifth anniversary in the summer of 2003. Comedy was its original forte. It cut the campaigns for films like *Porky's* and *Bachelor Party*. More recently, it has worked on titles as diverse as *Vanilla Sky* and *Spider-Man*. Aspect took the lead on *Legally Blonde 2*, but by no means was it the only vendor. There is always an elite cluster of postproduction companies jockeying for every piece of Hollywood business, places with names like The Ant Farm, Craig Murray Productions, Trailer Park, Seismic, Giaronomo and Cimarron. The *T3* trailers were cut by Mojo and Interlink. In some cases, as with the misbegotten 2003 action sequel *Lara Croft: Tomb Raider: The Cradle of Life*, several firms' work is stitched together to make one trailer in a tactic called "Frankensteining." The same project is often given to several houses at once, who compete in "bake-offs" to see whose approach will be embraced by the studio. It is not unlike the process of doctoring a screenplay, which often results in a conga line of writers endlessly covering each other's tracks. *Charlie's Angels* famously burned through seventeen writers. Don Roos, who rewrote *Legally Blonde 2*, was one of at least four writers known to have done a draft. "You have no idea if what you're reading is one writer's opinion, or if it's a committee," he said. "I was never able to tell whose work I was actually working on. I had no idea how much of what they had contributed was in the script."

The sand-colored, industrial exterior of the Aspect office complex on Homewood Avenue, tucked between a historic Los Angeles firehouse and a fifteen-screen multiplex, belies the frenzy within. A faded Champion Sparkplugs billboard has been left atop one of the buildings—a clue to the ethos of the place. Trailer specialists can be considered the car mechanics of Hollywood, flushing out the hoses, lubricating the pistons and making the feature purr. Over the last several years, the mechanics have gone from waving from the garage as the car drives off to being on call in the pits at the Daytona 500, ready to make any necessary adjustments before or during the race. "The stakes became so high," Aspect CEO Mark Trugman said, twirling a business card in one hand. "They used to ask for four trailers. Now they ask for forty." As filmmaking itself has evolved, turning ad agency refugees like Ridley Scott and music video auteurs like McG into filmmakers, the aesthetics of the medium have changed. And trailer houses, in their work with studio marketers and NRG, are constantly striving toward a more finely honed pitch aimed at a highly specific demographic. Roughly $1 million is shelled out on a typical trailer effort, though the cost can rise far higher in extreme cases. Equipped with razor-thin laptops and state-of-the-art theater systems, trailer house employees are engaged in a relentless process of evaluation. Sitting in the Aspect lobby, you can hear the constant rumbling of sub-woofers, the squealing of tires. Then silence. Then the same sequence of noises again. "Trailer editor is a bit of a misnomer," Trugman said. "What we've done is train a generation of highly skilled movie industry advertising specialists. When I compete on a movie like *Tomb Raider*, I want to obliterate the competition. If they're going to finish eight TV spots, I want to do six of them." In a quest to sex up the trailer for the 2003 Angelina Jolie sequel, *Lara Croft: Tomb Raider 2: The Cradle of Life*, Paramount used elements from seven vendors in an especially desperate Frankenstein maneuver.

Directors usually have little to do with the process. David Sameth, head of creative advertising at DreamWorks, likes to tell the story of first-time director Sam Mendes excitedly insisting on editing the first trailer for *American Beauty*. What he came up with was a true representation of the film that was unplayable in any theater—Kevin Spacey smoking pot and lusting after a teenaged blonde, Thora Birch shown exposing her breasts. Mindful of MPAA rules and the principles of enticing consumers, trailer cutters often emphasize elements that are not particularly key to the film. Sometimes, scenes appearing in the trailer are cut out of the film altogether. The trailer for *Snow Dogs* was full of talking dogs, even though that footage came from one short dream sequence in the film. Disney marketing president Oren Aviv spoke for many when he told *The New York Times*: "In a trailer, you want two or three great moments. When a film has ten great moments, you're lucky."

The struggle to find those key moments hit home for Cameron Crowe with the trailer process of *Almost Famous*, a widely admired DreamWorks release he wrote and directed that flopped in the autumn of 2000.

"A lot of people took very passionate shots at how to sell it," he recalled. "We settled on one trailer that was pretty nice." A year later, Crowe was sent copies of trailers that film school students had crafted for *Almost Famous,* entries in a contest administered by the *Hollywood Reporter.* He popped the winner into his office VCR and sat there stunned. "I made the movie, and I wanted to go see the movie. It was perfect," Crowe said. "I saw this trailer and it was like, 'That marlin of a trailer was out there.' That's the thing that I'll always carry with me. From now on if there isn't an idea that strikes you to your very core, use every waking hour to try to find it, because I believe that trailer would have opened the movie."

Elle Woods snapped her compact shut and cried out, "Excuse me!" The trailer editor rolled back to the beginning of the sequence again, scrutinizing every element, looking to create the perfect rhythm. This was to be the first beat of version ten of a trailer known internally as "America's Favorite." There would be at least two dozen more versions to come, differentiated only by an extra word of dialogue, the lift of an eyebrow, a cutaway shot of Bruiser the Chihuahua. There would also be several completely different trailers and dozens of versions of each of these. One called "Look Good" would open with a shot of the scales of justice and a voiceover explaining: "In the American justice system, there are those who make the law and those who make it look good." That was the opening that would appear in the final trailer.

When the trailers were shown to the Taylor Research focus group of ten-to-twelve-year-old girls, one of them called out, "Oh yeah!" after Elle's pert "Excuse me!" in "America's Favorite." When the trailer had finished, another declared, "That one is definitely better [than "Look Good"]. It didn't have as much of the lady in black." She meant Sally Field, whose character another focus group member derided as "really boring." Among thirteen-to-fourteen-year-olds, the "Look Good" trailer fared better. "An additional direction to consider is the focus of support Witherspoon gets from her friends, which appealed to the thirteen-to-fourteen-year-olds," concluded the NRG moderator in her report on the sessions. Older and younger groups preferred "America's Favorite," which "delivers more story detail." In the ten-to-twelve-year-olds, a chatty group with names like Samantha, Bianca, Jessica, Sierra and Luciana, one member offered this unexpectedly adult opinion: "I liked that it showed longer parts and they got to finish sentences."

Bridging the gap between these microdemos would be a marketing challenge that would dog MGM until opening day. Complete sentences were not the issue. Characters and plot were—and those elements were more difficult to overhaul. This was not *Kangaroo Jack,* which producer Jerry Bruckheimer Frankensteined from a straight-ahead action movie into a PG-rated family movie with a cuddly marsupial—*after* principal photography was completed. Elle had moved to Washington and she was there to stay.

Eric Kops explained: "We found that young girls wanted

more of the same. As they got older, they wanted new and different. So you're walking a fine line because we showed those first trailers, some of the twelve-year-olds said, 'Where's Selma Blair? Where's Matt Davis? They wanted the first story and what happened to every character and why aren't they in this? Then, as we got older, it was, 'Who are the new characters?'"

Adee agreed. "That was a real problem," he said. "We had a movie that was wildly popular with girls. When we said we had *Legally Blonde 2* coming, one hundred percent they wanted to see it. They could see it in their mind's eye how great it was going to be. We could have shown them a Rembrandt and they would have said, 'It's not what I thought.' Because it wasn't brand-new we were never quite showing them anything up to their expectations."

Reliving the frustration of the campaign's early days, Adee sat back on a white cotton–slipcovered sofa in his tenth-floor corner office in the MGM Tower. The company had moved in the spring to this newly constructed Century City skyscraper, a distinct upgrade over its previous five-story Santa Monica office park in terms of sleekness and visibility. MGM's famous lion logo looks down on its neighbors from atop the building. Inside, column-lined hallways and Louis XIV lobby décor recall the Las Vegas lineage of the company (owner Kirk Kerkorian, pushing ninety, also controled casino firm MGM Mirage). Executive offices have tan sisal-like carpet; the cubicles are made of real wood. On a flat-panel display in the lobby, the *Legally Blonde 2* trailer played in an endless loop. From

Adee's office, normally panoramic views of the Hollywood Hills and Palos Verdes peninsula were shrouded by clouds. On one wall was a large poster of the scene in Harold Lloyd's 1923 silent classic *Safety Last,* in which Lloyd plays a department store clerk who dangles precariously from the hand of a clock high above a city street as part of a PR gimmick. "You are a goddess!" Adee raved as his assistant delivered cashews, Jelly Bellys and an array of espresso drinks from Starbucks. Before taking a break for our interview, he had aimed a remote control at the VCR, rewinding and playing TV commercials for *Uptown Girls,* another blond teen movie that was slated to follow *Legally Blonde 2.*

"It's the state of sequels," he said. "We saw it so strongly with this, and it scared the living bejeesus out of me. I thought, '*Aaauughh!* What are we gonna do?' There are some movies where you show them one frame and the audience goes, 'No!' It's just an outright rejection. We didn't have an outright rejection. We had, 'Prove it. And strongly prove it, because we loved that other movie.'"

The conflicting data from Taylor Research was a puzzle yet to be solved, but MGM took considerable solace in going through the process, a comfort that NRG had always been happy to provide. "Focus groups are really cool," enthused Adee. "The coolest one I went to was in Japan. It was amazing. It was like testing me. I'm pretty sophisticated when it comes to advertising—not about anything else. But these people were like, 'Do *not* talk down to me.' Give them an impression [of what the movie is] and they will go."

An impression is all the teaser trailer was aiming to create. MGM had a can't-miss opportunity with *Die Another Day*. The company expected a huge opening weekend and it needed to tell audiences about its big movie the following summer. In October 2002, with ink still wet on the contracts for Witherspoon and Herman-Wurmfeld, the star and director found themselves on a soundstage at L.A. Center Studios in the first of the film's many races against the clock. They would have just a few hours to shoot and would be doing so without a proper crew or the film's eventual cinematographer. The concept was deceptively simple: Convey the fact that Elle Woods was going to Washington. But how to accomplish that in an appealing way in just thirty seconds?

On Halloween night, up against the following day's deadline for getting the teaser attached to prints of *Die Another Day*, Adee drove from MGM's old Santa Monica offices to Aspect Ratio in Hollywood. Never an easy drive, the trip was lengthened to a two-hour ordeal because of the annual costume parade through West Hollywood. "When I got there, I was so irritated!" Adee said. "We had a rough cut, but Reese had a problem with it, Mark had a problem with it. And the deadline was then. I went to Aspect Ratio and met Charles and hammered it out for hours." Opinions were exchanged. No one held back. "I am a giant handful when it comes to creative advertising," Adee said. "If I don't like something, I really don't like something."

Herman-Wurmfeld recalled, "There were questions

about what takes we were going to use and we didn't have a lot of material to work with, so there weren't that many decisions to make. There were some big go-rounds about the [teaser] script and I think that was probably more dramatic than meeting over the cut [of the movie]."

The result of the late-night editing session, which ended in the wee hours of Nov. 1, was a piece that began with footage of Washington monuments and a solemn voice-over: "Washington, D.C. The heart of democracy. The center of power. And this summer, the land of the free and the home . . . of the blonde?!" Cut to Elle Woods against a backdrop of the United States Capitol. "Two parties, one mall . . . I love this town," she says. "*Legally Blonde*," the announcer intones. "Two!" cries Elle, holding up two fingers (or is she flashing a peace sign?). The final image plays up one of the first film's most beloved characters. Elle sits facing the audience, munching popcorn in a darkened movie theater. "Shh, Bruiser," she stage-whispers to her dog. "The movie's about to start."

No one connected with *Legally Blonde 2* would defend the teaser as high art; it was about establishing a presence and achieving what NRG calls "unaided awareness." After *Die Another Day*, the teaser also played before the December 2002 hit *Maid in Manhattan*, which starred Jennifer Lopez. By the time the full trailer was shown to the girls at Taylor Research in March, twenty-nine out of thirty of them already knew a *Legally Blonde* sequel was on the way.

All of the squabbling and hand-wringing over the full-length trailer caused MGM to miss its goal of getting it in the can with *What a Girl Wants*. Instead, it opted for *The Lizzie McGuire Movie*, a very similar picture which would deliver the same young girls, as well as subsequent May releases *Daddy Day Care* and *Bruce Almighty*. But the blown deadline showed what a struggle it was to strike the right compromise between bubbly comedy and self-empowerment story. The spirit expressed by the film's theme song, "We Can" was "the one thing they weren't getting when they cut the first trailers," Kops said. "It was just joke, joke, joke. They missed the whole transition from the first movie, that montage of her buying the computer, raising her hand in class. The empowerment aspect."

The struggles with the trailer and TV campaign are particularly evident in this case when compared with the ease of coming up with the movie's print advertising—one-sheets, billboards, newspaper ads and the like. Print, though long ago eclipsed by television in the overall movie marketing budget, is often the clearest distillation of the studio's intended message. Instead of relying on stills, studios will often commission a special photo shoot in order to arrive at the best selection of images. In the case of *Legally Blonde 2*, a one-day photo shoot would yield an image of Elle Woods—in her pink Chanel suit, standing on the Capitol steps—that would remain constant in all print material. The studio came up with a tagline that read, "Join the party."

"In my entire career, I have never seen an easier process

in developing a one-sheet than that one," Adee said. "It just worked. We mocked up some ideas. Marc Platt had it in his head from the beginning that she'd be on the steps. Originally there were a lot of stodgy types looking at her, but that didn't work. We went for simplicity and quick readability. We put together seven or eight comps based on a photo shoot we did.

"It was not like the normal process where everyone debates the look and no one is really happy with the final poster. Reese came in. We had a number of ideas. She said, 'Oh, definitely that one.'"

The result was a pastel confection of equal parts pink and periwinkle. It was so perfectly evocative of the character that it never changed.

"Our image became a singularity," Adee explained. "When you look at a logo and you go, 'I know what it is.' Like a *Batman* logo. People try to do it all the time in print. With *Legally Blonde 2*, I think that's what we ended up with: her in that outfit, the pink and the blue. From a distance you knew what it was. We didn't have to try very hard and the moment you saw the image, it would be reminiscent of other stuff you saw about our movie or the fact that it was a sequel. So I think that we looked fresh. We looked simple."

Unlike *Terminator 3*, which developed a three-stage outdoor ad campaign, starting with a teaser and ending with the image of a battlefield teeming with robots and the tagline, "On July 2, the machines will rise," MGM opted to stick with one image. It bought highly concentrated sets of billboards on the west side of L.A. and in the southern San Fernando Valley. The single image also enabled MGM to strike an effective balance between Elle and her new milieu.

"In print, at least you have the environment of politics," Adee said. "In the TV ads, we found that we couldn't go down that road. So we went in and looked at a lot of our early trailers and TV spots and a lot of them have political jokes in them. And the audience just doesn't seem to care about politics. Sorry. They just want to be entertained. We tried a couple of political jokes and we realized we were spending way too much to get nothing. So what we did in the trailer and on television was to sell our character. We had a giant advantage over most movies. We were a known quantity. We were liked and desirable. And if we are saying that our character is in a new situation and is funny and is doing things you're going to love, if we can promise that—and that's all advertising is anyway, a promise—then the wish fulfillment of offering something they want to see and be entertained by, we've done it."

The road to wish fulfillment got a significant new curve during the development of the one-sheet. During her visit to MGM's offices to pick her preferred look, Witherspoon suddenly seemed to grow restless and out of sorts. The normally purposeful Southern belle whose company produced *Legally Blonde 2* and had a big stake in its marketing, displayed no patience for this brief transaction. Kops remembers her looking around and scowling at the buttercup-colored conference room, as if seeing it for the first time. "I need to go. I can't stand yellow," she said firmly. Her manager, Evelyn O'Neill, exchanged a look with Kops as they hurried out. Their hunch in that moment was soon confirmed: Reese Witherspoon, the $15 million queen of MGM's summer, if not its entire year, was pregnant.

The Beast of Burbank

The telltale sounds of helicopter rotors and machine-gun fire reverberated through the Stephen J. Ross Theater on the Warners lot in Burbank. The house lights flashed, revealing a *Terminator 3* banner dangling from the rafters, and a familiar figure materialized onstage. "I promised I'd be back and here I am," he said. "I'm pleased to be back with such a great franchise. This movie is going to blow people's minds."

Arnold Schwarzenegger wore a crisp, dark blazer and a radiant smile. This was his element—a carefully controlled and choreographed sales conference in a movie theater packed with industry executives and policed by a small army of publicists with walkie-talkies and clipboards. Onstage were director Jonathan Mostow, actor Nick Stahl, who played the Terminator's protégé, John Connor, and actress Kristanna Loken, who played his lissome nemesis, the T-X. At moments like this, Schwarzenegger became a one-man infomercial, zinging the crowd with one-liners, delivering an impassioned, two-minute stump speech, heaping praise on the script, stunts and special effects, his director and costars. "I loved working with Kristanna," he said. "It's hard getting your butt kicked every day. But I'm used to it. I'm married."

It was a tough audience, full of people who held the key to a successful run at the box office for *T3*; exhibitors, among them Ray Syufy, co-CEO of Century Theaters, one of the West Coast's biggest circuits; and executives from Regal Cinemas and AMC who would book films for the fifty-two screens at the Ontario Mills mall. The occasion was a marketing event called the Big Picture, which percolated for two days at the end of April beneath the famous water tower on the Warners lot. It began with a *Loony Tunes Back in Action* breakfast on a dusty Western set called Laramie Street. Later, there would be a *Last Samurai* dinner on the rainforest set where the TV series *Fantasy Island* was filmed in the 1970s, and a *Matrix Reloaded* party on the studio's tallest soundstage.

The Big Picture was a surrogate ShoWest dedicated exclusively to the Warner Brothers release slate, orchestrated by Warners' domestic marketing chief, Dawn Taubin. Months in the planning, it was the equivalent of several junkets, scheduled back to back. Schwarzenegger's appearance at the Stephen J. Ross Theater capped a long presentation by the studio brass. As Taubin looked on, Warners Entertainment CEO Barry Meyer and COO Alan Horn beat the drums for the bottom line. Horn said he wanted Warners to be "the most major of majors," with a huge release schedule and an ongoing emphasis on "event" films like *T3*.

The next speaker was a man Horn introduced as "Dan 'The Man Once It's in the Can' Fellman." This was the studio distribution chief, considered almost as much of a star as Arnold Schwarzenegger to the assembled exhibitors. A caricature of Dan Fellman's face was painted on the wall at The Palm, a West Hollywood steakhouse and industry hangout. Everyone in the theater business called him Danny. The Fellman family has been in distribution for three generations. His son is Brett Fellman, the MGM executive who— unknown to most people in the *T3* camp—would spend the weeks leading up to July Fourth working at cross purposes to his dad, trying to stoke exhibitor enthusiasm for *Legally Blonde 2*. Dan's father, Nat Fellman, began his career in Warners' theater division in 1928 and went on to create one of the first box office tracking services, Exhibitor Relations. Fellman spoke the same language as the theater owners, and he knew how to butter them up. Onstage at the Stephen J. Ross theater, he hailed recent improvements in exhibition— the digital sound and projection, expanded food courts, online sales and customer service—which he said had resulted in record admissions for the industry. "Believe me," he said. "We're going to need your screens."

While Warners' production executives worked on the lot in elegant, Mission-style offices surrounded by manicured lawns and gardens, Fellman and Taubin worked in a bland Burbank office building across the street. In the 1970s, the studio's modest marketing and sales offices were scattered across the lot. But the wide-release era had conferred enormous power on these departments, which had outgrown their old quarters and were now several times the size of the production department. The geographic demarcation was also an emblem of Fellman and Taubin's separate roles at Warners. They each had one foot on the lot and one foot in the world outside. Equipped with voluminous research into market conditions, they bred demand for the studio's movies across a wide field of precisely targeted demographic niches, and pumped out the product to satisfy that demand weekend after weekend. Taubin's job was to massage the advertising materials that were shipped into thousands of theaters and beamed into millions of homes, using all the power of the five-hundred-channel cable universe, the Web, the print media and radio airwaves. Fellman's was to coax the theater circuits to deliver the right screens in the most lucrative zones. They were huge tasks. Fellman and Taubin released more than twenty movies a year. They had a new campaign to plan every two or three weeks. There was no time to come up for air. No executives in Hollywood had quite so many theaters to book, so many advertising offensives to oversee, so many junkets and premieres to orchestrate, executives to accommodate and filmmakers to mollify.

T3 was a natural fit for this system. Fellman honed his distribution skills under Warners' longtime cochairmen Bob Daly and Terry Semel, who transformed the studio in the 1980s into a franchise factory, parlaying wide-release blockbusters like *Lethal Weapon, Batman* and *Superman* into steadily profitable cable and home-video commodities. When the first *Lethal Weapon* opened much bigger than expected, Daly and Semel summoned Mel Gibson and others from the movie to the lot, presenting them with the keys to a fleet of Range Rovers in a rainbow of colors. Wide-release blockbusters were in Warners' DNA. It was one of the first studios to abandon traditional roadshow release campaigns in the 1950s in favor of national, saturation-style distribution. In fact, the first films that Warners opened wide had an almost uncanny resemblance to *T3*.

In the summer of 1953, Warner Brothers released *The Beast from 20,000 Fathoms,* a low-budget monster movie based on a Ray Bradbury story and directed by French auteur Jean Renoir's longtime art director, Eugene Lourie. The film begins with an atomic blast in Antarctica. Ice shelves crash into the ocean, and a mushroom cloud rises into the sky. Unbeknownst to the scientists monitoring the explosion from a nearby bunker, they've disturbed a Rhedosaurus, a fictitious dinosaur the size of a football field, which had been asleep for thousands of years. The Rhedosaurus makes its way to New York, squashing buildings, swatting at cars and shrieking pedestrians, leaving a trail of poisonous germs in its wake. In the first scene, a technician with a clipboard points to the blast and announces, "Every time one of these things goes off, I feel like we're helping to write the first chapter of a new Genesis."

The Beast from 20,000 Fathoms would help write the first chapter of a new era in film distribution. Warners supported it with saturation TV and radio advertising—an unusual gambit in the early days of television. And the film opened wide, starting in New York and Los Angeles on June 24 and spreading to fifteen hundred theaters within its first week.

The Beast from 20,000 Fathoms cost $210,000 and required just twelve live-action shooting days. Its stop-motion animation techniques were invented from scratch by effects wizard Ray Harryhausen, using reverse projection and scale-size models, including a forty-foot dinosaur puppet that the film crew called Herman. Warners, which bought *The Beast from 20,000 Fathoms* for $450,000 from producers Hal E. Chester and Jack Deitz, could afford to gamble on an aggressive release pattern driven by a marketing blitz, not by reviews or reputation.

The film grossed $5 million, opening the floodgates for a huge outpouring of 1950s monster movies. In June 1954 Warners released *Them!*, a film about killer ants the size of passenger trains—"crawl-and-crush giants crawling out of the earth from mile-deep catacombs!"—unleashed by the first atomic tests in the New Mexico desert. In *Them!*, the queen of the ants flies to Los Angeles, and takes refuge in the sewers. *Them!* went even wider than *The Beast from 20,000 Fathoms*, opening rapidly in two thousand theaters, driven by a "day and night" advertising blitz that the studio press book described as "the largest TV and radio campaign ever to support a motion picture."

The Beast from 20,000 Fathoms and *Them!* were products of the new distribution landscape created by a series of Justice Department anti-trust lawsuits in the 1940s, which brought an abrupt end to the golden age of the studio system. One of those lawsuits was brought against Paramount in 1948. It prohibited the studio from engaging in block booking, a longstanding practice in which a distributor sold blocks of inferior product to theaters, sight unseen. Paramount settled the case by signing a consent decree, agreeing to sell its theater circuits. The rest of the studios soon followed suit. After the consent decree, exhibitors became independent contractors, and blocks of mediocre movies could no longer be crammed down their throats. But if the consent decree allowed theaters to be more selective, it also gave studios incentive to open films wide. Rather than releasing films vertically through a single circuit, they could exploit a horizontal network of major theater circuits. Unconstrained by the old rules, studios began experimenting with aggressive release campaigns and flooding the market with prints.

The consent decree also created a new market for independent studios, like Samuel Arkoff's American International Pictures, founded in 1954, which specialized in exploitation movies like *I Was a Teenage Werewolf, The Beast With a Million Eyes* and *How To Stuff a Wild Bikini* that played suburban drive-ins and filled out double-features at downtown theaters. These companies in the 1950s formed a down-market parallel universe within the film business, turning out a bewildering array of horror, drug and sex-ploitation movies. They were hit-and-run operations, which pumped out shoddy product at a fast and furious pace, often pulling their films from circulation before there was time for word to get out about just how bad they were. Driving through Hartford in the early 1950s, a regional distributor for Arkoff named Joseph E. Levine, saw people standing in line in a snowstorm to see a sex hygiene film called *Body Beautiful.* "It made me sick, so I got the New England rights, played it up big and did really well with it," he recalled years later. In 1956 Levine spent $1 million marketing a Japanese monster movie about a four-hundred-foot-long Tyrannosaurus Rex called *Gojira*. He dubbed it into English, removed twenty minutes of Japanese footage, hired the actor Raymond Burr to shoot a few extra scenes playing a U.S. newscaster who reports that Tokyo has come under attack by a giant monster, and renamed it *Godzilla: King of the Monsters*. For Levine, it was an extension of the brash methods he developed early in his career with films like *Duel in the Sun*, a 1946 western produced by David O. Selznick and distributed in abnormally large clusters of theaters thanks to heavy radio advertising. Levine made sure posters took the then-unusual step of promoting the release date: "Remember the day, the 7th of May."

The monster movies were also the product of a flush postwar economic climate. The sprawling suburban neighborhoods with their bulging automobiles, which sprouted from factory assembly lines in record numbers, the proliferating shopping centers, drive-in theaters and hard-top, wide-screen movie houses, gave B-movie distributors extra incentive to deliver product rapidly and widely. Their target audience was teenagers who craved the Next Big Thing in a recreational market suddenly saturated with novelty trends and pop ephemera. Warners releases like *The Beast from 20,000 Fathoms* and *Them!* demonstrated the potential of tapping into a suburbanizing landscape increasingly defined by TV. That new box in the living room that had so worried 1950s movie moguls was becoming an agent of transformative power. It hastened the obsolescence of exclusive engagements in downtown movie palaces and window displays in surrounding department stores. In a 1954 *Variety* column, Terry Turner, who helped devise the ad campaign for *The Beast from 20,000 Fathoms*, exhorted his peers in the industry to reach out to as many moviegoers as possible, to provide convenience along with entertainment: "What is the sense of a smash TV campaign for a lone, first run in the downtown area of a city when 40 good-grossing keys are right within the primary orbit of that TV station and get the campaign with just as strong an impact as the lone downtown theatre? . . . I am more convinced than ever before that television (as a solid sales instrument and not as an exploitation gimmick) is here to stay."

The Beast from 20,000 Fathoms, Them! and *Godzilla* could be sold to the public in simple, sensational images and taglines; they were equally adaptable to mass-media advertising and to old-fashioned carnivalesque PR stunts. Warner Brothers scheduled a number of personal appearances around the country for Herman. The studio even wrote to Scotland's Loch Ness Tourist Union, offering to loan it out as a stand-in for Nessie. Fabled press agent Marty Weiser also nabbed the front pages of the local papers by staging a "sighting" of a sea monster off San Pedro, in the South Bay section of Los Angeles. Warner Brothers tried to arrange for a photograph of Albert Einstein standing next to a model ant from *Them!* The studio underscored its approach in a memo to *Them!* director Gordon Douglas before shooting began: "We want a picture with the same exploitation possibilities as we had in *The Beast From 20,000 Fathoms*. We all know this will not be a 'class production' but it has all the ingredients of being a successful box office attraction." It was a crucial distinction. *The Beast from 20,000 Fathoms* and its ilk weren't prestigious films like *Quo Vadis?* and the other colossals; they were action movies with formulaic plots and no-name stars. The distribution model for these films was a natural extension of their subject matter. They ran riot through the nation's theaters, much as Harryhausen's fictitious Rhedosaurus and the giant ants from *Them!* rampaged across America's cities, from New York to Los Angeles.

Variety had called *Quo Vadis?* a box office blockbuster, but these were the real thing. These films were all metaphors for the atom bomb. They were spectacles of destruction, visiting vicarious havoc on the American landscape. They tapped directly into, and neatly displaced, the country's Cold War anxieties. The saturation release campaigns, which firebombed the country with prints, may have succeeded in part because the viewing experience was cathartic. Such films, Susan Sontag wrote in "The Imagination of Disaster," neutralized a psychological trauma that was a new reality for America's consumer class in the 1950s—the threat of "collective incineration and extinction which could come at any time, virtually without warning."

Five decades later, Warners' marketing chief had the same mandate: put enough heat under the studio product to ensure that it arrived in theaters in a blinding flash. *T3* was perfect fodder for this approach—a high-spirited action vehicle about a nuclear holocaust. In 2001, when Taubin was named the studio's president of domestic marketing, saturation release campaigns were the rule, not the exception. Marketing was no longer a carnivalesque sideshow; it was a streamlined corporate function. But Taubin, who grew up in Hollywood, the daughter of a flamboyant agent and studio boss, Guy McElwaine, could appreciate the legacy of the job. Taubin was the closest thing to Warners royalty. Her father was production chief in the 1970s, and his old office now belongs to Taubin's boss, Alan Horn. Two of her five sisters and half-sisters work in the entertainment business.

In her page-boy haircut and stylish suits, Taubin appears unflappable—the quintessential corporate player in a studio sales culture still run like an old boys' club. Taubin was sometimes the only female executive in marketing meetings, a circumstance that had helped to harden her against creative disputes with talent. But the marketing campaign for *T3* would prove taxing in ways no one could have anticipated when Warners made the winning bid to distribute the film. It had so many moving parts, and so many producers and executive producers, it was like three films rolled into one, with three times the usual squabbling. "One of the problems with this campaign is there were too many cooks in the kitchen," Mostow said. "It was very rare that anybody had the same opinion about anything." The Big Picture came less than ten weeks before the Fourth of July, but the team behind *T3* was restive. The producers wanted Taubin to commit more gross ratings points to the TV campaign. A GRP is a Nielsen rating equivalent to 980,000 households, costing anywhere from $10,000 to $50,000 a point. The *T3* campaign would accumulate twenty-one hundred GRPs in the days leading up to opening weekend.

The biggest challenge for *T3* wasn't the size of the advertising blitz, but the message. Taubin summed up the campaign's main theme in a few words: "It's the *Terminator* that you know and love, but there's more. Arnold's back, but there's more." Months into the campaign, however, that message still wasn't getting through. The Christmas trailer and the Super Bowl ad hinged on the gimmick that Warner Brothers assumed was the film's chief sales handle: the battle of the sexes. They focused on the showdown between Terminator and T-X. Cut at Hollywood trailer house Mojo, they were a showcase for Loken, who oozed the icy sensuality of a 1940s film noir diva. She was sexy, to be sure, but the material was flat. There was scant special-effects wizardry on display; there was little evidence of the millions of dollars the producers had spent destroying buildings, fleets of cars, fire trucks and stretches of highway. There was no way to tell if the story was taut or baggy, engrossing or incoherent. The scenes of the rampaging T-X in a red leather bodysuit appeared campy—*Faster Pussycat Kill Kill!* meets *The Bionic Woman.*

The trailer was tested by NRG in mall intercepts and it got high marks. It was attached to *Lord of the Rings: The Two Towers* and screened in thousands of theaters in November and December, but the campaign remained stalled. Mostow went to a theater to watch it and was dismayed to find that people hissed at the end. The campaign desperately needed a jolt of fresh ideas. From the first announcement that Mostow, not Cameron, was directing the film, it had been dogged by a backlash on Internet fan sites, and even the appearance at Comic-Con hadn't succeeded at dispelling the cloud that hung over the film. As Web critic Smilin' Jack Ruby put it on Chud.com, "it looked like a big cash-in for all involved."

But in April the *T3* sales campaign finally started to hit its stride. Postproduction on the film was almost done, and the mood at the Big Picture junket was upbeat. In February, when the film was first screened in raw form for senior management at Warners and Sony, producer Moritz Borman said, "a sigh of relief could be heard from Burbank to Culver City." By March the campaign was rolling into high gear. No longer would Warners' marketing efforts depend mainly on trailers and ads. The talent was ready to press the flesh. On March 7 Schwarzenegger's co-stars Kristanna Loken and Nick Stahl flew to Seattle to attend the Association of College Newspaper Editors Convention and screened a new trailer for 250 undergraduate editors; on March 19 Schwarzenegger received a lifetime achievement award from the Hollywood Publicists Guild; the Sunday before the Big Picture event on the Warners lot, Schwarzenegger returned to the site of the Kaiser Steel Mill in Fontana, California, now the home of the California Speedway. The Mill is where James Cameron shot the final sequence of *T2,* in which the Terminator bids farewell to John Connor and melts in a swirl of molten metal. The California Speedway event heralded a new beginning. Schwarzenegger unveiled a NASCAR Terminator car at the Winston Cup Auto Club 500, and stood by the track waving a green flag to start the race.

In the months to come, Schwarzenegger would remain the public face of the *T3* campaign, but Mostow was the perfect foil. Onstage at the Big Picture, he appeared at least six inches shorter. Where Schwarzenegger was cool and detached, Mostow was soft and approachable. He wore wire-rim glasses, wasn't fussy about his clothes, and most days sported a thick layer of facial stubble. What he lacked in physical stature, however, he made up for in brain power. Onstage at the Big Picture, reading from index cards, he delivered a sales pitch ready-made for the visiting exhibitors. Mostow understood the theater business better than most directors. He was fascinated with multiplexes, projection technology and theatrical sound systems. When he began shooting first-unit footage of *T3*, he used the name York Street Productions—after the movie theater where he worked as a teenager—to disguise the crew and keep out spies who might put photos of the set online. "I started my career at age sixteen as an usher in a New Haven theater," Mostow told the crowd. "I took tickets, sold popcorn and soda and changed the marquee. I understand the importance of giving the audience their money's worth. We've pulled out every stop possible."

Mostow grew up a Yale faculty brat, son of G. D. Mostow, a mathematician who studied with John Nash and helped develop an esoteric branch of algebra known as rigidity theory. Mostow's grandfather was a professional violinist who was the concert master at the Boston City Music Hall. While other members of Mostow's conservative Jewish family became classical musicians and academics, Mostow majored in visual studies at Harvard, interned for Ralph Nader in the summers, and subsisted for years at the lowest rungs of the Hollywood ladder. He worked as a chaperone on *The Dating Game* and as a director of music videos before directing his first feature film, a straight-to-video horror comedy called *Beverly Hills Bodysnatchers*.

Mostow had turned his back on the conservatory, but in *T3* he would compose his own symphony of destruction, augmented by theater-rattling explosions and gunfire. The film opened and closed with an operatic flourish: missiles racing toward cities in what appears to be World War III. Mostow was so obsessed with the soundtrack, he would later enclose a letter with every print sent to exhibitors, exhorting them to play the film as loud as possible. At the Big Picture Mostow remarked that the eight-minute clip was just a two-track stereo mix (the final mix would have more than a dozen tracks). The soundscape of *T3* was being engineered by a first-rate team, Mostow said, with sixteen Oscars behind them. He implored the exhibitors to play the film at 85 decibels, the maximum volume theaters can play a movie without damaging the ears of its audience.

The footage screened at the Big Picture provided the best glimpse of the film anyone outside the production had seen to date. The storyline, kept in strictest confidence for months, was suddenly much more clear. So was the scale of the action, and some of the deadpan humor. The Big Picture clip showed the Terminator's first appearance in a Mojave Desert roadhouse, a rehashing of his trademark entrance in *T2*. The Terminator barged into a Ladies' Night party and commandeered his leather outfit, sunglasses and a pickup truck from a male stripper. The scenes that followed showed him manhandling the female Terminator, wrestling with her in the bathroom of an office building, and smashing her head through a toilet. It also showed a segment of a street chase involving a firetruck, cop cars and a crane that was the movie's most spectacular set piece, shot in a decommissioned Boeing factory in Downey, California. The female Terminator is at the wheel of a Champion Crane, with Schwarzenegger dangling from the crane arm several feet off the ground, swinging from side to side, demolishing cars and telephone poles. Finally, he is sent crashing through the facade of a building, which collapses behind him in a series of bright, concussive explosions.

The exhibitors liked what they saw, but they had reservations. Here was a thrill ride whose stunts and star power would ensure significant ticket sales over the long July Fourth weekend, and it was clear Warners planned to put its marketing guns behind it. But that's where the agendas of the studios and exhibitors diverged. *T3* had the ingredients for a big opening weekend, but the theaters were looking for a film with staying power. At a time when summer blockbusters were generating nearly half of their box office gross over opening weekend, exhibitors craved lasting summer hits. They didn't want another one-weekend wonder; they wanted that summer's equivalent of *Jaws*.

To many people, *Jaws* marks a turning point for Hollywood almost as decisive as the advent of talking pictures. "*Jaws* changed the business forever," writes Peter Biskind in his history of 1970s Hollywood, *Easy Riders, Raging Bulls*. After *Jaws*, Biskind laments, "every studio movie became a B movie." In *When Hollywood Had a King*, her fastidiously researched biography of Lew Wasserman, Connie Bruck notes that *Jaws* "was the first in a new genre, the summer blockbuster movie." Studio distribution records tell a different story. *Jaws* wasn't the first summer blockbuster. *Jaws* was a vindication of a distribution and marketing idea that had been a B-movie standard since *The Beast from 20,000 Fathoms* and *Them!*.

Jaws had a B-movie premise. But it was produced by David Brown and Richard Zanuck, the tandem behind prestigious hits *The Sound of Music* and *The Sting*. It was based on a national best-seller, and it was expensive. It ran over budget and cost $11 million, consuming 150 days of principal photography, most of it on Martha's Vineyard. Spielberg shot four hundred thousand feet of film; the final cut was just eleven thousand feet. Initially, the schedule called for a summer 1974 wrap, giving the studio an option of a Christmas release. Bruce, the mechanical shark, didn't cooperate, and the opening was pushed to the following summer. Crew members had taken to calling it "Flaws."

Test screenings turned perceptions around in a flash. Three months before it opened, a test in the Lakewood Shopping Center in Dallas had audience members "tearing the seats out," Zanuck said. Two days later, at a preview in Long Beach, reaction was equally rabid, even though the marquee touted the screening as *Big Fish Story*. "I only remember one thing: The cards were amazing," Brown said. "There were so many people going to the first preview, we had to schedule another one afterward, at eleven at night. We repaired to the local hotel with the cards. I remember one card where the comment was, 'This is a great movie, now don't fuck it up.'"

Steven Spielberg has often mused that *Jaws* could never be a hit in today's marketplace. "The audience would want more shark," he told the *New York Times*. Indeed, before the opening, he, Zanuck and Brown "all thoroughly agreed on at least one thing—the shark was to remain a mystery," screenwriter Carl Gottlieb wrote in his *Jaws Log*. That concept was to apply to the film itself, which doesn't reveal Bruce until the third act, and to all of the prerelease hype. No behind-the-scenes pictures of mechanical sharks. No stories about how the creature was brought to life. Just the "dah-dum, dah-dum" TV spots and a fearsome one-sheet that took six months to develop. (All of the earlier versions, artist Tony Seiniger recalls, looked like dolphins.)

Universal spent $2.5 million promoting *Jaws*, about $1 million more than the average film of 1975. That figure included $700,000 in network television ads. Universal's parent, MCA, was a TV-oriented company well-positioned to take full advantage of the medium. Unlike today's wall-to-wall TV buys that begin six to eight weeks ahead of the opening, *Jaws* was more selectively targeted, with the initiative starting just three days ahead of the opening. "We also went for quality network programming instead of sheer tonnage, which is still the way most of the media services seem to go," said G. Clark Ramsay, the studio's head of advertising and publicity. Universal had an internal name for its strategy: "*Jaws* consciousness." There were *Jaws* T-shirts, jigsaw puzzles, board games, Zippo lighters, Matchbox cars, hand towels and beach towels. The summer of 1975 was renamed "the summer of the shark."

Until the start of the 1970s, studios had been using television sporadically to advertise their films, rarely even spending extra money to produce color spots. Sid Sheinberg, who was chief of Universal Pictures at the time, describes the era as "a two-and-a-half-network world. ABC didn't even count." Scant on-air options, however, also meant a highly consolidated mass audience. If you could tell viewers of *All in the Family* or *M*A*S*H* about your movie, you could reach tens of millions of viewers and turn even a pedestrian movie into an event. Television had the multiplier effect of thousands of full-page ads in the *New York Times*. Not insignificantly, it also held out the chance of a rapid return on investment. Since the 1950s, studios had occasionally made saturation buys in certain markets, snatching up cheap fringe time to announce the newest *Flipper* or Elvis or monster movie, an inexpensive technique that usually paid off at the box office. That investment in television surged as the decade progressed. Media spending shot up 40 percent in 1978 compared with 1977, and 34 percent more in 1979, when studios spent $175 million to plug 452 films on TV. By contrast, in 2003 the average marketing cost of a single studio film was $39 million.

When *Jaws* was booked into theaters, Universal had a take-no-prisoners approach to distribution. Any "A" theaters who balked at the film's rental terms were bypassed in favor of suburban B and C locations which were easier to reach with TV anyway. To help minimize the risk of the TV buy, Universal put a clause in the rental contracts requiring any theater playing the film to pay into a fund that would defray some of the advertising costs. After a wildly successful preview screening on March 26, 1975, Universal boss Lew Wasserman met with Sheinberg, distribution chief Hi Martin, and producers Zanuck and Brown in the theater lobby. He chose restraint over a roll of the dice. "Hi was all excited and he told Lew, 'I've got it booked in 600 theaters!'" Zanuck recalled. "'And Lew told him to get rid of two hundred of those runs.'" He correctly assumed that lines around the block would further stoke demand. The final theater count was 464 in North America, 409 of those in the United States. Wasserman's goal wasn't to blow the windows out on opening weekend. He wanted *Jaws* to have legs.

Jaws opened the weekend of June 20–22, 1975 and smashed box office records from Los Angeles to New York. A front-page ad in the next week's *Variety* (with a close-up of the shark) crowed "'JAWS': OPEN FOR BUSINESS," noting the opening-weekend total down to the last dollar: $7,061,513. But that was just the beginning. *Jaws* did have legs. It sold 25 million tickets in its first thirty-eight days. "We didn't obsess about being number one in our first weekend," Zanuck said. "We wanted to own the entire summer. And we did."

Even after *Jaws,* skepticism about wide releases persisted. "Audiences seem to tire not only of trends in subject matter, but of distribution methods," Stuart Byron wrote in *Film Comment* in 1976. "My suggestion is that after being burned a few times by movies being distributed in a certain way, the public grows suspicious of anything being handled in such a manner. Right now, multiple openings, with attendant saturation advertising campaigns, convey a certain freshness, but this will change after the public is exposed to two or three real clinkers."

All of the evidence indicates otherwise, of course, and is easy to see with the passage of time. Transcripts of Universal's television ads for its *Airport* franchise show which way the business was headed—toward even wider releases, more aggressively front-loaded, engineered to generate maximum profits from Friday to Sunday. Spots for the first *Airport*, in 1970, ended with the announcer's tagline: "Rated G." Those for *Airport 1975* teased "Soon at your local theater or drive-in." *Airport 77* ads finished with a telling reflection of the opening-weekend imperative: "Starts Friday at a theater near you."

The first *Terminator* was a saturation release—it opened in October 1984 on 1,005 screens—and it had legs. It grossed $4 million in its first three days; the following weekend, ticket sales rose by five percent. But two decades later, *T3* was hard to predict. Warners was selling it like it was the summer's first blockbuster. But few people had seen the film. It wasn't finished yet; nobody knew how well it would open, or whether it could hold its own after opening weekend.

The Big Picture screening was followed by a *T3* lunch on the studio's New York set, which was decorated to resemble an urban war zone. A police car was converted to a bar and DJ booth, its turntables concealed behind a flashing siren and rows of cocktail glasses. The exhibitors ate prime rib and swordfish at tables wrapped in yellow and black hazard tape, as waiters hired from a modeling catalogue to resemble the Terminator circulated in black T-shirts with gray-and-white Cyberresearch insignias. Animatronic robots built by Stan Winston studios were stationed on one side of the event. On the other was the blue-and-yellow, 160-ton Champion crane used in the film, its hook and pulley rising one hundred feet in the air to hold a giant steel rafter over the street.

Soon after the Big Picture, the trailer rotation in theaters would change. Warners hired another trailer house, Interlink, to cut a new spot. It was a hard-hitting, 150-second spot with more mayhem, more special effects, and a heavy emphasis on the storyline, with its slow countdown to nuclear Armageddon. "Judgement Day, the end of the world, is today, three hours from now," John Connor says at the end of the trailer. The timing of the trailer was pivotal. It was attached to *The Matrix Reloaded*, which arrived in packed theaters May 15, and it delivered a big bump in Warners' internal estimates of opening weekend. But the producers were still antsy. At lunch a few weeks later, Mostow ruminated over the minutiae of the marketing campaign, fretting that competition might have more exposure heading into opening weekend. "*Legally Blonde* is everywhere," he said.

More troubling to Mostow were the still unresolved struggles to arrive at a signature image that could pull together their marketing efforts. "There was no coherent visual motif to the movie," he said. The image of the Terminator's face that was used in the Warners one-sheet was a close-up, not a studio head shot. "His face was sort of lopsided," Mostow said. "It wasn't a strong look." What the campaign lacked was a single iconic motif, like the mouth of the shark from *Jaws*, the egg in *Alien*, the baby carriage in *Rosemary's Baby* or the shot of a UFO atomizing the White House from *Independence Day*.

Dawn Taubin didn't think it was a problem that *T3* lacked a single visual signature. "Few films do," she said. Taubin, who was a publicist for a decade before taking up marketing—a far more abstruse science—was graceful with the press. Her office was cozy with chintz patterns, and a glass coffee table was piled with books and candy. A pink ceramic mug bore the hand-painted message, "I love you, Mommy."

But she had a steely edge. In an interview in her office a few weeks after the Big Picture, Taubin wore a fashionably tapered black ensemble, and a studio security badge dangled from her neck. Asked about an uncomfortable conversation with Schwarzenegger—he'd been promoting the film in New York, which was saturated with bus-stop ads and billboards promoting Reese Witherspoon in *Legally Blonde 2*—Taubin stared impassively at the notebook in her lap before answering, slowly sketching the petals of a daisy.

"There were issues," she said finally. Taubin's chief issues had nothing to do with Schwarzenegger's willingness to promote the film, however. They came from other things: the perception in some corners that the Terminator was old hat; the struggle to arrive at the right advertising material; the frequent and endless meetings with *T3*'s myriad producers and consultants; and the difficult juggling act she faced in releasing, in the same summer, *The Matrix Reloaded* and *T3*—two violent, R-rated science fiction films about machines taking over the world. *The Matrix* came first, and it was wholly owned by Warners and Village Roadshow, an Australian company that co-financed several Warners movies. Warners had only licensed domestic and home-video rights to *T3*. Compared to *The Matrix*, the studio's profits on *T3* had a ceiling. The studio wouldn't milk the TV rights and other ancillaries in perpetuity. Those rights still belonged to C-2 and Intermedia. Taubin bifurcated her staff, devoting entirely separate creative teams to each film. "When we made the deal to make this, the marketing group defined the target audience, developed a strategy and refined it as we went," she says. "I didn't treat this movie any differently than I treated *The Matrix*. With our event films, I never look at it on a profitability basis. It was just like every Warner-released, Warner-funded movie."

Nobody would argue that the schedule of publicity events for *T3* wasn't ambitious. After the Big Picture, several similar events would follow in quick succession: a Cannes junket, a Los Angeles press junket, a premiere and an international tour. These events would have an almost uniform style and script. There would be robots and other *Terminator* props, sales patter by the producers, and the climax would always be a short appearance by Schwarzenegger. He would step out from behind a curtain or doorway, shake hands with the crowd and deliver his signature line, "I'm back."

A few weeks later, Atari threw a party at the Raleigh Studios soundstage during the annual Electronic Entertainment Expo, or E3, to celebrate its *T3* videogame. C-2, Intermedia and Atari recognized the upside of such cross-promotion. If the movie did well in July, it would only help sales of the game in November. As videogame sales have eclipsed annual box office totals, Hollywood and game designers have become willing bedfellows.

The red carpet was lined with about seventy-five members of the media, many from broadcast outlets. Conspicuous in their absence were marketing and publicity executives from the studio. Access to producers, director and stars was better than at any movie premiere; fans walked right up to Stan Winston, Jonathan Mostow and C-2 partners Andy Vajna and Mario Kassar. The atmosphere was that of a well-funded college dorm study break. Winston ate fried jalapeno peppers and plugged a low-budget horror movie he produced called *Wrong Turn*, which Fox would release May 30. An exterior wall of the sound stage was illuminated by a giant *T3* logo. Two squat, animatronic robots stood guard at the end of the carpet.

Guests who walked through the twenty-foot-tall stage door found themselves in the midst of a military complex. Props used in the film shoot were deployed in every corner: a helicopter, a bullet-riddled hearse. Black netting and sandbags surrounded the central bar. Vajna tried to get the evening jump-started by introducing the man of the hour. The crowd was still a bit sparse, however. At Vajna's cue, the spotlight came on and there was a smattering of applause. Then a lengthy pause. Arnold was still in promotional mode on the red carpet and had not heard his introduction. "This is very well coordinated," he muttered sarcastically upon reaching the stage. "I was in the middle of my interviews when I was pulled by my left sleeve and told I was being introduced. I hope that the sales of the actual videogame are better co-ordinated than this."

It was clear that the Terminator was displeased. His orderly world had been disrupted by dilettantes who were still in short pants when he set the standard for movie-star promotion. But he soon regained his composure. Reflecting on the limits of computer animation, Schwarzenegger observed: "It is the first time I liked myself, the way I looked." The *T3* game, after all, was no simple tie-in; it marked the first time Arnold has licensed his image, likeness and voice for such a purpose. "Be the Terminator!" implored the voiceover on the videogame's trailer. Be Arnold. It's a concept his fans would find hard to resist.

Who's Bad?

S pike now had a much bigger role in *Sinbad,* but the dog still wouldn't hunt. Eight different dogs in a recording studio had licked mayonnaise off of plates, growled on command and whined for pieces of rawhide held just out of their reach, all in an effort to make Spike more than merely a Burger King toy. Spike occupied a significant portion of the movie's trailer, which appeared in mid-March. "If he starts humping your leg, it means he likes you," Sinbad quips to Marina. Later, amid the pitching and rolling of the open ocean, Spike's cheeks fill up and he vomits over the side. Aside from giving Spike more of the spotlight, the trailer desperately sought to make *Sinbad* sound hip. It begins with a voiceover straight out of a Mountain Dew ad—"No wave is too huge!"—as Sinbad's galleon comes skittering over an ocean swell. The final flourish is a series of split-screens with shots of Brad Pitt, Catherine Zeta-Jones and Michelle Pfeiffer hamming it up in the recording session.

The trailer did nothing to revive the spirits of Dream-
Works executives, who were confronting yet more mediocre
results from test screenings. The filmmakers may have been
enchanted by the notion of a canine sidekick and an array
of menacing monsters, but neither did much to raise scores
with a crucial segment: young girls. And boys were too easily distracted. "If boys want to see monsters, they'll go see
T3," predicted one person involved with *Sinbad*.

The trailer hit screens at an inopportune time. Dream-
Works' only spring movie was a Chris Rock misfire called
Head of State, whose audience was almost exactly the opposite of *Sinbad*'s. So much for MGM marketing chief Peter
Adee's notion of speaking to your audience all year long.
And there wasn't a major family hit to which the trailer
could be attached, unlike the year before when Fox's computer-animated *Ice Age* had become a sensation in March.
Mindful of all this, the DreamWorks marketing team still
managed a few meaningful thrusts. They engineered a segment on the April 13 edition of *Entertainment Tonight* that
featured clips from the film and interviews with Pfeiffer and
Brad Pitt. A similar interview was arranged for the *Los Angeles Times*' annual "Summer Sneaks" issue on May 4. Positive
reviews of test screenings had popped up in March and April
on fan Web sites like Ain't It Cool News and Dark Horizons.
"This movie will bring 2-D animation back to life," predicted a review signed by "Big Brother." Terry Press and her
team were still playing a crafty game of poker. Unlike *Treasure Planet*, which was rattled by negative press long before
its release, *Sinbad* was escaping serious media scrutiny.

The inoffensiveness of the film may have suppressed test scores, but it also kept any harmful word of mouth from spreading. That Sinbad was originally a sailor from Baghdad was a fact that never registered in focus groups, according to those who saw the feedback. In fact, the problem was more serious than that. Nobody seemed to know exactly who Sinbad was. In an interview with a fan Web site conducted at DreamWorks' Glendale campus, codirector Tim Johnson explained, "We sort of chanted, 'Magic and gods and monsters'—that's the world we were going to visit, an alternate history a thousand years ago." But what was in that world for the modern audience to connect with? Unlike *T3*, which faced a gauntlet of rumors and cynicism from longtime fans of the franchise, or *Legally Blonde 2*, which risked becoming an emblem of sequel fatigue, *Sinbad* was operating in a frictionless environment. Terry Press clearly had reckoned with that dawning reality on the spring afternoon when she phoned Peter Adee's office at MGM. He put her on speaker phone. "Are you cooperating with this book?" she asked him. "I don't know yet," he said. Press declared: "I know I'm not going to have anything to say because I already know I'm going to finish third."

Meanwhile, *Sinbad*'s crew entered a full-scale push to put the finishing touches on the film's grueling three-year production process. They were aiming for a style some in animation call "tradigital"—meaning a meticulous blending of two-dimensional and three-dimensional techniques. Michelle Pfeiffer's character, the malevolent goddess Eris, had been the most complex animated creature in any of

DreamWorks' seven animated features to date. The ocean, long a formidable challenge for animators and special-effects teams, required the creation of eight layers of computerized textures influenced by the nineteenth-century seascapes of Russian painter Ivan Konstantinovich Aivazovsky. Ships, monsters and human characters were then laid on top. A four-minute sequence in which the ship *Chimera* is set upon by three-dimensional Sirens took six months to animate.

If animating an ocean seemed formidable, the publicity campaign was positively Byzantine. After some down time in the spring, Pitt was off to Morocco to film his lead role in *Troy*; Catherine Zeta-Jones was having a baby and Pfeiffer was, well, too available. Of the three, she was the least potent star when it came to opening a movie. Normally, animated movies are not viewed as star vehicles, but Katzenberg had used stars to sell *Shrek,* running ads with live-action clips of Mike Myers, Eddie Murphy and Cameron Diaz. Katzenberg believed passionately in the value of promoting star voices as he would live-action players. It even bothered him to read criticism of one of his actors concerning projects he wasn't involved in. On May 24 he fired off a letter to the *Los Angeles Times,* which the paper printed. It ripped critic Manohla Dargis for her review of the Eddie Murphy comedy, *Daddy Day Care,* a Revolution Studios film that Katzenberg had nothing to do with. Murphy, the voice of Donkey in *Shrek* movies, also had a producing deal at DreamWorks. "Eddie is one of the most brilliant comedic talents of our time and his track record speaks for itself," the letter read. "His career should be judged in its entirety, not just on a few titles that might not have fully delivered on his talents. After all, what Hollywood star hasn't had a miss? For more than twenty-five years, Eddie has consistently been making audiences laugh—and for that we should all be a little more grateful, and maybe just a little less judgmental."

The trailer and TV spots for *Sinbad* focused on its star wattage, and a "Summer Preview Reel" sent to journalists in early April also showcased the vocal talent. In the preview reel, Pitt called making the film "fantastically fun." There's footage of a recording session, in which Pitt stands at a microphone, dressed in a T-shirt and backward baseball cap. A crew at the mixing board, including Katzenberg, crack up at his line reading. "Who's bad?" Pitt asks rakishly. "*Sin*bad." Pfeiffer's distended reading of the phrase "glorious Chaos" also reduces the room to giggles.

The problem with relying so heavily on movie stars to promote the film was that personal appearances were not an option. Even holding a press junket was a near impossibility given the schedules of the major talent, so DreamWorks conducted several mini-junkets. Unlike *T3,* which had Schwarzenegger methodically plowing the publicity field from the time of the Super Bowl to the film's premiere in Japan, *Sinbad* would not have a consistent spokesperson in the media.

A June screening of the film for employees on the DreamWorks lot was filled with foreboding. According to several people in attendance, Katzenberg sought to rally the troops, including many of the animators who had spent years on the film, by reading a rave review from Joel Siegel. It would turn out to be one of the only enthusiastic reviews the film would get. At the very moment when *Finding Nemo* was redefining all that was witty and innovative in animation, the man arguably most responsible for ushering animated movies into the blockbuster era was saddled with a throwback. In pop music and sports apparel, throwbacks were hip. Not so in animation. "The atmosphere in the theater was leaden," recalls one of the DreamWorks employees in attendance. "There was no applause afterward. People just filed out shaking their heads, like, 'This is what we're releasing after *Shrek*?' "

Realizing they were sailing into a tempest, and with positive word building for live-action rival *Pirates of the Caribbean*, DreamWorks tried in the eleventh hour to shift the release date. Studios, though mindful of the appearance of collusion, often negotiate directly with competitors about release dates. Katzenberg had famously jousted with Harvey Weinstein when DreamWorks' *The Road to Perdition* and Miramax's *Gangs of New York* were slated for the same summer date. After a twenty-minute phone conversation, Katzenberg declared, according to DreamWorks' version of the story, "I've got Tom Hanks and I'm not moving!" Indeed he didn't, though *Gangs* wound up opening December 20, just five days before *Catch Me if You Can*, putting Leonardo DiCaprio, star of both movies, in competition with himself.

Katzenberg and distribution chief Jim Tharp talked informally with Paramount, a co–finance partner on several other major productions, about moving *Sinbad* up to June 27. Going later in July or August was not feasible. Kids, especially in the South, would be heading back to school by August and *Pirates* was firmly planted on July 9. But the June date worried Paramount, which had grabbed June 13 for *Rugrats Go Wild!,* the synergistic melding of two of Nickelodeon's successful animated series, *The Rugrats* and *The Wild Thornberrys*. Unlike live-action films, which were squeezed cheek-to-jowl in the summer because of their potential for massive openings, animated films generally opened to more modest numbers and enjoyed a better "multiple," or ratio of opening-weekend gross to the total. Consequently, Paramount insisted on more breathing room for *Rugrats*. The studio would not budge.

Resigned to the July 2 date, DreamWorks attempted a last-ditch sales maneuver a week before the opening. In a story planted atop the lead page of *USA Today*'s Life section, DreamWorks announced it would give a free read-along CD-ROM called "Shrek and Fiona's Honeymoon Storybook," an elaborate plug for *Shrek 2,* to purchasers of children's tickets to *Sinbad* during opening weekend. The translation to those attuned to the telltale signs: This movie has zero traction, but come and see it anyway if you want a free gift that reminds you of one of our better animated movies. Two years after the directors gave studio executives their first glimpse at the goods, the film had never transcended the limitations of an old-fashioned story that was hopelessly unsuited to the mercurial interests of twenty-first-century children. It was still, as one insider described it, "two guys, a girl and a boat."

To execute the speedy release of what Katzenberg referred to as "Shrek 1½" (the CD-ROM), DreamWorks would marshal the resources of a marketing operation on the smog-licked Eastern fringe of Los Angeles: the Technicolor depot in Ontario, California, a few miles from the megaplexes at the Ontario Mills mall. Prints from most of the major studios heading for theaters west of the Rocky Mountains pass through Ontario, as do marketing materials bound for all of North America—everything from trailers and posters to standees and logo merchandise. Turnover is quick. The depot never closes.

Jeffrey Katzenberg, Terry Press and the rest of Hollywood's opening-weekend architects have never set foot inside Technicolor's ninety-thousand-square-foot Ontario warehouse. Thanks to its mechanized efficiency and its proximity to two interstate freeways and a major airport, they don't have to. They can drastically alter their marketing strategy with one phone call. It took roughly twenty-four hours to pack three million *Shrek* CD-ROMs into the crates containing prints of *Sinbad* and ship them to theaters. Studios routinely demand overnight turnaround for such marketing initiatives, and Technicolor does its best to comply. When DreamWorks called to fast-track a trailer for Will Ferrell's summer 2004 comedy *Anchorman*, the trailer reached projection booths the next morning.

The depot is a Willy Wonka–like ostinato of activity illuminated by yellow fluorescent light. A small portable stereo blasts the distorted strains of Mexican pop music from a tall shelf reachable only by ladder or forklift. Towering rows of orange metal shelves brush the thirty-six-foot ceiling. Forklifts scuttle about, using hydraulic lifts to shelve and retrieve stacks of posters, banners, T-shirts, caps and standees. Materials from older films are kept locked in a caged area, lest any enterprising Technicolor worker want to augment their income on eBay. Five of the fiberglass Bruce sharks from *Finding Nemo* sat for several months on a bottom shelf, awaiting a benefit auction. On one side of the warehouse, an elderly woman uses a rolling-pin-like machine to spin a dozen movie posters into a neat cylinder, which she slips into a mailing tube headed for a theater. In a small, windowless room off the warehouse, a dozen middle-aged Latino women take two-thousand-foot reels of duplicated trailers and cut single trailer reels that are the size of library microfilm spools. An experienced operator can process 130 trailers an hour. Colored labels are affixed to trailers and they are sent back out to the floor. Twosomes of "pickers" and "packers" steadily fill cardboard boxes with 45 trailers, sending them down a chute of metal rollers toward a loading dock, where trucks are loaded for transport to theaters.

Trailers for previous versions of the Sinbad story, like those starring Douglas Fairbanks or Gene Kelly, would have been handled by the National Screen Service, a monopoly that controlled the creation and distribution of studio marketing materials for decades, until the 1970s. The NSS established a network of depots connected by rail, each located in an urban center like Cleveland or East St. Louis or Downtown Los Angeles, near the movie palaces of traditional city theater districts. Technicolor quickly overtook the NSS, whose records were never computerized and whose hubs had all deteriorated into crime-ridden zones with few vibrant multiplex theaters.

Technicolor's facility in Ontario is one of several dozen off-white boxes rising fifty feet from the city's desert scrub, like beige boulders with loading docks. They house shipping hubs and warehouses for companies such as Wal-Mart, Target, Costco, United Parcel Service, Procter & Gamble and USCO Logistics, a large firm that stores and tracks everything from olive oil to migraine pills to golf shoes. From a distance, these distribution hubs resemble megaplex theaters like the dueling pair at the Ontario Mills mall, the Edwards Palace 22 and 30-screen AMC. Like the Technicolor depot, they're clearinghouses for products manufactured elsewhere.

About half of Ontario's annual sales tax revenue, or nearly $2 million, now comes from distribution. These way stations for companies with no local ties occupy the same land where aerospace plants, an appliance factory and the Kaiser Steel Mill anchored and defined community life a little more than a decade ago.

Sinbad wasn't all that different from olive oil or pills or shoes—it was a market-tested and efficiently packaged item shipped to national retail chains through what a local economist calls "the distribution economy" of Ontario and the Inland Empire. Unlike those products, the success or failure of *Sinbad* would be dramatized and analyzed by a voracious media fixated on opening weekend box office receipts. A month before July 2, its shelf life was impossible to predict.

The Running Man

"The movie looks fantastic," Arnold Schwarzenegger said, lighting his cigar with a miniature blowtorch that emitted a low hiss and blue flame. "No, there is another word for it, I think: extraordinary. 'Fantastic' is not the right word. Because with the music and the sound, it's becoming, like, complete. Spectacular."

Schwarzenegger agreed to sit for an interview with us, but only in the context of a cover story for the May issue of *V-Life*, a glossy magazine spun off from *Variety*. Making *Terminator 3* had taken its toll on the fifty-six-year-old man of action. He had needed rotator cuff surgery after tearing a tendon while driving with one hand and repeatedly cocking a four-and-a-half-pound shotgun with the other. He spent the next eleven months in physical therapy. For the cyborg who once tossed off lines like, "I'm a cybernetic organism, living tissue over a metal endoskeleton," the experience proved eye-opening.

"It's tedious, painful and long," Schwarzenegger said. "With my heart surgery [in 1997], a week later I was home, another week later, I was hiking up in Will Rogers Park with my dogs. But this is, like, unbelievable the amount of time it takes."

The *T3* campaign promised to take even longer, but this was work Schwarzenegger clearly relished. Leading up to opening weekend, Schwarzenegger would appear on the covers of *Esquire, Entertainment Weekly, Popular Mechanics, TV Guide, Parade* and *Cigar Aficionado.* Warner Brothers would secure nearly twenty magazine covers overall for the cast of *T3,* and the publicity department's clipping service would record more than a hundred other early magazine hits. In one twelve-month period, *Newsweek* alone ran a story on Hollywood's new action heroes that mentioned *T3,* a piece on the twenty-fifth anniversary of *Pumping Iron,* a summer film preview with a story on the breakout performance of costar Kristanna Loken, a separate feature entirely devoted to *T3* and still another feature on Schwarzenegger himself. The star's public flirtation with political office undoubtedly helped to whet the media's appetite for the Terminator's return.

Schwarzenegger was also warming up for a marathon of TV appearances scheduled for the final weeks before opening weekend. He would tape more than a hundred interviews and make more than a dozen appearances on network and cable TV programs, including four *Tonight Show* appearances before the end of the summer, culminating in the August 6 announcement before Jay Leno's millions of viewers that he would run for governor of California.

Schwarzenegger first came to international notice when visiting the Cannes Film Festival in 1977 to promote *Pumping Iron.* The bodybuilding documentary was marketed with a stunt along the Riviera in which the seven-time Mr. Universe flexed his famous muscles while surrounded by bikini-clad women. In New York, the film would use a legendary "living sculpture exhibit" at the Whitney Museum of Art to brand Schwarzenegger among the city's cultural elite. Since observing the potent results of that film's campaign, the star has been drawn to up-close, bicep-flexing, hand-pumping, baby-kissing publicity stunts. Arnold's first-name-only fame and personal outreach to his fans were perfectly suited to the films that made him a major star—heroic dramas, stuffed with spectacular action sequences built around his own bulging physique. Big male Hollywood stars of the 1970s like Robert Redford, Al Pacino and Robert De Niro shrank from the limelight. That would not be the case in the 1980s, as Schwarzenegger, Sylvester Stallone and Bruce Willis brought heightened public profiles to their roles as action heroes and muscular pitchmen for the films in which they starred.

"He recognized his star power depended on getting butts in seats," said Peter Gruber, the onetime head of Sony Pictures Entertainment, whose TriStar division released *Terminator 2.* "He was being paid to create that interest. He was a bodybuilder, so he knows that it takes repetition and sophistication, both." Bodybuilders are judged on how well they hold a pose—front double biceps, front lat spread, back lat spread, front abdominal-side isolation, and so on. (The heavy bronze trophy given to the winners of the Arnold Classic, his annual tournament in Columbus, Ohio, depicts one of his patented poses, the "three-quarter back.") Pros call posing "staying in your shot." As Schwarzenegger would step onstage in search of another bodybuilding title, usually to the strains of Richard Strauss' *Thus Spake Zarathustra*, he managed to stay in his shot longer than anyone.

When *T2* came out, director James Cameron sized up his leading man this way: "He's never gonna play a character where he sits around in an office and wrings his hands. He is about direct action. He's about being decisive. He's about knowing what you want and going for it. He's very clear."

For that very reason, the role of a lifetime for Schwarzenegger was the Terminator. It allowed him to be what Cameron once called "the ultimate rude guy," coolly neutralizing any obstacles in his way with a stiff-arm shove, one-liner or shotgun blast. Bill Zehme, in a memorable profile for *Rolling Stone*, wrote, "When Arnold wants to pay a man a compliment, he says of the man, 'He's in control.' There is no higher praise than this." The Terminator was the ultimate expression of self-control. Upon the release of *T2*, he reflected on the popularity of the character. "Everyone would like to be a Terminator," he said. "Everyone would like to be a person who can take care of the job.

Whoever makes you mad, you can get even. There's a tremendous amount of frustration in human beings, and I think this is a way of fantasizing to get rid of those frustrations. To think, 'I can do this too.' It's a release, especially when you throw in a few cool lines of dialogue that always signal that you're not even concerned about the danger. You make fun of danger, like John Wayne. You never heard John Wayne talk hectic, even when the bombs went off around him. You think, 'Wow, how can he be so cool? The guy is standing in the middle of a bombing and he's in control.'" At a *T2* convention in Los Angeles in 1991 Zehme described an Arnold look-a-like contest moderated by the original T-800 model. Schwarzenegger had the crowd eating out of his plump, beringed hand. "Jim Cameron and I have just decided backstage that we're going to do another Terminator after this one," he said to a roar of delight from the assembled. "The title will be The Sperminator. 'I'LL COME AGAIN!'"

Twelve years later, resurrecting the Terminator was hardly a joke. Making the character relevant again was a mission whose first step was addressing the audience's doubts about how the story would avoid franchise fatigue. Jonathan Mostow began trying to solve that puzzle in 2001, meeting Schwarzenegger at the star's home in Pacific Palisades and spending two hours in the den laying out his vision of the sequel. He felt grateful to be pitching a star who relished the sales part of the movie business as much as the acting. "He had such an intuitive understanding of how the audience understands and enjoys the character," Mostow said. "So few actors are able to take a step back and clearly see those considerations."

In the auteur 1970s, when the current action-sequel industry did not even exist, his physique was considered a liability. Pausing during our conversation by a waist-high bronze statue of Eugen Sandow, father of bodybuilding, he recalled the years of struggling to move from gym to screen, when he was billed onscreen as Arnold Strong in films like *Hercules in New York* and Robert Altman's *The Long Goodbye.*

"Bodybuilding got me to America. When I saw my idols—Steve Reeves, Kirk Douglas, Charlton Heston, John Wayne—all those guys were these very heroic guys," he said. "But what fascinated me the most about guys like Steve Reeves was that they won Mr. Universe first and then got into movies. They never really trained to get into movies. They trained as bodybuilders. I was thinking the only way I would ever get to America or get into movies was that route. So I, like a fanatic, started training. Then, after I won all of those championships and came to Hollywood, people said I was twenty-five years behind the times. There were still guys like Clint Eastwood and Charles Bronson, but the guys who were really cutting-edge were Dustin Hoffman, Warren Beatty, Jack Nicholson. I had to expand my dream. I was programmed to be a star."

Rather like the embattled Terminator, Schwarzenegger now saw himself as fighting an entrenched opposition, so he had ample reason to apply more than his usual amount of muscle to the *T3* marketing campaign. Industry cynics considered him the guest who had stayed too long at the party. Since his last solid hit, Cameron's *True Lies* in 1994, worldwide grosses of his movies had nose-dived.

Schwarzenegger had long drawn strength from adversity. "One agent said to me, 'No one who ever did a movie with an accent was successful,'" he recalled in our interview with the same impassive trace of a smile he wears when terminating someone onscreen. "Someone else said, 'It'll never work with this name.' Other people said, 'This body is totally off. Why don't you get out of the business and go make some health food stores?' But I felt that I could turn all of those obstacles into assets."

Since September, when shooting wrapped in L.A. on *T3*, Schwarzenegger had been in more of a PR comfort zone. He switched agencies, from William Morris to CAA, and reports began circulating about big-budget sequels to *Conan the Barbarian*, *True Lies* and *Total Recall*. Dismissive headlines about *Collateral Damage* and a nasty takedown attempt by *Premiere* magazine had since faded away.

One of the key weapons in Schwarzenegger's 2003 arsenal was his simmering political aspirations. Schwarzenegger resolved early on to remain coy about his political ambitions while promoting *T3*. But that will-he-or-won't-he factor opened up possibilities that might not have existed if the storyline was just "Arnold's back in a summer sequel." The *V-Life* cover showed him in the same pose as Redford in *The Candidate*, blowing a bubble in front of an American flag. He told the studio audience in an appearance on *The View* on July 2, "I'm trying to stay on message.

Right now, I'm running for the *Terminator*." *Esquire* put him on its July cover with the headline "Arnold: California's Next Governor. Really." There was no leather jacket or cigar. Instead, Schwarzenegger wore a navy suit with a conservative red tie. Inside were two cover stories, one about the movie, the other following him to Detroit, where he made an appearance on behalf of his Inner-City Games Foundation. "My entire life over here in America, it became a big asset for me, I have to say. I mean, it's just, it sells," he told the magazine. "It's a great advantage in many ways when people expect less. You can only surprise them."

His candidacy had been gathering momentum for months. In November, the after-school funding initiative Proposition 49 was approved by California voters by a convincing margin. His stewardship of the campaign fed speculation that the Austrian Oak (as he was dubbed in his bodybuilding days) was poised to run for governor in 2006. In the April interview, he remained coy about his future political plans, saying only that he had not yet committed to start shooting another film. "Of course I haven't made a decision, otherwise I'd be out there running," he shrugged. "Right now, I'm very focused on promoting the movie and on show business"—pronounced "cho business"—"and if I decide to switch over to that other thing, then I would have to make the announcement that I was retiring." Though Republican strategists applauded Schwarzenegger for taking on a ballot initiative before trying his hand at a full-fledged campaign, he scoffed at the notion.

"They think that everything you do is calculated," he said. "When I did Prop. 49 they said, 'This is his way to get into the political arena.' When I sold my Ferrari, they said, 'Oh, he's getting rid of his European car.' If you run, you run. Ronald Reagan didn't have any proposition and he ran. Bill Bradley never had a proposition. He came from basketball and ran for Senate."

The template for film promotion in the blockbuster era, one that Schwarzenegger had helped to invent, would transfer remarkably well to the political arena. "He is about a release date and working backwards," recalls his former agent, Lou Pitt. Even the announcement of Schwarzenegger's entry into the race was made from a distinctly show-business setting, the movie star–friendly *Tonight Show* couch. As the gubernatorial campaign ramped up later in the summer, information and access was carefully withheld. Appearances were carefully selected, staged and scripted. Having done thousands of what weightlifters call repetitions in his career—at press junkets, he might do two hundred interviews in a weekend—the idea of staying on message politically was as intuitive as a bench press. Literally translated from the German, his surname means "black ploughman." He knows how to keep tilling the soil, covering the same ground with relentless purpose. Nearly every interview included his proud note that he worked his 6-foot-2, 218-pound body back into the exact same shape it was in for *T2* in 1991, down to the identical body-fat percentage.

Then, of course, there's that bust of Lenin. Schwarzenegger's Santa Monica office—three floors up from his restaurant, Schatzi on Main—is suitably vast. Gas-fed flames illuminate a white marble fireplace big enough to stand in. Its mantle is crammed with framed photos of Schwarzenegger with world leaders like Mikhail Gorbachev and Bill Clinton. The decor blends beachfront, sandstone tones with the trappings of a traditional, all-male club-room.

The office contains busts of Lenin, Reagan and John F. Kennedy (whom Schwarzenegger admired, he says, long before marrying Kennedy's niece Maria Shriver). A group of Russian bodybuilders from St. Petersburg brought the three-foot-tall Lenin head into the United States after the Soviet Union dissolved and presented it to Schwarzenegger. Upon their return next year, they wanted to outdo themselves with another bust. "When they unveiled Stalin, I said 'NO.' I had to explain to them why," he said. "Lenin was not as evil. He was just in the right place at the right time. But Stalin was evil. He was a dictator beyond belief. There were questions of who was more evil, Hitler or him." At the time of the interview, images of statues of Saddam Hussein toppling in Baghdad were flashing across the news. The possibility of a Saddam Hussein bust appearing in the office seemed remote. But this political novice, whose signature movie role was a crypto-fascist fantasy of the ultimate rude guy, wasn't shy about expressing his admiration for other political demagogues. "Saddam didn't start anything great," Schwarzenegger said. "But Lenin started communism and the whole Karl Marx thing. He started something that lasted seventy-something years."

Almost every square inch of wall space in Schwarzenegger's office is covered with totems and trophies. A Warhol dominates one wall. On another is an oil painting of Schwarzenegger striking a pose. Another wall displays an intermingled array of prizes, from his bodybuilding titles to a Golden Globe for best film newcomer for his role in Bob Rafelson's film *Stay Hungry* to a handful of clear plastic awards from ShoWest. Around the reception area are looming eight-foot-tall replicas of Terminator robots and the beast from *Predator*. There is a pair of imposing marble legs from a five-hundred-year-old Hercules statue he got in Italy because he admired the definition of their calves. It didn't take much prodding for Schwarzenegger to offer us a tour of the impressive space. He held his cigar like a flashlight, careful not to spill ashes on the stylish carpet. He chuckled at the memories each piece of memorabilia inspired.

"At the time, *Terminator 2* was groundbreaking. But there hasn't really been that much done since then," he contended. Special effects "have been used more. But the things that we're seeing—like *Lord of the Rings* and other movies, like *Jurassic Park*—have some groundbreaking things. It gives you a chance to make people feel like they're part of the story because you don't have to cut away all the time."

The process of releasing a blockbuster, he argued, is "not any more competitive today than it was ten years ago." In the *T2* era, "one released a movie on fifteen hundred to two thousand screens. Sometimes, it was a revolutionary kind of release that made everybody open their eyes and say, 'Wow,' maybe it was twenty-eight hundred. Today it's understood that you release on five thousand screens, six thousand screens, seven thousand screens. So a movie's life is shorter. You're putting out on so many screens so more people see it and you can accommodate people in a short period of time for everyone to see the movie in the first week, second week, third week. That means if the movie stays in there six weeks and you're doing well and then, of course, it fizzles out. You have a winner on your hands. In the old days, ten years ago, you were counting on a slow drop, twenty-five percent, thirty percent. Today, the only movies that do that are the ones that don't open on all those many screens. . . . Now, it doesn't matter if someone opens two weeks later, another big movie a week later because you're cashing in much more on the opening weekend. So the competitiveness is the same; it's just different. It's more compressed. There are more sequels, more monster movies, more epic movies with effects."

From the Terminator's standpoint, not a lot has changed. The movie's old-fashioned stuntwork, done on a sky-high budget, was a calculated bet that traditional action movies still mattered. "I said I'd be back and I'm back," the star had intoned in countless interviews, appearances and campaign rallies. Unlike Reese Witherspoon and Brad Pitt, he had no more movies to shoot at present. He could spend six months traveling the world to promote himself and the character who had made him famous, and who would potentially catapult him to new heights. He would methodically wear his opposition down.

Wash. Rinse. Repeat.

Eric Kops scoped out his spot. He eased his tall frame into a Louis XIV bergère in the lobby of London's Dorchester Hotel. It gave him a direct line of sight to the front desk, the restaurant and the elevator. "This is my favorite place," he said, "because I can see who's coming and going, and I can smoke." Relishing the absence of laws prohibiting smoking indoors, he fired up a Marlboro Light.

The press junket for *Legally Blonde 2: Red, White & Blonde* had reached the halfway point. The date was Saturday, June 7. Kops served as the human hub of activity at the three-day event, directing traffic, chatting up talent and perfecting the art of ordering room service. He had been in London for almost a week, but it took barely a day for the event—and the eight-hour time difference—to take its toll. As the business day wound down in London, the action was heating up in Los Angeles. A front-page story in *Daily Variety* involving MGM had kept Kops on the phone until well past 3 A.M. the night before.

Two floors up from Kops' post, Reese Witherspoon, a wool-capped Ryan Philippe and their precocious daughter, Eva, roamed the hallways with a sizable entourage of family, manager and personal publicist in tow. While his wife promoted her movie, Philippe took Eva to nearby Hyde Park. By the end of the junket, Witherspoon's retinue would rack up tens of thousands of pounds in hotel expenses. Given the total cost of a junket, in this case estimated by MGM to be nearly $300,000, the studio would not squawk too much about the tab. The company knew that the junket was central to the private process that gives movie stars a public profile heading into opening weekend. A logistical feat involving a dozen studio publicists and a host of videographers, lighting technicians and makeup artists yields the crisp, enthusiastic sound bites that convince television viewers and newspaper readers that they are getting an intimate look at their favorite stars.

The *Terminator 3* junket would be held a week later on Arnold Schwarzenegger's home turf, at Los Angeles Center Studios, the production facility in which long segments of both *Legally Blonde 2* and *T3* were shot. Warners' choice of junket locations was a boon for Schwarzenegger. It was a thirty-minute drive in light traffic from his home on the Westside. He'd shot his previous film, *Collateral Damage* there, and the facility had arranged to dedicate a soundstage to the actor as the *T3* junket media snapped pictures.

Under normal conditions, the junket for *Legally Blonde 2* would have been held in L.A., likely at the Four Seasons Hotel, in Beverly Hills. But Witherspoon was shooting her next movie, *Vanity Fair*, in London and also happened to be five months pregnant. MGM pulled off the high-wire feat of securing two days off during the shoot for Witherspoon to return to America, coordinating appearances on *The Tonight Show* and at the film's New York premiere, so getting her to a junket in L.A. was impossible. The company was amortizing the cost of flying junketeers across the world by busing them out to visit the sets of the studio's forthcoming *Agent Cody Banks 2: Destination London* and *De-Lovely*, a Cole Porter biopic. These sorts of midproduction junkets, accounted separately on each film's budget and therefore boosting MGM's total costs well past the $300,000 ascribed to *Legally Blonde 2*, are increasingly common. They started in the 1990s and then mushroomed once it became clear how quickly a film could become an event thanks to the Internet. In the digital age, an online Pied Piper like Harry Knowles, who runs Ain't It Cool News, can spread more meaningful buzz than the traditional busload of middleweight TV correspondents. Studios have even started holding special "trailer junkets" expressly for movie Web sites to get an early look at a trailer and post their reviews. New Line's mother of all junkets, held in New Zealand for *Lord of the Rings*, raised the bar for set-visit junkets. So did a series of Disney blowouts over the last decade. The million-dollar *Pearl Harbor* junket took place on an aircraft carrier in Hawaii. For *Aladdin*, the studio flew junketeers and their families down to Orlando, handed out free passes to its theme parks and transformed an entire park into an Arabian bazaar. The eighty-five print and broadcast journalists attending the *Legally Blonde 2* junket were not being treated to a theme-park party but they were not exactly digging ditches, either. Two-thirds of them had been flown to

London at the studio's expense and put up at the Grosvenor House, a luxurious prewar hotel just three doors down Park Lane from the Dorchester.

Other studios capitalized on the fact that so many journalists were in London for *Legally Blonde 2*. Warner Brothers threw a party for its Mandy Moore movie, *Chasing Liberty*; Universal held a set visit at Pinewood Studios for *The Thunderbirds*, in which actors in full costume gave interviews during their breaks from shooting. And, on different floors at the Dorchester, junkets were held for *Swimming Pool* and *28 Days Later*. One floor up from *Legally Blonde 2*, Jeffrey Katzenberg and Brad Pitt were offering interviews to a cluster of TV and print journalists at a sparsely populated junket for *Sinbad*.

In cases like this, studios often appreciate being able to share costs. But they still keep track, of course. When Dream-Works abruptly insisted that Pitt be interviewed in a large suite by a crew from *Access Hollywood*, delaying a long-scheduled interview with Witherspoon, Kops told his colleagues, "The whole day for that suite is going right on their bill."

Having worked more than a hundred junkets, Kops knows well what a bizarre Hollywood ritual they are. But they remain a startlingly efficient marketing tool, especially for all of the midsized newspapers and TV stations in America, or the legions of foreign media outlets. Peter Adee described the central theme of *Legally Blonde 2* as "innocence triumphs over all." In three days, the junket allowed that message to get shotgunned out to hundreds of millions of potential ticket-buyers.

The mechanics of the process do not vary much. On one

day, junketeers are shown the movie, in this case at a frumpy screening room inside the British Academy of Film and Television Arts. Another day is set aside for broadcasters; a third for print journalists. Food is served throughout. A tenor of barely contained chaos prevails. Though the interviews aren't technically scripted, the same questions are repeated endlessly. Stars, directors and writers rotate from one suite to the next. Some broadcast entities like *Entertainment Tonight* or MTV, or print outlets like the *New York Times* or *Newsweek*, will be accorded extra time for one-on-one interviews. But many esteemed outlets shun the junket process, believing its bounteous buffets and carefully orchestrated interview arrangements constitute a grave violation of journalistic principles. Shepherding the interviewees is a phalanx of studio publicists, personal publicists and managers, who make sure that neither the five-minute time limit nor the bounds of decency are ignored.

The ritual dates back to the 1930s. But the recent explosion of broadcast and Internet outlets, and the studios' relentless focus on opening-weekend, saturation TV coverage, has brought the exercise to a new level of absurdity. Ground rules are clearly established—no asking Tom Cruise about rumors that he is gay, no asking Lindsay Lohan about her dad's criminal record. Offenders are sometimes ejected from the junket; others are simply crossed off the studios' invite list for next time, a ban that for many Hollywood correspondents is a professional death penalty. Since junketeers make their living on access to stars, they not only tend to conform to the ground rules, but also to go out of their way to fawn over the celebrities. "Two kids and your career's taking off like a rocket," one said to Reese Witherspoon. "Do you ever wake up and think, 'How do I do it?'" Another TV regular on the junket circuit tapes his name to his shoe in the hope that the star will say it on the air, suggesting a personal connection to the viewer at home. On the junket for *Almost Famous,* Mark Ramsey, representing the Web site MovieJuice.com, quoted a line from *Jerry Maguire,* telling Kate Hudson, "You complete me." He later said, "She laughed hysterically, but the rest of the reporters went after me like I crossed some serious news line. You'd think you were in a room with Morley Safer and Mike Wallace."

The overall effect is disorientation, numbness and fatigue. It's ShoWest on one floor of a hotel. Director Jean-Pierre Jeunet has said he "very nearly went mad" during a junket in Japan for *Alien Resurrection.* "After one particularly bad interview, I remember running into the next room to just scream. I wanted to cry. Making a film takes a long time but not as long as the interviews if you are making one for a big studio." A slap-happy Charlie Herman-Wurmfeld, though proud of his film *Kissing Jessica Stein,* laughed out loud when one junketeer began a question by calling it "a modern-day *Annie Hall.*"

From his perch in the Dorchester lobby, Kops kept one eye on the door, waiting for Kelly Clarkson. The *American Idol* star was set to interview Witherspoon for a popular MTV show called *Movie House.* Fifteen minutes later, well after her appointed time, Clarkson entered the lobby. "Sorry I'm late," she said, unconvincingly. "Lost my dang passport." Kops ushered her into a suite on the broadcast floor, where he could prep her for the interview. Clarkson wore all black: boots, silk bell-bottoms and a short top that revealed a navel ring. Doe eyes darting around the suite, she asked for a pot of hot water. ("I only drink hot water."). Noting her raven-colored bob, the pop-culture-obsessed Kops observed, as if to an old friend, "You got rid of your extensions!" She explained that they're great only to "throw around" while performing. Plus, she filmed the summer movie *From Justin to Kelly* sans extensions, so she wanted to provide continuity in her public appearances.

Clarkson had missed the screening the night before, so Kops showed her trailers and delivered a three-minute synopsis of the film so tight and informative it belonged in Cliff's Notes. ("I've seen the first one twenty times and this one fifteen times and I like this one," he concluded.) He made a point of mentioning that Witherspoon is a direct descendant of John Witherspoon, one of the original signers of the Declaration of Independence. "Cool!" Clarkson enthused, offering a sense of her interviewing style. Kops ushered her into a suite down the hall and the awkward love-in began.

Clarkson: I'm such a huge fan, by the way. You're, like, one of my favorite actresses.

Witherspoon: I'm a huge fan of yours, too.

Clarkson: Really? Oh, cool. I'm not good at this. I'm used to being interviewed. I saw the trailer and it looks so good. I'm actually kind of wary about sequels, but that looks better, so I'm very excited about seeing it. Was it fun to work on?

Witherspoon: It was fun, and the clothes got even better.

As the conversation went on, TV crews hired by MGM manned simultaneous interview locations in ten other suites, clogging the plush-carpeted hallway with electrical cords and steel-case equipment boxes. High-intensity lights created a suffocating heat that could not be quelled with air conditioning. In the middle of the hall was the Hospitality Suite, where a dozen or so MGM staffers communicated with each other by walkie-talkie, helping junketeers procure goodie bags and monitoring all of the TV interviews happening in the various suites.

Many of the local broadcast personalities seemed like understudies to the national network correspondents. From certain angles, they display a bit of the sheen and bounce of those they are interviewing, but their careers exist at the margins of the small screen. They kept the chatter in between interviews light. "I love my show," one told a publicist waiting outside a suite. "It's on Fox." Another marveled at a location by the Thames River that MGM had secured as a picturesque backdrop for TV reports. "Thank you for boosting my Nielsen ratings!" The Parliament and Tower of London tableau would be perfect accompaniment for lines like, "I caught up with Reese here in London."

When the junket interviews began, conduct got even more dubious. One reporter showed Witherspoon a small journal containing notes he took while watching the screening: " 'Reese and her character are intelligent and rise above.' . . . Isn't that cool?" Kops would hardly blink at the dozens of exchanges like that shown over the weekend on a control-room monitor set up in one suite. His main focus that day was keeping tabs on the Clarkson-Witherspoon colloquy. In the control room, a mixing board modulates the volume and a bank of small monitors show both interviewer and interviewee. The studio hires the crew and equipment and even owns the tape. If anything objectionable is ever said, the studio can halt the interview and then tape over the offending question and answer. The MTV session was innocuous enough not to require Big Brother oversight; Kops just wanted to see if the seeds he'd planted in Clarkson's subconscious had sprouted. The fusillade of "happy talk" emanating from the mixing board suggested otherwise. "The first *Legally Blonde,* apparently, did really well. Now how about this one? Projections are looking well," Clarkson ventured. As the dialogue continued, Witherspoon looked at once relieved by the soft questioning and perplexed by Clarkson's inability to let her get a word in.

"She talks faster than I do," muttered Kops, sprawled on a nearby couch. "Should I tell her to slow down?" wondered a colleague. The interview was scheduled to last twenty minutes, which at that point seemed an eternity. "Unless we want to give her a minute to see if she settles in," said Kops. She didn't exactly "settle in," but in an unexpected way her frenetic pacing gave the interview more potential sound bites to choose from. MTV would manage to splice together a workable package. That's all MGM was after.

Marketing chief Peter Adee drifted into the control room. He wore a leather jacket and ran a hand through his shaggy hair. "Can I hear Reese?" he asked, boosting her volume on the mixing board before anyone could answer. Narrowing his eyes, he concentrated on her responses, which were indistinguishable from those in the twenty-two other interviews she had given that day. Assessing her floral-print dress, he concluded, eyes never leaving the screen: "She looks so much better than yesterday. I don't know why she wore that thing." Adee is a clap-on-the-shoulder, how-you-hittin'-'em kind of guy, given to sudden outbursts and eye rolls and poisonous darts of gossip. Asked months before opening weekend about the poor advance word on *Sinbad,* he grimaced. "It doesn't matter about the movie," he said. "They're going to spend like crazy." Initially, Adee may come off as arrogant and more than a little withholding. Interlopers are regarded with suspicion. His style occasionally prompted clashes with studio bosses, though his creative abilities and charm usually came to the rescue. MGM was his fourth studio job in the past decade, following stints at Disney and DreamWorks (where he worked with Terry Press) and a year at Universal. Such moves were not unusual given the rampant turnover in the marketing game. Marketing executives are convenient studio scapegoats. Streaks of poor opening weekends often end in the ouster of those guiding the campaigns even as the production executives behind the flops keep their jobs.

As Adee surveyed the monitors, one broadcaster stood out. She was an extremely round, buxom and glad-to-meet-ya woman no taller than five feet. Her name was Maria Salas and she worked for Telemundo. For this occasion, she wore a homemade tribute to Elle Woods: a pink lace skirt with a black top and a pink flower. She beamed a broad smile while traipsing through the hallways between interviews, eager to explain the origin of her dress. Kops called Salas "the Charo of junkets." He elaborated with a conspiratorial look: "Sometimes I strategically send her in at the end of the day and the energy in the room goes right up."

Print junketeers throw off less heat and light than broadcasters and are generally a more irascible lot. These are the people whose names you read underneath fulsome quotes in movie ads, like Earl Dittman of an obscure publication called *Wireless Magazine.* He called Paramount's disastrous remake of *Four Feathers* "exquisite, breathtaking," "astounding, unforgettable" and a "phenomenal cinematic achievement! You will feel compelled to see it over and over again!"

Print interviews are conducted in "roundtables," clusters of six or seven reporters around a table in a hotel suite. Over a two-hour period, subjects are herded over to roundtables for short intervals. Every few minutes, they switch, so that every table gets every subject. In between interviews, there is the inevitable down time, which jaundiced junketeers fill by complaining, about the air-conditioning in the room, about the shabbiness of their hotel, about the long flight from the United States. After Witherspoon has left the room, a vigorous debate breaks out. The topic: What to do with the per diem provided by MGM? Save it? Spend it all? Since most studio per diems are in the range of $150–200, it isn't an entirely inconsequential discussion.

MGM hosted a cocktail party for the junketeers at a Mayfair bistro called Scott's, where Ian Fleming reportedly came to write his James Bond novels. Legend has it that a bartender there created the martini for him and he, in turn, popularized the drink in his 007 books. Dimly lit and spacious, the venue has three levels: a reception area, a bar and a restaurant. The MGM party took place on all three. Liberated from a grueling day under the TV lights, Charles Herman-Wurmfeld made a brief circuit around the room, shaking a few hands and smiling when the situation demanded it. For the shiny-headed, goateed director, making the film had been a mixed blessing. *Legally Blonde 2* was his big break, but he was visibly uncomfortable with the process. In several of his interviews during the junket, Herman-Wurmfeld was asked about the competition between *Terminator 3* and *Legally Blonde 2*. He usually gave the same "Kumbaya" reply: "People have a choice on July Fourth weekend between guns and explosions and death or pink and love." Later, at the party, he reflected on the intensity of fine-tuning the film to meet the studio's demands. "I wonder why I'm up at night playing bongos and then I realize, 'Oh yeah, I've been immersed in commerce.'"

Across the room, Kops was still coping with sleep deprivation, but he deemed the junket a success. "No major disasters" was his characteristic assessment. It was true. The event had not created another one of the junket horror stories swapped by publicists, involving a star showing up drunk or muddling the carefully scripted publicity message. It would take a couple of weeks for the junket interviews to gestate, but when they did, Reese Witherspoon would be ubiquitous. Admiring profiles would be written about Bob Newhart, Sally Field and Moondoggie, who played Bruiser the Chihuahua. The reshoots, the anxiety-laden test screenings, the script issues and the infighting over the soul of Elle Woods that had Herman-Wurmfeld beating the bongos—all of it would be buffed with fine pink polish. As a bonus, the London setting, the cocktail party at Scott's, and the *De-Lovely* and *Agent Cody Banks 2* set visits had allowed MGM the chance to promote itself as a company. It didn't have a Big Picture event like Warner Brothers did—with Arnold, robots, fireworks, *The Matrix* and Tom Cruise—but it would always have London.

Adee, ever mindful of the summer's competitive landscape, chatted at the party with a couple of international distribution executives. Everyone marveled at the spectacular $70 million opening of *Finding Nemo* the week before. As one of the architects of the campaigns for *The Lion King, Aladdin* and *Prince of Egypt*, Adee understood that one of the biggest pop-culture events of summer 2003 was at hand. Someone asked him whether the film's one-sheet, which depicted a close-up of Bruce the Shark's razor-toothed grin, risked scaring young children. "No-o-o," he said, his eyes widening into his teasing, you-just-don't-get-it expression. "As soon as I saw that image, I saw a hit."

The *T3* junket on June 16 and 17 wasn't a touristy boondoggle for the Hollywood press. It was a model of industrial efficiency at a production facility on the post-industrial outskirts of downtown Los Angeles. But the mood of the filmmakers and studio executives was decidedly upbeat. In the early afternoon on June 17, producers Andy Vajna and Mario Kassar trailed by a small entourage, piled out of a blue Bentley and a silver Mercedes which gleamed in the bright sunlight. The producers were crowing about the first reviews of the film, which had appeared a few hours earlier on Web site Ain't

It Cool News, posted by people who'd attended one of the junket screenings. "Wow . . . wowee wow wow . . . and another wow!" screamed one review. "This film . . . is way cool! What can I say, other than, thank you for not screwing this movie up!" "Check out the scene of Arnie smashing a toilet over Kristanna Loken's head. ROCKIN!" said another. These were fans, not major critics; their endorsements didn't carry much clout. But they lent the marketing campaign momentum at a pivotal moment. Warners employees in the press check-in area clutched photocopies of the reviews, as broadcast journalists meandered between the soundstages. A makeshift commissary in front of Soundstage 2, cordoned off with yellow police tape, was strewn with other movie props. Red Styrofoam bricks were piled on black tablecloths. A waiter in black tie and jacket, half his face disfigured with purplish Terminator makeup, served cappuccino and hot chocolate. Leather biker jackets wrapped in plastic spilled out of a cardboard box in the press room—gifts for the junketing media that could fetch hundreds of dollars on eBay. A makeup artist was on hand to provide Terminator face paint to complete the look.

The *T3* junket was a homecoming for Schwarzenegger and the cast. The *T3* production had been headquartered at Los Angeles Center Studios for six months in 2002 (*Legally Blonde 2* began shooting there just as *T3* wrapped). Weeks before principal photography, Schwarzenegger and the producers had reached a deal to shoot at the sprawling production factory—with its six sound stages, twelve-story office tower and more than twenty-five thousand square feet of offices, dressing rooms, production and screening facilities—scrapping their original plan to shoot more than half of the film in Vancouver, Canada. The switch from Vancouver to L.A. allowed Schwarzenegger to position himself as an adversary of runaway production, the large-scale shift of Hollywood moviemaking from the United States to foreign locations. Fueled by cheap labor costs and tax incentives from Canada and other regions, runaway production had bled money from the L.A. economy throughout the 1990s and was estimated to have cost the United States $4.1 billion and twenty-five thousand jobs between 1998 and 2002. A production on the scale of *T3* was a big boost for the region. "The local economy thrives because of it," said L.A. Center Studios co-owner Chris Ursitti. "Every [production] dollar that's spent in town radiates in the community by ten."

A rumor circulated in the press that Schwarzenegger had taken a pay cut to bring the budget in line with the heightened expense of shooting in L.A. The rumor didn't hurt Schwarzenegger's nascent political career. The actor's pledge to restore California's economy by luring businesses back to the state would become his mantra in the months to come. The decision to shoot *T3* in L.A. was also intended to simplify the complex production logistics. The one-hundred-day shoot was one of the biggest film productions of 2002. Roughly $70 million of the $175 million budget went to "above the line" costs—the rights and development of the property, the salary of the talent and filmmakers. Crew wages, effects work and incidental costs during production were classified as "below the line" expenses. In *T3*'s case, the $105 million below the line would have to cover a shooting schedule that was mind-bendingly complex. The only easy part of Jonathan Mostow's day would be making the manageable commute from the San Fernando Valley. He would be captain of a film shoot occupying, at times, all six of the eighteen-thousand-square-foot soundstages, plus twenty-five thousand square feet of office space. More than one thousand workers, many of them unionized, were used during the shoot. The production rented out additional office space in an adjacent twelve-floor tower. During the filming, Stage 2 caught on fire. The black dubateen material masking one of the lights used to illuminate the scene in which actors Nick Stahl and Claire Danes were chased through a military compound by an airborne robot burst into flames, setting off the sprinkler system. Shooting on the stage had to be canceled for two weeks.

The decision to shoot *T3* in L.A. was a coup for the production facility. Parts of Steven Spielberg's *Catch Me if You Can* and Tim Burton's *Planet of the Apes* remake were shot at the facility. Studio personnel have fond memories of the *Apes* production, when hundreds of extras, dressed in monkey suits and prosthetic makeup, wandered the corridors of the studio, sipping liquid meals through straws and talking on cell phones. But the *T3* production was on an even bigger scale. The facility cut its fee to make the deal work, so the film's producers had only to shave two percent off the budget (usually, it costs ten to fifteen percent more to shoot in California rather than Canada). All of the profit participants took a cut. Schwarzenegger, knowing how much his fortunes were bound up with the film's, decided to pay out of his own pocket for the scene in which the Terminators do battle in a claustrophobic office lavatory—the scene in which he memorably appears to bash Loken's head into a toilet. For a burgeoning production complex located in one of the city's most blighted neighborhoods, the huge *Terminator 3* shoot provided a timely tonic. Facility managers had blocked out an hour of the June 14 schedule to show their gratitude to Schwarzenegger by dedicating Sound Stage 2, the one that had caught fire, to the star.

Los Angeles Center Studios sits on the former site of the Union Oil Company's global headquarters. The company fled to Texas in 1996, continuing the turnover that defines downtown L.A., that symbol of urban renewal, the rise of the automobile and the sprawling modern city without a center. The studio, the first one built in the city of L.A. since the 1920s, helped satisfy Hollywood's urgent need for soundstages. It forms, with Frank Gehry's nearby Disney Hall and the Staples Center arena, an "entertainment campus," as Ursitti enthused. "In five minutes, we can go sit on the floor of a Lakers game."

The streets of downtown L.A. would remain a distinguishing feature of the entire *Terminator* franchise, and serve as the staging ground for some of its most outlandish stunts. In the first *Terminator,* Schwarzenegger commandeers a police car on South Broadway and pursues Linda Hamilton and Michael Biehn through downtown's trash-strewn streets. In *Terminator 3,* a 100-ton hydraulic crane and a fire engine appears to stage a high-speed pursuit through downtown L.A., crushing cars, toppling telephone poles and ripping apart a glass building. Los Angeles Center Studios offers a bulwark against the urban wreckage of downtown L.A. If you stand, as Schwarzenegger did for a *USA Today* photographer on June 14, on a bridge spanning the lot's office suites and gleaming soundstages, you may as well be standing in tidy Burbank. The photo of Schwarzenegger would appear in *USA Today* three months later at the height of the gubernatorial campaign in a story that traced his ambitions to the 1960s, when the actor was a gym rat and bricklayer, under the headline, "Brick by brick, an immigrant builds a life of fame, fortune and power."

The field marshal of the *T3* junket was Warner Brothers marketing executive Marc Cohen, a well-scrubbed New Hampshire native with years of experience on movie junkets. For most of the day, Cohen prowled Sound Stage 2 and its surrounding offices. A stairwell led from the street to the bowels of the building, where floor-to-ceiling curtains created a long corridor illuminated by a pair of flashing red lights, and a set of interview suites where, in five-minute time allotments, TV reporters interviewed Schwarzenegger, Nick Stahl, Claire Danes, Kristanna Loken, robot designer Stan Winston and director Jonathan Mostow. The junketeers moved on a rotating schedule from one micro-interview to another, biding time between appointments by waiting in a line of black folding chairs arrayed outside the interview suites. Publicists with clipboards and headsets roamed quietly among them.

The interviews were recorded by a film company hired by Warner Brothers, whose personnel reviewed each tape before releasing it to the appropriate journalist. Beneath a flat-screen monitor at one end of the corridor, with a digital display of each interview in progress, a Warner Brothers official kept tabs on the action. The operation was as efficient as a factory assembly line. The actors each had stylists, who performed makeup touch-ups between interviews, and various hangers-on. Loken wore a flouncy red dress with cutaway sleeves and a plunging V-neck. She sat in a room that was outfitted like a scene from *Terminator 3*. ILM had created a video segment depicting an army of marching robots that played in a loop on a video screen behind her. A waiter arrived with five cans of Red Bull on ice in a silver bowl. She vamped between interviews. "I learned not to speak at all in my daily life. Now I just sign," she said to her manager gesturing to him in sign language. Swooping into the interview chair, the manager began massaging her feet and flashed a mischievous smile. "Could you just spread your legs a little for the camera?" he said.

The raw materials of the production—charred and wrecked cars, steel beams, a bullet-riddled coffin and hearse—were arranged in the street outside Sound Stage 2, next to a row of golf carts. There was a battered Toyota Tundra, painted with the insignia of the Emory Animal Shelter, the veterinarian's clinic where the Terminator first grapples with the T-X. A blackened steel rampart lay across the crumpled hood and shattered windshield of a Lexus SC 430 hardtop convertible, the car that the T-X snatches from a surprised Rodeo Drive shopper in one of the film's opening scenes.

His interviews done, Mostow made a final stop at the press room, where Marc Cohen helped him try on a Terminator jacket, one of the pricey leather replicas being given out to junketeers. He slipped on a couple different sizes, checking his reflection in a mirror wearing the very garment he often said made the Terminator the most recognizable film character in the world. Cohen handed him a report from the Warner Brothers box office database that gave a snapshot of the top dozen movies in the marketplace. *Finding Nemo* continued to top the charts, but Mostow's eye was drawn to the minuscule $3.8 million Friday gross for the Harrison Ford cop movie *Hollywood Homicide*. One of the summer's big disasters had arrived. What did that mean for next weekend's *Hulk* or, for that matter, *T3*? Mostow didn't hang around to speculate. "I think my wife and I are going to try to go see *Nemo*," he said on the way out the door. Consumed with the final push toward opening weekend, he wouldn't make it to the movies, at least not that night.

Late in the afternoon, it was finally time for the Stage 2 dedication. Schwarzenegger took a break from the final spate of interviews, emerged from the bowels of the soundstage and strode toward a makeshift platform on the south side of the lot. The star's black Mercedes SUV was parked right in front of Sound Stage 2. At the end of the day, he would fire up a cigar, climb into the driver's seat and slip anonymously into L.A. traffic.

The actor was outfitted in Western wear—blue jeans with an oversize Western belt buckle, a tan blazer and custom-designed cowboy boots with silver heels and silver-capped toes. He looked at first glance like his unflappable hero John Wayne, staying in control as the bombs dropped around him. As a crowd of some fifty onlookers gathered near the platform, Schwarzenegger slowly approached. While it may have eluded the obsequious junket cameras, upon close inspection his lips were curled into a tight grimace, his face showing for the first time his dwindling patience for the act of smiling for photographs. He was followed down the street by a T-1 robot on treads, the tank-like menace from the movie that would accompany Schwarzenegger to many of the promotional events for *T3*. A technician with a goatee used a steering wheel strapped to his chest to maneuver the T-1. Schwarzenegger was introduced by Chris Ursitti and other studio personnel, then mounted the platform and pulled a cord, which lowered a curtain on the exterior wall of the soundstage revealing a sign that said, "L.A. Center Studios honors Arnold Schwarzenegger for outstanding achievement as an actor . . . for spectacular use of Stage 2."

A cake in the shape of Stage 2 was wheeled out, and Schwarzenegger cut the first slice with a large sword. The Terminator looked unusually drained. He'd done more than one hundred interviews in three days, and his legendary brio was on the wane, the façade showing the wear and tear of a promotional spree every bit as repetitive and wearing as cocking a heavy shotgun during filming. Standing at the podium next to Stage 2, he recited a short and familiar speech, applauding the studio for bringing production dollars back to Los Angeles, and urging everyone to see his new film, *Terminator 3: Rise of the Machines*, on July 2. "I said I'll be back and I'm back," he said to the small cluster of reporters and L.A. Center Studio employees. "Thank you, and I'll be back."

Schwarzenegger posed for more photographs, standing next to the T-1. Improvising without a script, he had nothing to say for the first time all day. Pondering the robot for a moment, he concluded finally, "He has the right attitude."

Robots on the Riviera

The lobby of the Carlton hotel in Cannes usually opens onto a grassy lawn planted with palm trees facing the French resort town's long beachfront thoroughfare, the Boulevard de la Croisette. But in early May, a construction crew built an elaborate movie set between the hotel and the beach. They toiled for several days in the bright sunshine, hammering together a metal structure designed to resemble a high-tech military bunker from *Terminator 3*. There were plastic gun turrets and corrugated metal walls decorated with red neon *T3* logos. There was a giant steel door that looked like it was meant to withstand a nuclear blast.

For most of the year, the InterContinental Carlton Cannes is the epitome of French Riviera elegance. Its sumptuous suites cost thousands of euros a night. On a clear day, the view from the twin cupolas, said to be inspired by the breasts of nineteenth-century courtesan La Belle Otéro, stretches unimpeded across the coast. But when the fifty-sixth annual Cannes Film Festival opened on May 12, the hotel shed its Old World demeanor. The belle epoque exterior was swathed in more film advertisements than the lobby of a suburban multiplex theater. The entryway was flooded with flyers and festival broadsheets. Enormous banners promoting *Charlie's Angels 2, Pirates of the Caribbean, Bad Boys II* and *The Matrix Reloaded* were hung from the roof and terrace. The *T3* bunker was the most ostentatious of these efforts. And on Saturday, May 17, it sprang to life.

The press had been notified that an event, referred to as "Carlton Photo Call" in internal memos distributed to the *T3* producers and cast, would take place May 17 on the stage in front of the Carlton, featuring robots and special guests. It was an audacious stroke of old-fashioned film festival PR, the sort that was a trademark of producers Andy Vajna and Mario Kassar, perfectly tailored for their flamboyant superstar, Arnold Schwarzenegger. It was expensive. It didn't look much like a movie prop. It looked more like a flamboyant four-car garage with aluminum siding. It occupied what was arguably the most commanding patch of real estate on the waterfront. And until 1 P.M. on May 17, nobody knew exactly what it was.

Kassar and Vajna had been using Cannes as a showcase for their films for more than twenty-five years. Their goal this year was to promote *T3* both to the assembled entertainment press and to the tourists who thronged the streets of Cannes during the festival and congregated in front of the entrances to its hotels, hoping to glimpse the stars emerging from their lodgings. Few stars were as potent a symbol of

Hollywood's global box office hegemony as Schwarzenegger, who drove a gas-guzzling Hummer and had served as fitness advisor to the first president Bush. But if an anti-American mood lingered in France in the aftermath of the invasion of Iraq, it evaporated under the bright glare of Schwarzenegger's personal magnetism and the carefully calibrated hype that surrounded him in all his public appearances.

In the days leading up to May 17, local radio stations began to spread the word that the actor would appear at lunchtime in front of the Carlton. At 1 P.M. on May 17, the mayor of Cannes closed the Croisette. Nearly one thousand people swarmed in front of the hotel. An open-air, two-story bus was parked across the street, its lower deck lined with international news crews. A swiveling remote control camera attached to a white blimp hovered one hundred feet off the ground. Fifteen minutes later, the first portentous stirrings of the *T3* score swelled from loudspeakers onstage, punctuated by pounding kettle drums. Vajna, Kassar and a large ensemble of executives from the film's foreign distributor, Sony Pictures Entertainment, appeared on a Carlton hotel balcony above the stage. Kassar could be seen bobbing his head in synch with the music. Clusters of curious onlookers peered down from the hotel roof. Two plasma screens on either side of the stage screened *T3* trailers.

For fifteen minutes, nothing happened. The music grew louder; and security personnel in black suits milled in front of the stage as the crowd became restless. Suddenly two garage doors slid open and out came robots, moving on long ovular treads. These were the T-1s, created by Stan Winston,

that careen through the third act of *T3*. They were animatronic Terminators, with tiny heads and gun turrets extend-
ing on auxiliary pumps. Onstage at Cannes, they didn't look
like killing machines; they were cute, like *Star Wars* droids. A
few minutes went by and a silky female voice announced
over the loudspeakers: "Alert, alert. Intruder in sector three."
Smoke began wafting from behind the stage. There was the
sound of screeching metal. The giant steel door parted and
out strode Schwarzenegger, dressed in a beige suit and sunglasses, a handkerchief folded elegantly in his right breast
pocket.

The crowd pressed forward; dozens of arms lifted digital
cameras above the crowd, aiming them at the stage, and the
air filled with shouts of "Ahnold." The actor held a microphone. "I love the Cannes Film Festival," he said. "I have
been coming here to promote my films since 1977, for my
first film, *Pumping Iron*." He wandered across the platform
and grinned. "This is the capital of promotions for movies,
because there are thousands of journalists and photographers from around the world [who] come to Cannes. So
make sure you urge all the fans to see *Terminator 3: Rise of
the Machines* in your country, because we have the best
stunts, and visual effects that you have never seen before."

Schwarzenegger posed with the robots. He gave a thumbs-
up sign to the photographers. "You're getting all your shots?
Very nice, good." He repeated the full title of the film, *Terminator 3: Rise of the Machines*, several times. "This is a fantastic
story," he said. "It has incredible stunts that are absolutely gi-
gantic. . . . And remember, as I always say, I'll be back." With

that, the actor disappeared offstage, and the giant steel door closed behind him. The *T3* soundtrack faded, replaced by reggae music. The robots remained onstage. As the crowd dispersed, they slipped out of character, and began to bob and weave to the reggae. The whole production, which lasted less than thirty minutes, was pure burlesque. Little had changed since 1977, when Schwarzenegger posed on the beach at Cannes in a publicity stunt to promote *Pumping Iron* surrounded by bathing beauties. The event recalled the carnivalesque exploitation stunts of the old B movie promoters—men like Marty Weiser, who planted fake news stories about *The Beast from 20,000 Fathoms* or Kroger Babb, a distributor of sex-hygiene films in the 1940s who blitzed newspapers with fake protest letters to whip up attention for his films and once buried a man alive in front of a movie theater. The only difference was that *T3* wasn't a low-budget exploitation film. It was a $175 million corporate machine that was both a movie and a licensing vehicle with its own video game, media spinoffs and sponsorship deals with Toyota, Coca-Cola, Nokia and Shell oil. The Carlton stunt nevertheless had the desired effect. It was covered by seventy-nine news outlets in France alone and by hundreds more throughout Europe.

There are two sides of the Cannes Film Festival. One side is the festival, with its black-tie receptions, its ceremonial screenings at the Palais du Festival for highbrow movies in competition for the Palme d'Or, an award still redolent of the tastes of the postwar European cinema's high priests who presided over Cannes in the 1960s and 70s. The other side is the market: a bustling, lowbrow trade show, concentrated in the basement of the Palais and its adjacent casino, in hotel suites and yachts parked in the harbor. The market is populated by an eclectic blend of legitimate sales companies, fly-by-night cable buyers, B-movie producers and porn distributors who hold their own awards ceremony at the festival, the Hot d'Or.

Vajna and Kassar were on intimate terms with both sides of Cannes. They approached the market like riverboat card sharks. They were on a first-name basis with the film buyers from fringe territories like Taiwan, Singapore and Egypt. In previous years, rumors circulated that the duo gave away jewelry, oriental carpets and expensive watches to foreign distributors who bought their films. They were willing to spend money to make even more back. And they showed the same bold insouciance to all foreign buyers, whether they were selling a finished movie or preselling an idea on paper, using their sales receipts to finance production. They arrived at Cannes in private jets or fancy yachts and threw stylish celebrity parties for their clients. They stayed at the area's most posh accommodations, such as the beachfront Eden Roc suites at the cash-only Hotel du Cap, fifteen kilometers up the coast in Cap d'Antibes.

"Mario and Andy's whole business was always to make the movie with their money and take it to Cannes," Schwarzenegger told us. "They'd say, 'We are here to raise money, but look who we have here: Arnold. While you're making your commitment to us, while you're signing up to buy France, to buy England, to buy this and that, we have the guy here who will sell it for you. Tomorrow, we're going to make a big presentation and he's going to talk about your company or his company. So it's up to you whether you want to put the money down.' And everyone would say, 'Oh, wow, I could be the start of something big.'"

But in 2003 the agenda was different. *T3* was in postproduction, and rights to the film had already been sliced and diced around the world. The duo were in Cannes to publicize their film, not sell it. Kassar flew to Nice first-class on British Airways the evening of Wednesday, May 14; Vajna met him at the Hotel du Cap. Almost immediately, they began priming the publicity pump. They did their first print interviews at the hotel on Thursday morning. By Friday, when Schwarzenegger arrived in Cannes, their schedules were booked in hourly intervals, with the occasional ten-minute grooming or cigar break.

The Carlton event was one of three publicity events at the Cannes Film Festival paid for by Sony. Like Warner Brothers in the United States, Sony had to overcome the prejudice in its international campaign that the film was old news. Even overseas, where Schwarzenegger was still a big box office draw, *T3* seemed like a film trapped in a time warp. This was Schwarzenegger's eighth trip to Cannes. Several years earlier, he had appeared at the premiere of Planet Hollywood's Cannes franchise. The restaurant closed shortly thereafter. But, generally speaking, in 2003 it was as if nothing had changed. There were the same back-to-back European print and TV interviews. There was a yacht party, sponsored by Anheuser-Busch, on the night of May 16, on the 150-foot-long pleasure craft, *Perfect Persuasion*, docked at a crowded pier in the town's old port. Guests were asked to remove their shoes before mounting the gangplank. They were given white athletic socks with *Terminator 3* printed above the ankle, and black Budweiser slippers. Schwarzenegger spent most of the party below deck, but he appeared topside for a half hour stretch, doing interviews and shaking hands. The next day was wall-to-wall press for the cast and filmmakers. There were TV interviews with *Entertainment Tonight, Access Hollywood,* the BBC, TF1 and France 2; and roundtable interviews at the Carlton hotel casino with print journalists. In twenty-minute intervals, the cast spoke to *Journal du Dimanche, L'Ecran Fantastique, Australian InStyle, Italian Marie Claire, Elle Russia* and Poland's *Super Expres.*

Schwarzenegger would next materialize in public, along with the rest of the cast and crew, at a late-night *T3* party hosted by MTV at Pierre Cardin's futuristic estate, the Palais Bulles, in the hills above Cannes. A vast residential whimsy designed by Hungarian architect Antti Lovag, the Palais Bulles is built out of huge concrete bubbles. It has pod-like rooms with giant glass portholes, colorful cushions and round swimming pools. Cardin has loaned his house to film studios before. The previous year, MGM commandeered the place for a party to promote the James Bond film *Die Another Day*. For the *T3* party, the house was decorated with Terminator mannequins, white police netting and steel ramparts. Schwarzenegger, along with the rest of the talent and the filmmakers, arrived shortly after 11 P.M. A thick fog created by smoke machines enveloped the party entrance. The actor did a lap through the space-age estate, surrounded by swarming, shrieking fans, before retiring to a VIP area. An hour later, he left for the airport in Nice to fly back to L.A. The rest of the cast flew to Berlin for another press junket.

If the *T3* principals had doubts about Warner Brothers' U.S. marketing commitment to the film, Europe was a different story. Sony saturated the continent with *T3* advertising and held publicity galas in a number of the major cities. "Every single one of these premieres—in intensity and scope and showmanship—blew away our L.A. premiere," one of the film's producers complained. "In Spain, there was huge outdoor advertising everywhere."

The Palais Bulles party may have been the most extravagant party of the film festival. But it was just one of several superhyped Hollywood events there. The flamboyant Cannes launch for *T3* unfolded in the shadow of another film that was, for a short time, spellbinding news. On Thursday, May 16, Warner Brothers' *The Matrix Reloaded* opened in thirty-six hundred theaters in the United States. By Saturday morning, film executives and the press in Cannes were projecting that *The Matrix Reloaded* would gross $150 million by the end of its opening weekend—a new box office record. Those predictions missed the mark. The film would face a storm of negative reviews, amassing $140 million in box office receipts over its first five days of release, before fading quickly from theaters. Its final box office haul wasn't record-breaking, amounting to less than *Harry Potter, Spider-Man* or *Star Wars, Episode II–Attack of the Clones.* By the end of the summer, its $280 million domestic gross would be considered a disappointment, eclipsed by a pair of even bigger blockbusters, *Finding Nemo* and *Pirates of the Caribbean*.

In the first days of Cannes, however, the *Matrix* backlash hadn't yet materialized, and it appeared to be a runaway hit. One of the reasons that Intermedia and C-2 sold U.S. rights to *T3* to Warner Brothers was to ride the *Matrix* bandwagon by attaching their trailers to prints of *The Matrix Reloaded*. But now they found themselves outstripped at every turn by *Matrix* hoopla. On May 16 *The Matrix Reloaded* had its European premiere at the black-tie, opening-night ceremony at the Palais. Five thousand fans and tourists massed behind police barricades as Keanu Reeves and assorted cast members stepped from their limos in evening wear and ascended the red-carpeted steps of the Palais, flanked by French police in formal attire. After the screening came a party in a giant barn-shaped tent at the tip of the Quai Laubeuf in the old section of the city, throbbing with high-decibel *danse musique*. Some two thousand guests were bathed in green light and served green food on tables decorated with green roses and bamboo. Afterward, a noisy, fifteen-minute fireworks display reverberated across the waterfront, its green and silver plumes descending in rivulets across the night sky like the computer squiggles of the *Matrix Reloaded* posters that were plastered across the Cannes waterfront for the duration of the festival.

T3, by contrast, didn't screen at all during the festival. On the morning of May 17, Vajna and Intermedia's Moritz Borman sat on a panel moderated by *Variety* editor in chief

Peter Bart in the basement of a beachfront café. They defended their decision not to show footage from the film. It wasn't quite finished, the producers said, and the script was a carefully guarded secret. They wanted to be sure to keep it out of Internet chat rooms, where a few early reviews might damage its reputation before opening weekend. Vajna recalled the production of *First Blood*, in which he and Kassar tried to sell the movie to Warner Brothers after putting together eighteen minutes of footage; the studio passed. "We later showed an hour and ten minutes at the [American Film Market] and got a standing ovation," he said. "You might as well show the whole movie or show nothing."

There was another reason it didn't screen at the festival: unlike *The Matrix Reloaded*, it wasn't invited. That didn't stop Vajna and Kassar from comporting themselves as if they were the city's newly appointed ministers of culture. At the *Variety* panel, Vajna appeared unruffled by the punishing regimen of interviews, panels and parties. He wore a baggy blue sweatshirt and sunglasses pushed atop his head. With his white beard and sleepy voice, he looked the way Santa Claus might if he got a makeover from hairdresser to the stars Frederic Fekkai. Next to him was a paper bag containing seven or eight cigars; in the midst of the panel, he put one between his teeth and lit it, blowing acrid cigar smoke into the room and into the adjacent *Variety* press room.

Vajna's cool disdain for corporate decorum, his fondness for stunts and grand displays of starpower and his impatience with the small details could all prove infuriating to the studio executives charged with keeping him happy. Vajna insisted at the *Variety* panel that studios needed passionate producers like him. "Every movie star in the world wanted to make *First Blood*," he said. "No studio put it together. We did. We believed in it." Vajna leaned forward. "Hollywood has made a terrible mistake not supporting producers, but supporting stars and directors."

It was a striking admission from a producer who seemed at times to regard the studios as a necessary evil. In the minds of Vajna and Kassar, the real visionaries in the film business were its maverick, globe-trotting entrepreneurs. That, in a nutshell, was why Cannes was so important to them. Here, at the world's biggest sales bazaar for film, independent producers had the real power. They knew the buyers, and they knew how to work the international press. Here was a place in which their money talked, and the world listened. They, not the studios, were the kings of Cannes.

Vajna and Kassar weren't the first producers to realize the benefits of throwing their money around the French Riviera. In the 1970s and '80s, producers like Dino de Laurentiis and Cannon Films partners Menahem Golan and Yoram Globus helped transform the Cannes Film Festival into a frenzied deal market. Today, the studios would seem to have the upper hand. Cannon Films went bankrupt years ago, and de Laurentiis has a first-look deal on the Universal lot. But Vajna and Kassar were for years living proof that a small group of international, independent producers have done as much as the studios to make the blockbuster film business what it is today.

In a sense, today's great innovators in Hollywood are still

the gutsy showmen who turn studio conventions upside down. In 2004 it was Mel Gibson and Newmarket Films distribution maven Bob Berney, who financed and released *The Passion of the Christ*, a new interpretation of the Christian gospels that became one of the biggest box office hits of all time. In the 1990s it was Bob and Harvey Weinstein, who turned independent film into a blockbuster business. All of these men owe a debt of gratitude to Joseph E. Levine, the producer of *Godzilla: King of the Monsters*. Levine stood five feet four inches tall, but he cast a long shadow. Decades before the consolidation of the Hollywood studios made big-budget film distribution the exclusive province of a few far-flung global media companies, Levine taught the studios how to open a film wide.

Levine clawed his way up from the slums of Boston's West End. Born in 1905, the youngest of six children, he shined shoes, sold newspapers and carried suitcases for North Station commuters, dropping out of school at age fourteen to work in a garment factory. He rented vacant stockrooms, built his own racks and sold ready-to-wear women's apparel under the name LeVine's. In 1938 he became a film exhibitor. With borrowed money, he bought New Haven's Lincoln Theater, the Round Hill drive-in in Springfield, Massachusetts, and the Park Square Cinema, a repertory house in Boston's Back Bay. His first double bill in New Haven was Julien Duvivier's Proustian drama, *Un carnet de bal*, and an exploitation cheapie called *How to Undress in Front of Your Husband*. Levine later claimed that the university audience pelted the screen with trash.

Like Vajna and Kassar, Levine put his chips behind movies that were highbrow and lowbrow, deftly eliding the differences between art and trash in the name of showmanship. He became a sub-distributor for the studios and began licensing New England territory rights to movies and booking them into other theaters: B westerns, war documentaries, reissued Universal horror films, Abbot and Costello comedies, and Italian neorealist classics like *The Bicycle Thief* and *Open City*. He specialized in Italian imports, picking up *Divorce—Italian Style* and *Marriage—Italian Style*, and Federico Fellini's *8½*. In the 1940s he rented the upscale Shubert Theater in Boston to show *The Scorched Earth*, a documentary about the Japanese occupation of China, and draped the theater with posters that screamed "Jap rats stop at nothing—See this. It will make you fighting mad." For the French documentary *The Sky Above, the Mud Below*, a serious study of New Guinea tribesmen, he stationed registered nurses in theater lobbies to provide oxygen to anyone who passed out from fright.

Legendary documentary directors Albert and David Maysles made their first film about Levine, titled *Showman*. The Maysles brothers followed Levine from New York to L.A., where he campaigned for Sophia Loren's 1961 Oscar in Vittorio De Sica's wartime drama, *Two Women*. Levine took an eight-by-ten still photo showing Loren kneeling in the dirt in a torn dress after she'd been raped by Italian soldiers, and ran it in a two-page ad in the *New York Times*. He screened the film in every city where a member of the Academy lived, and spent lavishly to promote the film in the Hollywood

trade press. Levine was one of the first producers to lobby for
an Oscar, and his efforts were successful. Loren was named
best actress—the first time that trophy was given for a performance in a foreign-language feature.

Levine made his first big mark on Hollywood with
Godzilla in 1956. But Levine's biggest breakthrough came
three years later with *Hercules,* a film he bought on the cheap
in the European market. Until *Hercules* most of the sword-
and-spear epics in American theaters were lavish studio
productions like *Quo Vadis?* and *Ben Hur. Hercules* was a
shoddy Italian knockoff. Levine first watched the film in a
freezing screening room in Rome; several Hollywood studios
had already passed. "But there was something about it that
made me realize there was potential fortune tied up in it,"
Levine told Hollywood gossip columnist Louella Parsons. He
claimed that he bought it for $150,000, then "took it apart,"
spending an additional $120,000 on sound effects and titles,
and $250,000 on promotional trailers.

Like DreamWorks' modern-day *Sinbad, Hercules* was a
jumble of ancient myths, teeming with warriors in loincloths
and statuesque amazons, starring one of Arnold Schwarzenegger's bodybuilding heroes, a former Mr. Universe named
Steve Reeves. Levine decided Reeves's voice didn't have the
proper godlike resonance, so he had an Embassy employee,
George Gonneau, dub his lines. Levine also turned around
and sold the film to Warner Brothers in an unusual deal that
put him in charge of "advertising, publicity and exploitation," all areas in which Levine excelled.

Levine began his media campaign three months before

Hercules hit theaters. He hosted what he called "an explodation luncheon" for twelve hundred exhibitors and journalists in the Grand Ballroom of the Waldorf Astoria. The invitation was a fake bomb with a fuse. More than a dozen *Hercules* banners were draped from the balconies promising endorsements from national magazines like *Look* and *Seventeen*. A forty-foot-tall, two-dimensional model of Steve Reeves, wearing a loincloth and holding a banner that read "*Hercules, Mighty Saga of the World's Mightiest Man,*" reached the ceiling. The guests were summoned to the tables by a trumpeter sounding the "helicon of Hercules," and served food and cocktails by handmaidens in Roman frocks. Levine hired Mae West to judge a Mr. Hercules contest at a Hollywood health club. He created chocolate *Hercules* novelties. He advertised Reeves's well-oiled physique in comic books and in gay beefcake magazines. "This tremendous entertainment—supported by a tremendous promotional campaign—will have proven again the vitality of motion picture industry," blared the *Hercules* press book. "The annals of boxoffice history will have opened wide to welcome a new champion!"

Open wide they did forty-four years to the day before *T3* opened. The distribution deal with Warner Brothers called for "day and date" saturation booking of six hundred color prints from coast to coast in the last week of June. On July 2, 1959, Warner Brothers distribution memos reported that the film was booked into 126 theaters in the Boston area and 95 theaters around Philadelphia. It had generated "the biggest single day's gross ever recorded by a single picture in these territories." In the first week of release it played in 156 "smaller situations throughout the country, and was smashing house records everywhere." In Baltimore, it was "out-grossing everything . . . by [a] ratio of five to one."

Hercules earned millions in its first theatrical run, racking up an estimated $20 million in theatrical grosses and TV licensing in later years. It also spawned dozens of imitators. Steve Reeves appeared in *Hercules Unchained* in 1959, a Levine import that was much less successful. In 1970, another winner of the Mr. Universe contest, an aspiring actor and bricklayer named Arnold Strong, later Schwarzenegger, got his first starring role in *Hercules in New York*.

Levine's long career is an encyclopedia of publicity stunts large and small. In 1960 he sponsored an exhibitors luncheon at the Plaza to promote a film about Jack the Ripper; he arrived with a phalanx of security guards and dumped $1 million in cash on a table, telling all assembled that he planned to spend the bundle on national advertising. In 1970 he held the premiere for *The Adventurers,* an adaptation of a Harold Robbins novel that he produced for Paramount, on a private jet.

In a profile of Levine in 1964, *Fortune* reported that the trend in Hollywood "was toward blockbusters—big, expensive spectaculars that can make or break the producer." These producers, *Fortune* continued, "have quit fighting TV and have joined it. They sell their old movies to TV without inhibition, and make an increasing number of films specifically for TV." In 1966 ABC radicalized the TV licensing business by spending $2 million for the right to show *Bridge on the*

River Kwai in primetime, from 8 to 11 P.M., on September 25. Sixty million people watched the broadcast, and competitive bidding by the networks for high-budget big-screen spectacles promptly shot through the roof. Levine, who was profiled by the *New Yorker* at the height of this frenzy, immediately began rethinking his business plan. "It's a whole new business now," he said. "Next year, we're going to make nothing but major pictures."

Levine's legacy is all but erased from the record books, but he survives today in the form of a freewheeling Jack Palance performance in Jean-Luc Godard's 1963 CinemaScope classic, *Contempt,* which Levine produced. Palance plays Jeremiah Prokosch, a crass American producer who hires a French screenwriter to pen an adaptation of Homer's *Odyssey,* then seduces the screenwriter's wife, played by Brigitte Bardot. It's a scathing indictment of Godard's American producer, who allegedly bridled when the French auteur refused to include nude footage of Bardot. "Every time I hear the word culture," Prokosch says at one point, "I bring out my checkbook." "We lost a million bucks on that lousy film," Levine later told the *New Yorker,* "because that *great* director, Jean-Luc Godard, refused to follow the script."

Vajna and Kassar would have sympathized with Levine. A few weeks before leaving for Cannes, the pair was in their office, prowling from room to room, surrounded by *Terminator* merchandise. *T3* was a worldwide phenomenon, and the duo was intent on exploiting the title to within an inch of its life. The headquarters of C-2 are a block from the old MGM office park, but the offices could not be more different. The interior of C-2 is industrial, with steel gates operated by winches separating the rooms. In April, the reception area was littered with technology magazines, free neighborhood circulars and copies of a publication called *Cruising World*. The exterior is a psychedelic swirl of colors that looks like a graffiti-covered New York subway car from the 1970s. Vajna hired artists to tag the building, and today every square foot is covered with spray-painted slogans and abstract images.

At Carolco, Vajna and Kassar shared an office, and worked facing each other across two adjoining glass desks. At C-2, they again share an office, sitting at a single, custom-built desk. Kassar's half is made out of glass, and Vajna's is made out of granite. Kassar says the jagged line which separates the two sides of the desk signifies the rift between the producers, which is now healed.

In May, there were *Terminator* props everywhere, and on a round granite desk at the center of their office sat a large can of Asahi beer bearing the half-human, half-robot face of the Terminator, covered with Japanese writing. Kassar was dressed in Army fatigues and faded New Balance sneakers; Vajna, in sand-colored warm-up pants and long-sleeved T-shirt, clutched a plastic lighter in one hand and twirled a slender cigar in the other.

When the producers auctioned off distribution rights to *T3*, they held on to a few lucrative components of the franchise for themselves. They kept the TV and animation spin-off rights. With Intermedia, they jointly own the licensing rights. The *Terminator* series wasn't a merchandising bonanza like *Star Wars* or *Harry Potter,* but C-2 had lofty ambitions for a new wave of *Terminator* toys and accessories. They hired a licensing expert named Paula Hoppe to oversee dozens of deals, including a Toyota contract to produce a *T3* edition of the Tundra pick-up truck, and a contract with Coca-Cola to promote the film in 4,600 retail and restaurant locations. There were *Terminator* sunglasses, T-shirts, leather jackets, model cars, comic books, trading cards and plastic lighters. But the U.S. licensing deals were just a fraction of the worldwide blitz. In Austria, they did deals with Nokia, Fisherman's Friend cough drops, and Manner Wafers, which would spend more than $200,000 on TV advertising; in Germany, they signed a deal with Shell, which would promote the film in 1,450 gas stations, spending $1.6 million on TV advertising; in Russia, they struck a deal with Pepsi to spend $1 million in TV advertising; in Indonesia, they did a deal with Gillette. Vajna and Kassar were as interested in these deals as in the film production.

T3 was the only film produced by Vajna and Kassar in 2003, but C-2 was operating like a tiny studio, franchising the title across every conceivable platform. Few producers are more entrepreneurial than Vajna. The former wig manufacturer still divides his time between Los Angeles and Hungary, where he owns two casinos, an international film sales outfit and a theater chain with dozens of screens. Vajna and Kassar are enamored of big sales ideas and marketing gimmicks, which made them especially hard to please when it came to the marketing of *T3*. "We're watchdogs for anything that might not be exactly on target," Kassar said.

Not all of Vajna and Kassar's plans for *T3* were acceptable to Warner Brothers. Vajna and Kassar had wanted to hold the premiere at the Shrine Auditorium or the Kodak Theatre, the past and present locations of the Academy Awards. They wanted to mount a "Terminator for Governor" campaign weeks before opening weekend, a plan that neither Warners nor Schwarzenegger endorsed. Vajna badgered Warner with so many ideas and complained so often if things weren't just right that one Warners executive ordered him never to call again. "We're here to argue with the studio," Kassar said. "We give them a lot of ideas. Some of the ideas are logistically impossible. It's hard to please us."

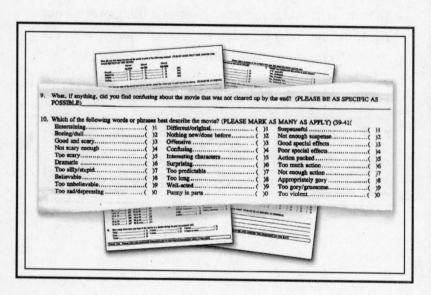

9. What, if anything, did you find confusing about the movie that was not cleared up by the end? (PLEASE BE AS SPECIFIC AS POSSIBLE)

10. Which of the following words or phrases best describe the movie? (PLEASE MARK AS MANY AS APPLY) (39-41(

Entertaining ( )1	Different/original ( )1	Suspenseful ( )1
Boring/dull ( )2	Nothing new/done before ( )2	Not enough suspense ( )2
Good and scary ( )3	Offensive ( )3	Good special effects ( )3
Not scary enough ( )4	Confusing ( )4	Poor special effects ( )4
Too scary ( )5	Interesting characters ( )5	Action packed ( )5
Dramatic ( )6	Surprising ( )6	Too much action ( )6
Too silly/stupid ( )7	Too predictable ( )7	Not enough action ( )7
Believable ( )8	Too long ( )8	Appropriately gory ( )8
Too unbelievable ( )9	Well-acted ( )9	Too gory/gruesome ( )9
Too sad/depressing ( )0	Funny in parts ( )0	Too violent ( )0

Finding Demo

On Thursday, June 12, studios got their first clear picture of the competition for July Fourth weekend. That's when *Terminator 3*, *Legally Blonde 2* and *Sinbad* appeared in the confidential telephone tracking survey published three times a week by Nielsen NRG, Hollywood's dominant market research firm.

The tracking report was assembled by analysts at NRG's Los Angeles headquarters. Working from a computerized phone bank in an office tower on Wilshire Boulevard opposite the La Brea tar pits, starting three weeks before opening weekend, they blitzed thousands of households in key media markets, measuring awareness and interest levels in new movies. Their results were based on interviews with four hundred people split into four demographic quadrants: men and women over and under the age of twenty-five. The Platonic ideal of a summer blockbuster by NRG's standards—what *Matrix* producer Joel Silver calls "the Valhalla of our business"—was a "four-quadrant" movie, one that scored an equal approval rating from all four demographic groups.

Tracking reports are published Monday, Thursday and Friday. They're copyrighted by NRG, and every page carries a stern reminder that it's illegal to provide tracking to those who aren't authorized to get it. But it's one of the worst kept secrets in Hollywood. Tracking data is circulated like the Soviet Union's underground Samizdat literature among producers, agents, exhibitors and journalists. Marketing information is a valuable currency, especially information predicting whether a competitor's film is a hit or a flop.

The brainchild of National Research Group founders Joe Farrell and Catherine Paura, film tracking used to be the purview of a few studio executives. But today it's one of the most entrenched—and divisive—mechanisms studios use to plan their assault on the national consciousness. It's the first public referendum on a film's prospects that carries the weight of empirical truth; more important, it provides a marketing context for the studio, situating each film in relation to the films that will share its billing on theater marquees. Months earlier, Warners and MGM had separately commissioned NRG to do pretracking surveys of *T3* and *Legally Blonde 2*. But pretracking measured only the public's awareness of the films; it couldn't assess the preferences of the general public on a particular weekend, given a finite set of choices about what to see at the multiplex. And most summer blockbusters in 2003 had only one weekend to burn their way into the fickle, super-saturated consumer consciousness before a new wave of movies shunted them to the side. That's why June 12 was such an important date. It marked the start of a new, intensely competitive phase of the campaign. It was a surrogate opening weekend. And it put *T3* well ahead of the pack.

T3 burst onto the tracking as the first choice of 15 percent of the survey sample. Even *Hulk,* which was due in theaters two weeks sooner, was first choice for just 13 percent of the sample. But *T3* also looked vulnerable. Only two percent of females under the age of 25 considered it a first choice, dealing a blow to its chance of becoming a four-quadrant movie. And unaided awareness for *T3* —the number of people who know of the film without prompting from an NRG tele-re-searcher—was just 4 percent. *Legally Blonde 2* faced a steeper climb. Although unaided awareness was also 4 percent, overall first choice was just 7 percent, most of it coming from women. The tracking on *Sinbad* was a virtual death sentence. The animated film's unaided awareness was 1 percent. And under the category of first choice, there was just an asterisk. Too few people considered *Sinbad* a first choice to rate even a single percentage point. DreamWorks' only solace was that tracking always has a significant margin of error. *Sinbad*'s prospects might be better than the tracking suggested; they might also be worse. Plus, children's movies were notoriously tough to track because eight-year-old cartoon fans could not be reliably polled. Two weeks later, *Pirates of the Caribbean* would appear on the tracking with a modest overall first-choice rating of 9 percent. Its success wound up serving as further proof of the limitations of NRG's forecasts. Despite such deficiencies, NRG tracking reports were coveted by the people shaping the release campaigns for July Fourth weekend. Distributed electronically to the studio marketing departments, they were immediately shotgunned to the producers and talent.

Hollywood market research is an opaque science. NRG tracking is published in a thick wad of data all but impenetrable to the untrained reader. Each page is an explosion of numbers—row after row of numerical rankings printed in so tiny a font that they look like columns of ants. The reports are modeled on rudimentary polling methods that have been in the political mainstream since the Kennedy administration. Until Farrell and Paura came along, however, they had never been tried by Hollywood studios. "The mainstay at the beginning of political polling was households," Farrell says. "You screened out anyone who wasn't likely to be a real voter. We took that idea. We focused on frequent moviegoers and we did random sampling by telephone."

It was a small but important step, and it would help spark a revolution at the box office, tipping the balance of studio power from the production department that created the movies to the marketing department that sold them on opening weekend. NRG was part of a groundswell of new thinking in Hollywood in the 1970s. As movies began opening wider, in bigger theaters supported by noisier marketing campaigns, a window of opportunity opened for a new generation of statistics mavens and data tinkerers like Farrell and Paura. These people didn't hold senior titles at the studios. They were self-taught mavericks, and lone-wolf, lower echelon executives. It's a group that included Marcie Polier, who started EDI, the first national box office tracking service, and Arthur D. Murphy, an erstwhile Navy lieutenant and movie critic who invented *Variety*'s box office index in 1984 and chronicled the rise of wide-opening movies throughout the 1970s.

These people perceived something at the grass roots that eluded the executives running the studios. They saw that the business of the box office was undergoing a profound tectonic shift, and they shared the assumption that there might be a more scientific system for building a movie into a mass event, and a more scientific system for rapidly measuring its success. NRG brought a new approach to an old problem. But it was predicated on an idea that even a producer like Joseph E. Levine, whose investments were based not on science but on gut instincts, would surely appreciate: With the right materials and sales pitch, NRG suggested, opening weekend could be bought.

Joe Farrell arrived in Los Angeles from New York in 1977 to open the West Coast office of Louis Harris & Associates. Harris was JFK's personal pollster and a pioneer in the fledgling field of market research. Harris & Associates handled both government research and image campaigns for industrial clients like Big Oil. "It was all about image building, image correction, or getting a score on an image," Farrell recalls.

Farrell's timing was excellent. In 1978, United Artists

founders Robert Benjamin and Arthur Krim, a steadfast Democratic party activist and John F. Kennedy crony, exited the company to create Orion Pictures, the company that would release *The Terminator* five years later. The new management at UA needed someone to organize the research screenings for *Apocalypse Now* and to help director Francis Ford Coppola plan the marketing campaign. Coppola clicked with Farrell, who had credentials that set him apart from the usual marketing crowd. He'd spent seven years in seminary studying to be a priest. He had worked as a street artist in Greenwich Village, selling charcoal black-and-white portraits for $2.50. He also had a Harvard law degree and had spent eight years working for the Rockefeller Brothers Fund, a philanthropic foundation. "Francis never wanted to take research literally," Farrell says, "but he had an instinct for what he heard."

With Coppola's support, Farrell founded NRG with Paura, a Harris employee fifteen years younger than him, and began to pitch the company to the studios. Their pitch was audacious—they were offering a virtual monopoly on Hollywood market research—but it suited cost-conscious executives seeking to outsource their marketing work. In 1967 the MPAA commissioned a study by Daniel Yankelovich which showed that publicity and advertising contributed little to the success of films, unless they were based on already popular books, plays or musicals. Studios, eager to cut overhead, used the study to justify their dismantling of "ad-pub" departments and in-house trailer production teams. This led to a reliance on outside ad agencies in the 1970s and, a decade later, on trailer production houses like Aspect Ratio.

But as the 1980s dawned, the business culture of Hollywood veered in a new direction, and movies began converging with the world of advertising and television in profound yet unanticipated ways. It was an era of shotgun corporate marriages and hostile takeovers; the studios suddenly had unlikely new parent companies and affiliates. Warner Brothers merged with Atari in 1976. In 1981 MGM and UA merged; five years later the combined company was acquired by Turner Broadcasting System. In 1982 the Coca-Cola Company bought Columbia Pictures. The corporate zeitgeist didn't take long to affect studio management. A memo was circulated at Columbia in the early 1980s banning Pepsi from appearing in the studio's films. Coke assumed it could succeed in Hollywood the way it won the cola wars—through market share. In 1983 Columbia's production output increased from ten to twenty films a year.

A new wave of directors who cut their teeth in the advertising world—Hugh Hudson, Ridley and Tony Scott and Adrian Lyne—began directing big-budget studio films. Emerging studio power brokers like Barry Diller and Michael Eisner had experience running TV divisions—as did veteran Lew Wasserman—where programming decisions were carefully tailored to Nielsen ratings and overseen by efficiency experts armed with demographic statistics and sophisticated financial projections. The TV audience was splintering, yet studios were embracing ever more widespread TV advertising campaigns for their films, and they were eager to adopt new techniques for capturing a broad audience. They were also eager to offset their marketing and production expenses through sponsorship deals with consumer products. In "Hollywood: The Ad," a 1990 cover story in the *Atlantic Monthly,* Mark Crispin Miller catalogued the product plugs that came to saturate Hollywood movies in the 1980s, from *E.T.,* the highest grossing film of the decade, in which a boy befriends an alien who eats only Reese's Pieces, to *Mac and Me,* an *E.T.* knockoff released six years later, in which a boy befriends an alien who drinks only Coca-Cola. A trip to the movie theater in the 1980s, Miller complained, offered "as much magic as you would find at Kmart or at Lord & Taylor." "Hollywood has changed," a Saatchi & Saatchi executive said to Miller. "Unlike the old days, the bankers and MBAs are calling the shots."

There were few people who understood that better than Farrell. In 1988 he sold NRG to advertising giant Saatchi & Saatchi. "Studios had to rationalize why things were being done," Farrell says. "Why were you opening a movie on a couple hundred screens when that other movie was getting on a thousand screens. Why was that person being promoted instead of that other person? Research gave them reasons. This person is well-known; that person is not. This is a movie that can be carried by a male. This is a movie that needs nurturing. The rationalizations got them off the hook."

From NRG's first headquarters in a low-rent Hollywood building that also housed a sex shop, Farrell and Paura began reaching out to consumers in ways that had never been tried in Hollywood. They got children to fill out surveys in parking lots, rewarding them with ice cream and candy. They yanked pedestrians off the street in New York City and interviewed them in a van outfitted with TV screens. In malls, they installed construction poles hard-wired with monitors to field-test trailers and other marketing materials. As the business grew, NRG began offering other services: white papers on global cultural trends, specialized reports on the marketability of certain stars and genres, lists of the words most commonly used by teenagers.

NRG standardized a business that before the 1970s was riddled with charlatanism and quackery. Under the direction of the Motion Picture Research Council, a division of the Academy of Motion Picture Arts and Sciences, scientists in the 1930s gauged audience reaction to movies by strapping medical devices like blood pressure meters, pneumographs, galvanometers and polygraph recorders to moviegoers. Gallup's Audience Research Inc. later conducted studies using devices like the Reactograph, which used electronic pens to record audience reactions on a moving sheet of graph paper, and tele-voting, a system of electronic dials controlled by audience members, connected to a control box resembling a giant typewriter. Mark Crispin Miller recounts an experiment at a New Jersey movie theater in 1957 by James Vicary, vice-president of a company called the Subliminal Projection Company. Vicary interspliced the William Holden and Kim

Novak film *Picnic* with ads one three-thousandth of a second in length, instructing audience members to eat popcorn and drink Coca-Cola. He held a press conference claiming concessions sales had risen dramatically as a result. His findings were later discredited.

Sneak previews have long been a staple of the studio system, but they were often wildly disorganized. Irving Thalberg was so obsessed with test screenings, according to historian Benjamin B. Hampton, he'd sit in different seats in a theater to observe the audience reactions, and ask restroom attendants to report back to him what audience members were saying. Producer David Brown remembers Gene Kelly, who directed *Hello, Dolly!* in 1969, flagging down motorists to persuade them to attend a sneak preview in Dallas. As late as 1975, the audience comments following a sneak preview of *Jaws* weren't collected at the end of the show; they were mailed to the studio, arriving in dribs and drabs two weeks later. "We closed all of that down," Farrell says. At the root of NRG's test screenings was a distinction between what Farrell called a movie's playability and its marketability. Marketability, Farrell says, "is all the efforts you make to get the movie into the minds of the public in the most positive way. That's how you open a movie." A movie could play well, but if it couldn't be marketed, it would be a lost cause. A movie could play badly, but if it could be marketed, a studio might still engineer a big opening weekend.

Sitting in his production company's spartan conference

room, Farrell has the detached but beneficent air of a re-
tired archbishop. He is soft-spoken, his skin is pale and his
neatly parted silver hair falls over one eye. He's an amateur
furniture designer; under the pseudonym Giuseppe
Farbino, he even crafted some of the desks, chairs and conference tables that decorated NRG headquarters when he
was there. But his reputation in the film industry is that of a
vicious competitor. When he was building the company
into a corporate powerhouse with international offices,
more than $30 million in annual revenues and exclusive
contracts at most of the studios, he had enormous influence
in studio marketing appointments. NRG's share of the market research business in Hollywood is now 80 percent, but it
reached as high as 98 percent under his watch. Farrell had
the ear of every studio chief, spoke at corporate retreats and
circulated discreetly between top-level studio staff meetings. In 1993 the *Wall Street Journal* published an exposé on
Farrell that accused him of cooking his data. He didn't lose
a single client. "You nurture a project for a year or eighteen
months," Brandon Tartikoff told the *Journal* "and then you
go to the first screening, and the lights come up and nobody
looks at you. Everybody's looking at Joe Farrell."

Why did the studios confer such power on Farrell?
"There was something about it that was strangely comfort-
ing," recalled Peter Guber, who ran Sony Pictures from 1989
to 1994. "The studios were all in the same boat together. It
was M.A.D.—mutually assured destruction. They equally
couldn't trust him, and in that, trusted him."

"When I first arrived, I saw that this was really a small community," Farrell says. "A few people controlled the whole thing. What I said was, 'We are capable of doing all of your research.'" Farrell and Paura created a clearinghouse of research data, which they used to make projections on films that were still in production. They even began forecasting opening weekend box office, but stopped in 1999 after studios complained it punished films that fell short of predictions.

Into NRG's voluminous database went research on trailers, fifteen-second and thirty-second ad spots, feedback on test screenings and NRG's new, proprietary mathematical equations measuring the popularity of specific actors and general trends. "What would be considered a successful-playing movie for an adult male?" Farrell asks. "There was a norm. How much could a movie make was a norm. All of a sudden the studios were getting information from hundreds of releases. We could say that if a film looked this popular and this playable, and that movie made this much money and if you had 100 of those cases, the 101st would probably do this."

Farrell and Paura are now independent film producers. They left NRG in 2003, six years after it was acquired by VNU, the Dutch conglomerate that also owns the Nielsens and EDI. Today NRG no longer has a virtual monopoly on studio marketing data. In October 2003 a rival research firm, MarketCast, owned by *Variety*'s parent company, Reed Elsevier, brought suit against NRG, alleging that NRG has sought to squelch competition in the movie industry research market. The lawsuit, since settled out of court, alleges that NRG contacted MarketCast's three primary vendors and threatened to stop doing business with them unless they agreed to exclusive contracts with NRG. The suit stipulated that NRG dominates a research market worth $90 million, consisting mainly of field research, customer surveys and focus groups. A new online market research firm, OTX, is also making inroads into the field by touting data derived from Internet surveys. Younger-skewing films often soar higher than NRG tracking, OTX and others believe, because those audiences are best analyzed online. In early 2004 Zelnick Media and Bob Pittman's Pilot Group acquired OTX for an estimated $30 million.

MarketCast and OTX are bringing Hollywood market research into a new era of deep polling, in which studio campaigns are built on an ever-expanding body of precisely calibrated marketing statistics. Farrell and Paura had opened Pandora's box. The norms and standards they pinpointed through market research and trumpeted in their trend reports became the bars that imprisoned the studios and filmmakers who used them. These tools that gave new power to marketing departments also limited their options, yoking them to an opening weekend system which made it hard for studios and filmmakers to look beyond the data to see the larger artistic and cultural ramifications of what they were doing. The marketing and distribution imperative became the most important one. It also boxed them into a single method of opening blockbuster films and judging their success or failure, and made it ever more difficult to assess the long-term financial health of the movie business.

Today, film tracking maintains a tight grip on the marketing process, influencing the shape and thrust of release campaigns for the summer's biggest movies, and the more than a billion dollars the studios collectively spend each year on TV advertising. One year after exiting NRG, Farrell and Paura still grow visibly uncomfortable when tracking data is casually cited. As with many of the research tools NRG brought to Hollywood, tracking is easily misunderstood, they say. "Tracking is a euphemism for many trackings that happen at the same time," Farrell says. "There was always Latino tracking, an African-American tracking, a parent tracking, a children's tracking. It would drive me crazy when people would say the tracking looks bad for a particular movie. The leaks were always considered *the* tracking." Different trackings, Farrell says, "mean so many different things."

But the mountain of data makes it hard for studio executives to focus on anything else. At Warner Brothers, Dawn Taubin keeps tracking reports on a clipboard that rarely leaves her side. At MGM, Peter Adee describes tracking as a buzzsaw that spins through his office at regular intervals. "In marketing, people believe you can change the impression at the drop of a hat," Adee said. "That's true to a certain extent. So what you have is a pressure cooker. You've made the movie. It is what it is. In marketing, on a three-times-a-week basis, whenever NRG's tracking comes in, you have either panic or delight or acknowledgment of defeat. Three times a week for three weeks until the movie opens."

And once it opens, the feedback comes every minute.

A Star Is Reborn

The procession seemed fit for a funeral, but in fact it was a resurrection. Two dozen extras made up to look like Arnold Schwarzenegger in black leather jackets and sunglasses formed two lines and escorted a forty-foot-tall cutout of the Terminator down Broxton Avenue toward the setting sun. There, amid a flurry of fireworks, the billboard was hoisted onto the stucco tower of the historic Mann Village Theater in Westwood. A technician flipped a switch, and the red, glowing eye of the Terminator became a radio antenna, beaming a short-wave signal for *T3* Radio across the city.

The fireworks marked the start of the Hollywood premiere of *Terminator 3* on June 30. Beneath the shadow of the Terminator, the streets of Westwood throbbed with activity. A red carpet flowed down Broxton Avenue, flanked by throngs of fans in bleachers. Photographers pressed against the police barricade. Radio and TV news anchors were stationed on pedestals with robots and other Terminator props, interviewing cast members as they emerged from the crowd. A cluster of Warner Brothers executives, including Alan Horn, Dan Fellman and Dawn Taubin, milled about in dark suits. A Toyota Tundra pickup truck dangled from a Champion crane twenty-five feet off the ground.

It was almost July Fourth weekend, the traditional midway point of the summer, but the story of the summer of 2003 had pretty much been written. The blockbuster season, which began with a burst of excitement in May, had hit a wall. Industry-wide box office revenues thus far were flat compared with summer 2002. More films were being released in three thousand or more theaters, and more films were suffering from steep second-week declines. *The Matrix Reloaded* had started a spell of antipathy toward big, bloated Hollywood spectacles. After scoring $134 million in its first four days, it had faced the scorn of critics and the indifference of the masses. It made more than 70 percent of its money during its first week of release. On its heels came *Hulk* and *Charlie's Angels 2,* two more expensive disappointments. *Hulk* set a record by plummeting 70 percent in its second weekend. The media determined that the audience was suffering from sequel fatigue as the studios prepared to release a glut of ultrahyped franchises to theaters: *Bad Boys 2, Tomb Raider 2* and the third installment of *American Pie.*

Into this malaise came *T3, Legally Blonde 2* and *Sinbad.* Fifteen miles from Westwood, at the very moment of the *T3* premiere, the distribution machinery that would set opening weekend in motion was humming. In Technicolor's film processing plant, concealed within an unobtrusive black building in North Hollywood, reels containing more than 100 million feet of *T3* and *Sinbad* prints were being readied for shipment to the Technicolor depot in Ontario. From there, they would be loaded in metal cans, given their full complement of trailers and shipped to theaters. (Prints of *Legally Blonde 2* got to the depot from Technicolor's main competitor, Deluxe.) The Technicolor plant was tucked away off Lankershim Boulevard, immediately next to the Universal Studios gate and in the long shadow of the black office tower where Lew Wasserman and his troops engineered "*Jaws* consciousness."

Stepping from the bright sunlight of the Universal lot into the office of Technicolor is like stepping into a darkroom. And that's what it is: a huge development lab, with room after room of chemical tanks, pulleys, high-speed printers and splicing tables. This is where blockbusters are given material form. Two-thousand-foot-long reels are produced from a continuous loop of celluloid. The raw material of a film print is recycled again and again by a complex network of machines, rooted in the nuts-and-bolts industrial age.

The studios were spending millions of dollars to give recycled franchises that were shipped to theaters on recycled film stock an aura of freshness and novelty. But even the splashy *T3* premiere in Westwood had a familiar air. It was the same cast of characters and the same movie props that had traveled from Warners' Big Picture junket to Cannes and back. Even the red carpet itself was recycled. It was supplied by a company called Entertainment Lighting Services, which installs red carpets at many Hollywood functions. ELS buys two thousand feet of carpet every eight months, washes vast swathes of it down with industrial chemicals between premieres and stores it in a warehouse in the San Fernando Valley.

The music at the after-party on the expansive grounds of the Wadsworth Theater unashamedly turned back the clock. The Dan Band, perhaps best known as the wedding band in the movie *Old School,* performed a repertoire of Laura Branigan and Toni Basil songs from the 1980s. A DJ spun vintage tracks by the Beastie Boys and Madonna. There were more extras dressed like Terminators, alongside a performer from Hungary named Istvan Kollar, attired in black leather and sunglasses, who did an interpretive *T3* dance. The event was styled in a décor that might best be described as industrial frivolity. Its dominant features were a series of twenty-foot steel spires encircled by metallic swirls and bordered by horizontal wildflower-shaped sculptures.

With opening weekend nearly at hand, the long-incubating sequel finally felt real. There would be no more fiddling with marketing materials. The movie itself was now the center of attention. "It's such a payoff," said Andy Vajna, standing with producing partner Mario Kassar. "We've been nervous wrecks all week." Director Jonathan Mostow spoke for many at the party when he responded to a guest's question, "How am I doing? Talk to me next Monday," and smiled. Mostow, Schwarzenegger, Vajna and Kassar would depart the party and immediately board a plane bound for Tokyo, where the

Japanese premiere would draw a fevered audience of six thousand. And on July 4 the star and producers would screen the movie for U.S. troops stationed in Iraq.

Schwarzenegger, of course, displayed no sign of awareness that this was anything but a spectacular time to be a movie star. Standing in a cream-colored suit and tan lace-ups with his wife, Maria Shriver, he basked in the attention of well-wishers at the Wadsworth Theater after-party, standing next to a statue of himself mounted on a pedestal near the party entrance. One of his handlers, personal publicist Sheryl Main, wore a badge around her neck with the inscription "Arnold's Army." The star gestured expansively around the open-air setting, pointing out props from the film. "It's one thing if you like a movie," Schwarzenegger told us. "Then it's another thing if the critics like it. And then it's really something when the *Terminator* fans get behind it. We have it all on this movie." Another irresistible thought occurred to him. "The really amazing thing is that I started out in the first movie as Goliath and now my character is David."

The third element of premiere week for *Legally Blonde 2* was also in Westwood, on July 1, the eve of the public opening. Premieres in the Hamptons and in New York City had been held the prior two nights. Witherspoon had flown from the London set of *Vanity Fair* to the New York event, but she had to leave the festivities early due to her pregnancy and travel schedule. She was absent in L.A., disappointing a small but vocal throng of squealing fans who had lined the street with cameras and autograph books in the hopes of joining the party.

Westwood Village, that barometer of opening weekends gone by, was more active than usual on this Tuesday night. Within two blocks of the *Legally Blonde 2* premiere at the Mann National theater, *T3* officially opened for business as many blockbusters do: with preview showings the night before the official opening. The movie played that Tuesday night in twenty-six hundred theaters across the country, including Westwood's Mann Village. The Village had three showings, which had resulted in a modest crowd of hardcore fans lining up to be the first to commune with Arnold. As they waited for the first *T3* screening, fans watched as select members of the media left the single-screen palace after an advance screening of *Pirates of the Caribbean: The Curse of the Black Pearl*. More than *T3*, they speculated obsessively about *Pirates*, which seemed to be the longest of longshots before it opened. Few people expected a pirate movie based on a theme-park ride to be very original. But word on the street was that it was a hit. This was opening-weekend mania in microcosm: Diehard *Terminator* fans lined up for their first look at their favorite robot, distracted on the way into the theater by a mega-budget movie opening just a week later.

The *Legally Blonde 2* event in L.A. was fairly subdued compared with the previous night's affair in New York, whose crowded after-party was held at Christie's. It had drawn a fashionable, black-clad crowd—except for director Charles Herman-Wurmfeld, who, in Schwarzenegger-like style, wore a cream-colored suit. Costar Jennifer Coolidge noticed a difference in audience reaction between the Hamptons and the city. Chuckling through tightly clenched teeth, she said, "The laughing in Southampton is like this." Then she relaxed her mouth. "Here it's more ah-ha-ha." Producer Marc Platt, who took a break during Broadway previews of *Wicked* to attend the New York premiere, observed "a difference between the East Coast and the West Coast. A lot of people got more of the thinking humor here."

In Manhattan, Reese Witherspoon, accompanied by her husband, Ryan Phillippe, had been met by adoring teens intent on an autograph, which she gladly supplied. She didn't stay for the postscreening party, however. "She's pregnant. She has to wake up early," a publicist explained.

In L.A., the only stars from the movie were Sally Field and Bruce McGill. A few pieces of white furniture were scattered around the open-air Armand Hammer Museum, which had been converted into a department store. Food stations were dressed up as designer boutiques for Tiffany's, Jimmy Choo and Paul Frank, and a functional beauty salon offered hair-styling and makeup. A few dozen revelers grooved on an upstairs dance floor to dance-pop pulsing out of a battery of speakers.

Peter Adee, Erik Lomis and Eric Kops never made it to the dance floor. They had jetted in from New York just hours before and between pure fatigue and opening-day jitters, they were hardly the picture of calm. "Andy Vajna called to wish us good luck," Adee said. At first it sounded like the setup to a joke. But it was just an update. "He also wanted a copy of that spoof TV spot we did," with Elle Woods promising, "I'll be back." There were fewer of the usual zingers from the MGM trio this time, just a sense of exhaustion, like they had made it to the finish line of a race that hadn't technically started yet.

On the way out, party attendees received a gift bag stuffed with freebies like scented lotion and hair gel, much of it bearing the brands of companies who had contributed to the promotional push. The lone token for men was a tin of styling clay from Frederic Fekkai, who has a cameo during the film's salon scene. And there were gourmet dog biscuits in honor of Bruiser.

Perhaps Sinbad the stand-up comic could have been brought in to enliven the L.A. premiere of *Sinbad*, which had been held to minimum fanfare on June 22, more than a week before *T3* and *Legally Blonde 2* held their premieres. As it was, no one seemed terribly interested in being at the five-screen Loews multiplex on a Sunday afternoon. The theater is entombed in the worn concrete and temperamental escalators of the ABC Entertainment Center. The entire structure—including the movie theater, the neighboring Shubert Theatre, a McDonald's and a restaurant with the unfortunate name Russian Roulette—would soon be razed to make way for more modern development, a modernist office park that would house the talent agency CAA. The void surrounding the theater only added to the feeling of impermanence about the whole affair. It was as if the movie had already come and gone.

DreamWorks saw a few small advantages to the West Side location: modest cost, generous seating capacity and the relative logistical ease of an enclosed mall. Under brooding, cloudy skies, the company rolled out a purple carpet, in keeping with the film's dominant color. A couple dozen photographers snapped away as an array of pint-size stars struck poses. TV crews and print reporters had all gone to the New York premiere, held five days earlier at the Ziegfeld Theatre. That event was slightly more elaborate, with Catherine Zeta-Jones and Michelle Pfeiffer attracting a modicum of media attention. Many of the paparazzi had focused on guest Soon-Yi Previn.

Despite Jeffrey Katzenberg's avowed commitment to centering the marketing campaign on stars, Joseph Fiennes and Dennis Haysbert were the lone voices in attendance in L.A. Fiennes, clad in a mismatched linen suit coat and pants and Nike hiking shoes, gamely pressed his lips into a smile for the photographers.

On the way into the theater, kids grabbed cups of Sinbad Sherbet, a fluorescent concoction from Baskin-Robbins, a cobranding partner with DreamWorks on many of its movies. Afterward, well-wishers flocked to Katzenberg. He received them gratefully but seemed more interested in dissecting the previous night's Lennox Lewis–Vitali Klitschko heavyweight title fight. Approached by a *Variety* reporter, he came up with a quote for the paper's society page: "It's a fun adventure ride. Sinbad has his flaws, like we all do. But you root for him."

Technicolor's lobby is a worn, wood-paneled space that could be a dentist's waiting room. One of the few clues to what is occurring inside is a *Wizard of Oz* poster hanging on one wall. Past the waiting room, there isn't so much a man hiding behind a curtain, but rather a Rube Goldberg–like series of pulleys, motors, chemical vats and dank, sharp-smelling hallways.

Technicolor's first facility, opened in the early twentieth century at the dawn of moving pictures, was located in a railroad car in Boston. The company's name derived from the innovative two-color camera it introduced in 1915 (two-color dye transfer processing followed in 1926). Its Los Angeles site has sprawled out in waves since the 1960s, with older machines being connected to newer models and new rooms being added on to increase capacity. There is constant demand for the plant's services; a dry-erase board keeps track of all of the movies, trailers and "dailies" (rough footage from a film in production) that are moving through the process.

A film's journey through Technicolor involves several meticulously executed steps. Negatives come out of development wet and are wrapped at ninety feet a minute around pulleys in dry boxes whose temperature remains a constant 100 degrees. The room has white brick walls. Tubes and cords snake along the floor. Four metallic,

residue-streaked tubs are filled with Technicolor's proprietary development chemical, whose exact ingredients are
as closely guarded as the formula for Coca-Cola. In between each tank of chemicals is a tank of water to rinse the
film clean.

The negative assembly room is a static environment
whose humidity level is rigorously controlled. Scenes of a
film are spliced together here, anywhere from one hundred
thousand to five hundred thousand feet per night. There are
eighteen splicing stations equipped with lamps, glue and
special tools. In another area, negatives are treated with
dry-cleaning fluid to remove any traces of dust.

In the negative printing room, a metal wall has computer panels that have been added at various intervals in the
plant's forty-year existence. Negatives move through a
twelve-foot-tall elevator at two thousand feet per minute,
emitting buzzing and whirring noises so loud that workers
wear ear protection.

At the completion of those stages, the first trial print from
the original negative is created, called an answer print. The
approved answer print is the last print before bulk production. The check print is the first print of the bulk production.
At these final stages, directors and cinematographers will
scrutinize the printing job, and Technicolor's own quality
control team runs films on projectors, looking for any tiny
processing flaws.

The process of creating film prints weekend after weekend hinges on the notion that materials can be reused. Fil-
ters extract chemicals from the rinse water and recover

silver from the photographic process. Technicolor works with Kodak, whose plant in Tennessee uses a device called The Chopper to cut up film stock so it can be melted down and reconstituted.

The endless loop at the Technicolor plant is representative of the open-wide process writ large. Recycling characterizes every aspect of the wide-release business. Westwood rolls out a recycled red carpet in front of decades-old movie palaces, adding tried-and-true enhancements like bleachers for the fans, the announcement of star arrivals and searchlights scanning the sky. *T3*, *Legally Blonde 2* and *Sinbad* existed as films because of the avid recycling of ideas that is a business imperative for everyone operating in sequel-happy Hollywood. NRG's research methods allow studio marketers to reprise successful campaigns that delivered big numbers in the past. What are press junkets but the recycling of interviews and sound bites on a massive scale? Exhibitors' megaplex concept, that revenue engine of opening weekend, has propagated across the country.

The machinery at Technicolor runs on an uninterrupted power source. Weekend after weekend, the pulleys, motors and chemical tanks keep churning out films. It is a manifestation of Hollywood's new mode. Nikki Rocco, the Universal distribution chief who works in an office building next to Technicolor, points out that the old custom of banking only on summer and holidays is giving way to a system in which big opening weekends come fifty-two weeks a year. Historical dumping grounds of February, August and October are now fertile soil in which to plant a hit. "Our goal is to provide good product year-round," Rocco says. That guarantee of electricity and Technicolor's mandate for efficiency mean the high-speed printers that yield thousands of film prints are never shut down.

Feeling the Numbers

The number felt big. Maybe not *Harry Potter* big, but big. Brawny. A set of digits befitting a muscle-bound action star who drives a Hummer, lusts for political power and takes several seconds to pronounce words like "extraordinary."

It was Wednesday, July 2. *Terminator 3* had been open for less than a full day, but Dan Fellman and three of his top distribution lieutenants at Warner Brothers were convinced it would surpass $100 million for the five-day holiday weekend. They based this gut feeling on a remarkably small sample of the film's 3,504 theaters and 6,400 prints. (The megaplex marketplace, in which five or six screens in a single location might be showing *T3*, necessitated the production of more prints.) About $1.5 million in matinee receipts had been officially recorded from 490 East Coast locations, following $4 million from Tuesday night previews. A small fraction of the weekend take was actually in the till. The rest was subject to interpretation. Such is distribution's lot: its executives serve as studio shamen, continually estimating results in an effort to soothe the anxiety that takes hold as a movie is sent out into the world. Others around town—at MGM, Dream-Works, and box office tracking services like EDI and Exhibitor Relations—were also predicting $100 million for *T3*, but the weekend would be extremely tough to call. Having the Fourth fall on a Friday confounded the usual three-day dynamic. Friday, which is often the most lucrative day of a three-day weekend, was likely to be the weakest day of receipts. The result would be an opening two-day burst, followed by a big dropoff, then up again on Saturday and then down again on Sunday.

In Fellman's well-appointed office across the street from the Warner lot, the quartet of executives did a rare thing. They let a pair of journalists into their weekend process at its most inchoate. The presentation of numbers to the media usually comes on Sunday morning, after all of the key players have signed off on the spin. This meeting was an immersion in the vicissitudes of calling the numbers.

The four men occupied black leather armchairs and a couch. A square glass coffee table was littered with printouts and projections. Joining Fellman were Jeff Goldstein, executive vice president and general sales manager; Richard Shiff, vice president of sales operations; and Don Tannenbaum, senior vice president of systems and sales operations. Fellman sat in a chair, reading glasses on, leading the meeting. He flipped through a binder, scanning for evidence to support his upbeat mood. Figures can offer optimism to all who seek it. Fellman, for example, felt particularly ebullient about the grosses in Canada. The Canada Day holiday on

Tuesday had propelled *T3* to $19,000 per screen, about triple what it averaged in the United States.

Suddenly, Fellman took off his glasses and sat forward a bit with a sober expression. "This is usually the point where we bet a hot dog," he said in his deadpan way. Gesturing to Tannenbaum, seated on the couch, he continued: "He owes me about five hundred hot dogs, but I think I owe him a barbecue."

Tannenbaum could only smile. If there was an over-under bet, he would stick with the over. "With rain, grosses from Boston down to Washington go up five to seven percent over what they would have been," he said. Rain indeed was falling on parts of the East Coast. It was a crummy forecast for fireworks but encouraging for the movie business. A gray-haired former high school statistics teacher, Tannenbaum had been at Warner Brothers for more than twenty-five years. One of his first weekends was *The Swarm,* an Irwin Allen disaster movie about killer bees which, Tannenbaum instantly recalled, opened on July 14, 1978, in twelve hundred locations, grossing less than $4 million. An exhibitor successfully sued Warner Brothers for misleadingly suggesting the movie was capable of much bigger grosses. Experiences like that, not to mention handling *Batman, Twister, Lethal Weapon* and *Harry Potter,* had rooted Tannenbaum in the numbers and, apparently, sharpened his senses. "I feel the numbers," he said, with the bemused half smile of a medium or an oracle. He held both arms out and pointed his fingers upward, making little twitching movements with his hands as if operating finger cymbals. "I can't really describe it, but it's just a feeling I get."

Because telepathy only counts for so much, the team had to come up with historical models to suggest where *T3* was headed. This is a fundamental exercise that every studio distribution department engages in during each phase of a film's life. Before a movie is green-lit, historical models are constructed to see what the genre, director, producer and star have done before. When a date is being selected, separate models are run using all studios' prior films to see how fertile certain release dates have proven in the past. The approach is another form of industry recycling, just like the bits of celluloid repurposed by Technicolor. If a date worked before, just use it again. When a film opens, modeling again enters the picture, giving a studio some notion of how the entire weekend will turn out. Distribution, in this way, is not unlike managing a mutual fund or a baseball team. Past performance may be no guarantee of future results, but it provides a welcome sense of protection for those doing battle in a risk-ridden business. As numbers flow in, making projections fluctuate, distribution and marketing executives follow them obsessively, knowing that agents, producers and talent will be calling continuously, seeking a measure of their newly created wealth.

In an essay in Jason E. Squire's *The Movie Business Book*, Fellman explained how Warner Brothers' "4 Star" computer database is used by the distribution department:

> Years ago, competing films would be listed on a wall chart in a conference room. Today, this information is contained in a sophisticated movie marketing system that tracks every Warner project, as well as our com-

petitors' projects, in development, production or release. Our customized system can display the box office history of any actor, producer, director or film in seconds; we can analyze a marketplace, release schedule, daily grosses, reviews, demographics, trailers, TV spots, print ads, posters, Web sites and year-to-date box office performance. Whatever information is needed regarding talent, box office receipts or research to aid in the decision-making process, it's in there.

The models selected for *Terminator 3* seemed odd on first glance, but they were not random choices: *Men in Black, Men in Black 2* and *2 Fast 2 Furious*. None was a Warner Brothers release. The latter two were action sequels like *T3*. The *Men in Black* films both opened on July Fourth weekends. Fellman had a table of projections examining in detail what those films did day by day. It was broken into three columns, marked "Wednesday," "3-Day" and "5-Day." If *T3* performed like *Men in Black 2,* posting a decent Wednesday but lacking a strong hold through the extended period, it would end up at $84.3 million. If it followed in the footsteps of *2 Fast 2 Furious,* which punched up a huge Friday in its June opening, *T3* could reach $103.7 million.

Warner Brothers was also running models for the whole weekend. It was basing its *Sinbad* estimate on Paramount's lackluster cartoon *Hey Arnold!*—and *Sinbad* was doing only a fraction of *Arnold*'s business. The group used data from the first *Legally Blonde* to calculate that *Legally Blonde 2* was on track for around $60 million over five days. Across town, MGM was using four analogs—the first *Legally*

Blonde, Sweet Home Alabama and the Julia Roberts summer releases *America's Sweethearts* and *Runaway Bride*—to arrive at a similar projection.

"I know in my heart and in this room with these numbers that we have an upside," Fellman declared. That is all anyone running box office numbers ever asks. The silver-haired Fellman had been through this drill for twenty-five years, all of them at Warner Brothers. He is an avid student of history, both because it is in his blood and because it is his job. Outside Fellman's office, a set of posters for the George Burns movie *Oh God!* were stretched out on the floor. Fellman explained that the studio had reclaimed some of its old marketing and publicity materials from a storage facility in Kansas City.

Fellman is known for his plainspoken feistiness. He was politic and prudent insofar as filmmakers and colleagues were concerned, but he wasn't afraid of mixing it up with his distribution counterparts. In the modern box office world, that often meant challenging them in the media. When he opened *The Green Mile* in December 1999, he criticized Disney for claiming the top spot in a hotly competitive weekend with *Toy Story 2,* the film's third straight weekend at number one. "When you're in your third week, you've got to let other people live," he grumbled to the press. The next summer, he reveled in *The Perfect Storm*'s landmark upset over July Fourth weekend, when it defeated Sony's heavily favored *The Patriot* in a rare mano-a-mano showdown. "I had a feeling we were going to take the weekend," Fellman told *Variety.* "It's what the people wanted to see. They wanted to be entertained."

Fellman waited years to get his post as president of distribution, serving patiently as the right-hand man to Barry Reardon, a venerable figure of decades past who guided Warners into the weekend-oriented era. He relished being the point man, especially on a movie as big as *T3*.

"The mall rats see so many movies in the summer," he said. "I needed to put my pole in the ground. I told Arnold we needed to go as wide as we can and on as many screens as we can. He liked that plan."

Confronting the early returns on *T3*, Fellman was a little more circumspect—but only a little. "There are a lot of variables that you don't know at this point," he said. "If Wednesday turns out to be $14.5 million, that would mean $88.5 million over five days. If it's higher, that would be over one hundred—and a lot of hot dogs."

It all came down to opening day. More than $450 million in total production and marketing costs among the three July Fourth films. The circuitous, twelve-year adventure of getting *T3* made. Mostow's efforts to deliver a hit that matched fans' feverish expectations. The comeback and political fortunes of Arnold Schwarzenegger. MGM's strategy of cost-conscious franchising. Charles Herman-Wurmfeld's legitimacy as a studio director. Jeffrey Katzenberg's ongoing battle with Disney and the ascendance of DreamWorks' animation unit as a viable rival.

That kind of was the endgame of every Warner Brothers event film in 2003. But the studio might never have streamlined the process if it hadn't been for a low-budget, misbegotten movie in 1971 that demonstrated what the meticulously primed marketplace was capable of delivering. The maverick visionary behind it was not merely interested in what happened onscreen. He was remarkably attuned to the realities of the consumer landscape, especially in flyover country between New York and Los Angeles. His name was Tom Laughlin and the film was *Billy Jack*.

The square-jawed Milwaukee native had struggled, during an acting career consisting mostly of supporting roles in films like *South Pacific* and *Gidget,* to make a film from a script he had written in 1953. Finally, in 1970, Laughlin directed, produced and starred in the $300,000 production. It blended elements of a traditional western, protest drama, vigilante thriller, martial-arts film, guerilla theater, Native American mysticism and New Age philosophy. The title character is a muscle-bound, part Indian loner who cracks the skulls of racists, rapists and anyone else who looks at him askance. As the tagline to the original one-sheet put it: "When you need him, he's always there!" One line of dialogue became Billy's signature. Squaring off against some goons in a public park, he declares: "I'm going to take this right foot and I'm going to wop you on that side of your face—and you know what? There's not a damn thing you're going to be able to do about it." Delores Taylor, Laughlin's wife, co-starred as the leader of a progressive school shattered by violence.

Desperate to tap into the youth market, Warner Brothers bought *Billy Jack* for $1.8 million and agreed to give Laughlin 45 percent of its profits and the right to make any sequels. That deal was struck after a previous distribution agreement with B-movie maverick Sam Arkoff fell through. The studio followed the traditional playbook, rolling it out a few theaters at a time, beginning on April 19, 1971, in downtown Cincinnati, not exactly a cinematic hotbed. According to Jorge Casuso's *The Untold Story Behind the Legend of Billy Jack,* the film "was dumped—in porn houses and drive-ins and B theaters—for a fraction of the rental price or double-billed with bombs the studio credited with the profits." It managed to collect $4 million over two years, but Laughlin insisted it had been mishandled. He filed a $51 million antitrust lawsuit against Warners. The suit prevailed and the studio was forced to rerelease *Billy Jack.*

This time, however, Laughlin would be calling the shots. He embarked on a "four-wall" reissue of *Billy Jack,* a little-used technique he had seen transform a film called *Bayou* into a surprise hit. A sordid romance set in the Louisiana swamps, it starred Peter Graves as a New York architect who falls for an underage local girl. The film flopped when United Artists released it in 1957. Producer M.A. Ripps bought it back and reissued it in 1961. He recut and retitled it, attaching a salacious tagline: "Somewhere, a 15-year old girl may be a teenager . . . in the Cajun country, she's a woman full-grown! And every Bayou man knows it!" Ripps changed the title from *Bayou* to *Poor White Trash.* He posted warning signs at drive-ins that armed policemen would prevent anyone under seventeen from buying a ticket. The film became a sensation that stayed on screens for years.

Under a four-wall deal, a distributor paid an exhibitor a flat rental fee and took care of all marketing costs, but also collected 100 percent of box office revenues. Theater owners favored such deals with unproven films because of the security they provided. Laughlin was a student of advertising guru David Ogilvy. He took to heart the adman's famous quip: "It took teams of scientists decades to create the molecule before us. And we in marketing get two weeks to give it an identity. But if we do our jobs right, we'll have as much to do with the success of this molecule as those teams of scientists and all those years." To give a movie an identity in the 1970s, Laughlin concluded, television was essential. Taylor-Laughlin Distribution, the filmmakers' company, supported Warners' reissue of *Billy Jack* with $2.5 million in TV ads. The spots targeted twelve of the twenty distinct demographic groups it deemed the film's target. As *Variety* reported, "T-L's spots covered all possible angles. The spots sold love angles, milked the counterculture, appealed to action fans, karate cultists, youth, the middle-aged, and the nonmoviegoer. It was, said one T-L exec, 'carefully calculated overkill.'" There was a "logorhythmic" aspect to the *Billy Jack* campaign, recalls Laughlin, a reflexively free thinker who eventually abandoned filmmaking for a career as a motivational speaker, presidential candidate and noted expert in Jungian psychology.

"We threw out the rule books," distribution president Ernie Sands told *Variety*. "We booked twins and theaters around the corner from each other. If the overhead was right and population density justified it, we rented the theater." The number of theaters, combined with the intense marketing, should "make it easy and convenient to see the movie," another Taylor-Laughlin executive said at the time. "A filmgoer should be able, after being dunned relentlessly

by the campaign, to fall out of bed and find a theatre where
Billy Jack is playing."

The strategy paid off handsomely, as *Billy Jack* piled up
roughly $75 million in additional grosses. It was a staggering
sum in 1973 and still one of the biggest returns ever for a low-
budget, independent film. "All of a sudden the whole industry took note," recalled Andrew J. Kuehn, a studio marketing
executive who founded the pioneering trailer house Kalei-
doscope. Agreed Barry London, former distribution head at
Paramount: "They showed what strong, fast-hitting TV advertising could do."

If *Billy Jack* had opened the door for regional saturation
supported by television, spawning a wave of four-wall imitators, the launch of its sequel, *The Trial of Billy Jack,* blew the
door off the hinges. Laughlin decided the sequel should open
on the same date across the country, November 13, 1974, in
twelve hundred theaters. The television campaign would be
even more ambitious, with $3.5 million in national ads.

At the center of *Trial*'s military-style invasion was John
Rubel, a former executive of Litton Industries and onetime
under-secretary of defense to Robert McNamara. Using feedback from repeated test screenings combined with charts and
demographic maps, the staff of seventy-five at Taylor-Laughlin laid the groundwork for studio marketing efforts to come.
"The *Billy Jack* people are detail and figure nuts," *Variety* concluded. Records from the film's rollout indicate as much.
Full-page graphs articulate the array of considerations in
each market used in planning TV buys, identifying the cost
per person, the breakeven, the direct cost, and so on. "Play-

dates were not selected willy-nilly," emphasized *Variety*, "but part of a complicated equation which included age-group audience potential, market potential, video umbrella penetration, and more than four months of pretesting the picture (it was previewed in rough, recut, previewed again, recut) to maximize impact."

Distribution was maximized by Laughlin's use of the industry's "80–20 rule," that is, 80 percent of a film's gross usually comes from 20 percent of the theaters. Taylor-Laughlin employed college students and part-time workers to fan out across the country and identify the country's top-grossing theaters. To circumvent the inefficient practice of opening in downtown "A" venues and widening from there, *Trial* would go directly to suburban houses normally accustomed to playing B and C titles. TV was a perfect way of reaching those audiences. Despite its nearly three-hour running time, *Trial* opened strong, racking up $9 million in its five-day opening and $11 million in its first week.

Like Joseph E. Levine, Laughlin is largely overlooked in most accounts of how blockbusters began. A character in *Trial* says, "Billy Jack's belief is that a man who doesn't go his own way is nothing." By going his own way, Laughlin reaped a vast fortune. He plowed a great deal of it into *Billy Jack Goes to Washington,* a sequel with a premise similar to that of *Legally Blonde 2,* which never got a theatrical release. It would be Laughlin's final screen appearance; his company dissolved in 1977 and Laughlin eventually moved with his wife to the hills above Ventura County, about fifty miles outside of Los Angeles. Since the studios decided his time was past, Laughlin's legacy has remained a well-kept secret.

Several of his attempts to remake *Billy Jack* have briefly gotten off the ground before falling apart. In a 2004 essay in *The Movie Business Book,* Paramount Pictures vice chairman Robert G. Friedman, who began his Hollywood career in the Warner Brothers mailroom, acknowledges that with *Billy Jack,* "the process began to change." But he gives sole credit to the studio, never mentioning Laughlin's name. "Warners refined this strategy for the national-saturation release of *Billy Jack,*" he writes, "spending unprecedented television advertising dollars to achieve an unusually high level of gross rating points, or GRPs."

Thirty years after he helped define opening weekend, Laughlin observed, "One of the things Delores and I have watched with amusement is that we don't seem to exist in Hollywood. My friend Lew Wasserman summed it up real simply. He said, 'The reason you're not considered the innovator is you're no one's son of a bitch. Hitchcock and George Roy Hill, those are *our* sons of bitches. There's no one to protect your image.'"

They may not have given credit to *Billy Jack,* but studios in the 1970s began to perceive that the wide release would be the wave of the future. "All it took," Ernie Sands said of *Billy Jack,* "was money and nerve." That would become an industry mantra. In May 1975 Grey Advertising, which had done the media buys on *Billy Jack,* helped Columbia craft a saturation campaign for *Breakout,* in which Charles Bronson plays a bush pilot hired to break Robert Duvall out of a Mexican prison. Columbia splashed the film across thirteen hundred screens amid $3 million of TV ad hype. One of the key weapons was a tactic called "roadblocking," in which every TV station in major cities ran the same *Breakout* ad at the same moment on a given night. The goal was to reach 92 percent of the nation's 211 million TV households and 84 percent of the target audience, 18-to-49-year-old males. Given its sizable outlay, Columbia wanted some way to gauge the return on investment. One distribution executive suggested installing a separate telephone system in order to speed the reporting of grosses to the studio. It was one of the earliest known initiatives to commodify opening weekend. The film proved a disappointment, however, grossing just $16 million in its entire run.

Lew Wasserman's Universal was one of the major studios grappling with wide-release economics in the 1970s. The company had seen Paramount execute a successful two-step wide pattern with *The Godfather* and *Love Story,* in which exclusive New York and Los Angeles engagements were quickly followed by nationwide openings. It had executed its own share of novel wide releases, among them 1974's *Earthquake,* whose Sensurround gimmick helped it open to $1.3 million in fifty-one cities. Wasserman, whose MCA had signed Laughlin as an acting client in the 1960s, talked to Laughlin several times about the innovative releases of the *Billy Jack* films, the director remembers.

Armed with that knowledge but mindful of the risks of opening wide, Wasserman opted for a relatively conservative release plan on *Jaws.* Seven months after *The Trial of Billy Jack,* the shark movie popularly credited with giving birth to the blockbuster opened on one-third as many screens.

There was no staying the hand of Warners' distribution

chief in 2003. Fellman was on a mission to deliver to Schwarzenegger the maximum screen saturation.

The phone rang in Fellman's office. Someone who understood the stakes was calling. It was Bob Daly, who had run Warner Brothers along with Terry Semel for twenty years until their exit in 1999. The pair became known for presiding over a franchise factory that rolled up sizable grosses by exploiting every tentacle of the Time-Warner empire. Under Daly *Batman* helped create an opening-weekend paradigm in June 1989, melding the bat-logo marketing image, savvy product placement, soundtrack sales and aggressive distribution to smash records in June with a then-stratospheric $40 million opening. Far more than *Jaws,* arguably, *Batman* created the modern opening weekend template for leveraging the machinery of a giant media company to achieve maximum on a single release date. Daly had become managing partner, chairman and chief operating officer of the Los Angeles Dodgers, a post he would leave when News Corp. sold the team in 2004. On July 2, 2003, Daly was in a different game than Fellman. But his heart—and many of his good friends—remained on the lot. When a big movie opened, he still called to check on the grosses.

Fellman shifted into shaman mode, reading off some of the numbers from the binder and assuring Daly, "We're in good shape." He had done likewise the day before with producer Joel Silver, who had called from the south of France to check on the dregs of *Matrix Reloaded*'s ticket sales. "275's in the bag," Fellman had told him. "I'm looking at 278, 280 is right there."

Dollars In Real Time

In honor of Elle Woods's arrival, the Cinerama Dome had gone pink. A network of high-intensity lights cast a rosy glow on the geodesic theater on Sunset Boulevard that made it look like an outsized jewel. Finally, on opening day, here was the aesthetic Charles Herman-Wurmfeld had strived to achieve. This was pure rock candy.

Dan Fellman's son, Brett Fellman, who heads MGM's exhibitor relations department, organized an event to mark the official opening of *Legally Blonde 2* at the Dome. The forty-year-old film landmark that used to be one of L.A.'s grandest single-screen movie venues was now part of a fifteen-screen complex called ArcLight Hollywood. The Dome party was one of two hundred such celebrations around the country, Fellman said. It was a far cry from Joseph E. Levine's "explodation luncheon," but carried an unmistakable whiff of showmanship. Stripped of the red-carpet glamour, free food and goodie bags of the industry premiere, the event was designed as an incentive for fans to check out the movie on opening night.

In the cavernous lobby, a special *Legally Blonde 2* gift shop greeted ticket buyers. Some of the merchandise specifically plugged the movie, but most was simply in harmony with it: beauty products, stuffed dogs, Barbie dolls, books like *Tiffany's Table Manners for Teens*. Behind a glass case stood several mannequins dressed in outfits billed as those worn by Reese Witherspoon in the movie. The designer accoutrements bore museum-worthy inscriptions. (MGM conceded later that they were replicas. Promoted as a touring exhibition, the display was actually occurring simultaneously at dozens of malls and movie theaters across the country.) The robin's-egg-blue Audi TT that Elle Woods drives in the movie was parked out front.

Presiding over the opening-night event was Jillian Barberie, the weather girl from *Fox NFL Sunday* and cohost of popular morning TV show *Good Day L.A.,* whose frothily populist sex appeal seemed in sync with the movie. Strangers approached her in the lobby to get photos taken. A helicopter circling overhead would get video of the pink Dome from above that would be used as a backdrop during Barberie's weather reports.

Inside the theater, a television camera followed Barberie for a local Fox News feature. She grabbed a microphone and introduced the movie with a mix of saucy attitude and earnest girl-power sentiment. "How many of you are legally blonde?" A few hands shot up. "Liar, liar, liar!" Then, in a more contemplative moment: "My coming-of-age movie was

Sixteen Candles. I just love a Hollywood movie that has a good message." After a thumbs-up for the film's pet-friendly point of view, she gave up the microphone and took her seat as the lights dimmed. It was a spirited sendoff, but a look around revealed a sign of the continuing summer box office malaise. The theater was only two-thirds full.

Across Sunset from the pink Cinerama Dome, on the nineteenth floor of an office tower known as Hollywood Center, a covert ritual was taking place to match the public spectacle below. A large room at one end of the floor looked out on the hills and famed Hollywood sign on one side and the twinkling of downtown skyscrapers on the other. No one working there had time to take in the view. They were too busy handling the load of calls to Nielsen EDI, the industry's dominant collector of box office data. Every night, theater by theater, grosses travel by phone, fax or email from 90 percent of the nation's thirty-five thousand movie screens to headset-wearing EDI operators, who rotate through six-hour shifts, punching grosses into Unix terminals that feed EDI's massive database. Studios and theaters are the company's core clients, so EDI goes out of its way not to alienate them. As the phone room collects raw grosses from theaters, it uses a tool called Boffo to transmit them at regular intervals to subscribers' handheld or desktop computers. Studios look at those returns and then calculate a "missing factor" to come up with an official estimate of the day's total business. Putting those numbers into a competitive context, EDI produces a hard-copy report of the day's activities and delivers it to the studio distribution chiefs at dawn on the following day.

The routine humming of that system would have been impossible for Marcie Polier to imagine when she broke into the movie business as a part-time secretary for Mann Theatres at age twenty-two in 1975. The job entailed gathering box office reports from theater managers by telephone, writing them up in pencil, typing them into reports and then sending them to a select handful of people. "I started around Christmastime," she says. "*Jaws* was still playing and the questions everybody had were, 'What were the grosses?' and 'Who can we share them with?'"

The more days she spent in her repetitious job, jotting down figures, typing them up, sending them out, the more Polier started to think about aggregating all of the numbers. There was obviously intense demand for the figures. Why not tap into it? She was young enough not to be dissuaded by the fact that for decades, box office had been divulged strictly on the basis of personal relationships. Studio executives and exhibitors would protect numbers fiercely, even from their own colleagues. Mann's information was given to just forty VIPs who clamored for info on double-bill screenings. The trade papers monitored film revenues, but reported it only in terms of exclusive runs in New York and Los Angeles and a smattering of other cities.

"Everybody said it wouldn't work. People were so competitive every second of every day," Polier remembered. "But there was one night when I couldn't sleep. I elbowed my husband in the ribs and said, 'I think it *can* work.'" Using a $400 loan from her father-in-law, a film booker with Fox West Coast Theatres, Polier created Centralized Grosses, which pooled information into a communal database. It later evolved into National Gross Service and finally was known as Entertainment Data, Inc. AC Nielsen, the company known for its TV ratings service and a music sales tool called SoundScan, acquired it in 1999 and, in turn, was bought in 2001 by Dutch conglomerate VNU. It is now known as Nielsen EDI.

Polier still has the company's first product, a green-and-white computer printout from August 1976. It hangs in a frame on a stairway inside her richly appointed, gated home in the hills of Bel Air. She cashed out of EDI in 2003 a multimillionaire, and now is Nielsen EDI's chairman emerita, focusing her energies on commercial real estate and charity work. Medium height, with curly brown hair that almost reaches her shoulders, Polier becomes warm and congenial once the conversation has reached a comfortable cruising altitude. On the ascent, she comes off as circumspect, even a bit strict, studying an interlocutor through reading glasses and hesitating before answering questions.

A native of the L.A. bedroom community of Ladera Heights, Polier was influenced from an early age by her father's business, an import-export operation that sold goods from the Far East. He had a central warehouse and three retail stores around the city. Every night at 9 P.M., without fail, he would get up and call in to get the closing sales for the day from his three stores. She studied art history at USC for two years, but soon migrated to the frontier of box office, whose customs held a curious appeal. Her natural business instinct kicked in.

"Everyone at Mann worked the phones and they were such outrageous characters," she said. "There was a gym next door to the Mann offices on Sunset and Ted Mann used to work out over there and then come to the office in his Speedo. He loved to sing." The realm of box office, she added, "is so unlike other industries. In other businesses, there are lines you won't cross. There is a form to a business letter. In distribution, if you have a little bit of a rough personality, they work with it."

EDI's impact was immediate. Polier knew it would be a success when she heard that Ted Mann had taunted William R. Forman, head of the competing Pacific Theatres chain, saying he knew all of the weekend grosses at Pacific Theaters. An outraged Forman refused to supply Polier's company with grosses for one year. It stung Polier's fledgling enterprise, but also demonstrated the power of EDI's numbers. Other clients remained loyal and Pacific's protest wound up being the biggest early hurdle she had to clear.

EDI's staunchest competitor is Rentrak, a box office tracking service launched in 2001. It operates on a distinctly different model from EDI, capturing box office grosses from the point of sale at a movie theater box office. That means there is no phone room in the company's stylish, loft-style offices in the San Fernando Valley, just a dozen workers with flatscreen monitors overseeing the flow of data. Unlike EDI's database, Rentrak's is continuously updated in real time, ticket by ticket. Most employees spend their shifts "cleaning the data" from theaters, in the words of senior vice president

Ron Giambra. Just as dirt is the enemy of celluloid at the Technicolor processing plant, statistical abnormalities are the bane of Rentrak's data collection. Giambra, a former distribution executive at the now defunct companies Orion, Polygram and Destination Films, started the box office arm of Rentrak along with Chris Aronson, who subsequently went to MGM to serve as second-in-command to distribution chief Eric Lomis. They asserted that EDI had become complacent, charging inflated rates and refreshing their data too infrequently for numbers-crazed clients. Aronson remained an acolyte of the service and made sure MGM was a loyal client. Several studios now subscribe to both EDI and Rentrak, but the latter has made significant inroads as the desire for around-the-clock data has intensified. Early in 2003, Disney, Fox and DreamWorks signed on. Giambra expected every other major to follow suit in 2004. Several studios, after a trial period, had abandoned EDI in favor of Rentrak. The innovations of this whisper-quiet new technology outfit may not be as dramatic as Marcie Polier's, but could end up transforming the box office game yet again.

EDI and Rentrak both formalized some of the innovations of A. D. "Art" Murphy, a longtime *Variety* reporter and film critic who, working from scratch, developed an array of new tools for charting box office grosses in the pages of *Variety*. The film business was a second career for Murphy, who spent a decade in the Navy, navigating destroyers and amphibious ships used to transport troops and tanks, while earning a masters degree in systems analysis and operations research. Honorably discharged in December 1964, he composed a letter analyzing the film business and sent it to Tom

Pryor, who was then editor of *Daily Variety*. Pryor immediately hired him. Murphy became the paper's chief film critic, known by the sobriquet with which he signed his reviews, Murf. Unlike Polier, Murphy was both an analyst and critic. He predicted how films would perform and then analyzed the results. Few at the studios dared confront him about his methods, lest he punish them with a damaging review of a future film. The Navy sailor was churlish and intimidating.

Murphy became fixated with the new release patterns and the box office performances of the films he was reviewing. When he started, *Variety* didn't publish a single regular report on nationwide grosses. Instead the paper ran a bewildering array of regional stories reporting ticket sales at particular houses—a system that prevailed well into the 1970s. On June 25, 1975, less than a week after *Jaws* opened, *Variety* ran thirteen separate stories analyzing its grosses around the country—it was "jumbo" in Portland; "sizzling" in Chicago; New York was "the perfect feeding ground." Murf sought to streamline that process, analyzing a film's total performance and how it would affect a studio. He compiled national numbers based on averages from key regions. In 1968 he began publishing a column called *Variety*'s Key City B.O. Sample. And he began to focus on first week ticket sales in the 1970s. *Variety* began publishing a weekly chart of the nation's fifty top-grossing films, which Murphy supplemented with his own statistical arcana. In 1984 he began publishing his own box office compendium, *Art Murphy's Box Office Register*, a slender almanac that listed films alphabetically and ranked their grosses, per-screen averages and a few other metrics.

The *Register*, which Murphy published and sold himself

(initially for $65 a copy), represented a kind of data mani-
festo of a new era. The introduction to a volume published
in 1985 read, in part:

> Nobody can truly participate in the motion pic-
> ture business without looking at numbers of all
> kinds, and especially those numbers which represent
> the collective and comparative decisions of paying
> customers. Box office grosses must be looked at con-
> stantly—on almost EVERY film, on almost EVERY
> day. Far from being mere numbers, box office grosses
> represent the responses of PEOPLE to films. To ig-
> nore those numbers—and those people—is to risk
> business failure and—worse—to inhabit the cata-
> tonic world of the compulsive aesthete. The concept
> of ART MURPHY'S BOX OFFICE REGISTER is to
> facilitate in some modest way a more convenient,
> more cohesive understanding of what makes moving
> pictures move.

Murphy was a maverick who used his institutional power
to create a unique role for himself in the industry. Like Farrell, he became the gatekeeper of an esoteric realm of the box
office business at a time when few national papers paid any
attention to it. In his later years at *Variety,* he was a gruff and
distant figure in the newsroom. He smoked two packs of cigarettes a day, and he was accompanied everywhere by a boxer
dog named Eddie, who sat outside his office. In 1979 Murphy
helped found the Peter Stark Motion Picture Producing Program at USC, the only accredited film school program for

students aiming to become producers. Peter Bart, who arrived at *Variety* as editor in chief in 1989, voiced objections to Murphy both reviewing films and interpreting their commercial performance. A few contentious years later, in 1993, Murphy moved to *The Hollywood Reporter* to continue writing box office analysis. He died on June 16, 2003, at the age of seventy. His memory was sustained by film business figures in academia and the studio system, many of whom spoke at his memorial service, acknowledging his pioneering work. Except for the fairly straightforward *Registers,* Murphy left behind a vast trove of trade journal articles full of densely constructed quantitative analyses. The significance of Murphy's work is unquestioned but the language of his reporting remains nearly impenetrable. It was so deeply influenced by systems analysis that it rarely looked beyond the minutiae to consider how the system was changing underfoot.

One of Art Murphy's best sources and fondest friends was Nikki Rocco, whose studio career evolved amid sweeping changes in the way films were released and tracked. Rocco was hired by Universal Pictures to work in the studio's road show department in 1967. She was a seventeen-year-old high school student from Flushing, New York, with a facility for numbers. She could swiftly operate a comptometer—a mechanical adding machine with columns of keys and a metal crank—with one hand, while holding a phone in the other. Rocco was both charming and ambitious. She was as comfortable punching up the grosses as she was fraternizing in the men's club of exhibitors and distribution executives. "I fit in," she says. "I could slap them all around." She endured countless sexual jabs—some petty, some not—as she worked her way up from the bottom, but betrays no bitterness about it.

"I was the little girl who knew box office from the night before," Rocco told journalist Mollie Gregory. "Lew Wasserman would call me into his office and I'd shake because I was so nervous. 'How'd we do at such and such a theater last night, Nikki?' he'd say. I'd give him the numbers. When I worked in New York, I volunteered to stay late and do the filing for the executive offices. The other women there loved the idea. I was reading the files and learning all about how to sell film . . . I was self-taught."

Wasserman, the long-presiding spirit of Universal Pictures in that era, invested major resources in his sales operation. Wasserman was obsessed with the grosses. Biographer Connie Bruck recounts the studio aides who delivered slips of paper to him throughout the day with updated box office figures, the Universal Tour head count, and stock market closing numbers.

Rocco was relocated in 1981 from New York to the Universal Studios lot in California. As the studio culture shifted and marketing assumed a larger role in studio affairs, Rocco was able to unite the realms of marketing, distribution and publicity. She was self-assured with journalists, and she was the quintessential loyal studio soldier. When former attorney Tom Pollock became chairman of Universal Pictures in 1986, he accelerated the tabulation of the grosses. At the time, the studio didn't run models for films. It didn't even keep a calendar of competitors' titles.

Pollock began calling Rocco at 4 A.M. Saturday mornings to secure her projections for opening weekend. "That's when my life ended," Rocco says. No longer was it acceptable to arrive at a gross at a leisurely pace on Saturday. She had to measure Friday's results instantly and interpret them for anxious executives and filmmakers. "We have conditioned audiences to believe that they have to be there on Friday night," Rocco says. "We've conditioned them to know when they get there, there will be a seat." So it also became necessary to know the numbers.

Box office trackers were also keenly aware of the expanding Hollywood press corps as the entertainment business became the lifeblood for a proliferating array of television, print and, eventually, Internet outlets, all of which were eager to publish weekend grosses. Box office plugged directly into the 1970s and 1980s culture of lists, from David Letterman's Top 10 to *People's Almanac Presents the Book of Lists,* which began its annual reign on paperback bestseller lists in 1979. Personal computers were becoming commonplace in people's homes. Free agency in sports made statistics an integral part of a big-spending new realm that brought championships to owners willing to pay players for every touchdown or run batted in.

In 1981 *Entertainment Tonight* aired its first satellite-delivered broadcast, ushering in a new era of saturation in entertainment news. That same year, CNN and MTV began broadcasting. On September 15, 1982, the first issue of *USA Today* appeared in the Baltimore and Washington, D.C., areas. By the following April, daily circulation had topped 1 million. Here was a newspaper that put a premium on short articles, charts and graphics. It was sold from street-corner receptacles which, cultural critic Neil Postman observed in

Amusing Ourselves to Death, resembled television sets. "The sports section of *USA Today,*" Postman wrote, "includes enough pointless statistics to distract a computer."

By 1974, Nat Fellman had already lived two professional lives, but by founding a company called Exhibitor Relations he embarked on a third. Officially the first company founded to keep track of box office grosses, it distinguished itself early on by dint of Fellman's decades of experience in exhibition. Ironically, what set Exhibitor Relations apart from Marcie Polier's Centralized Grosses was that it collected data only from the studios, never from exhibitors. It was a clearinghouse for those numbers but drilled no deeper. The father of Warner Brothers distribution president Dan Fellman and grandfather of Brett Fellman, Nat Fellman began his career at Warner Brothers' theater division in 1928, moving to top positions with Mann and National General. The early reports from Exhibitor Relations were anchored by Fellman's newsletter, which contained terse summaries of who was doing what kind of business where. Only rarely, as in the case of big openers like *Jaws,* did he inject emotion into the reports. The main commodity the company was selling was a sense of the competitive landscape, not just in terms of grosses but in terms of how films were being positioned. Exhibitor Relations was the first company to publish a competitive release schedule that showed when each studio was planning to release its films.

Jon Krier, another former exhibitor, joined the company in 1978 as a partner and executive vice president. He immediately began reaching out to the media, to some of the people at newspapers and wire services he had befriended over his years in the business. "The way Jon made the company bigger than the sum of its parts was through relationships with the media," said Paul Dergarabedian, the current president. By the time Krier bought out the other partners and assumed control of the firm in 1988, his efforts had borne fruit. The company was a key supplier of box office numbers to the Associated Press, *Los Angeles Times*, CNN and many more. When Time Inc. launched *Entertainment Weekly* in 1990, the magazine ran a top 10 box office list supplied by Exhibitor Relations. Just as important was Krier's constant presence in reports about the film business. "What I learned from him was being available," Dergarabedian said. "It's about accessibility and the quality of the data."

Today, EDI, Rentrak and Exhibitor Relations are part of a web of outlets beaming box office figures around the world. *Variety*'s decision in 1996 to begin publishing a chart of weekend estimates every Monday morning put pressure on other media outlets to match them on Monday. TV networks and radio stations built box office into their Sunday evening newscasts. In fact, studios don't always just battle for the number one spot; they also compete to be number five and thereby make the cut in a graphic that airs on local TV.

The latest variation on the 1970s concept of pooled data is the proliferation of Internet box office trackers, dozens of independently funded Web sites with names like Boxoffice prophets.com, The-numbers.com, boxofficeguru.com. Some allow people to bet real money on the outcome of a given weekend. The most prominent such site is Boxoffice mojo.com, run by Brandon Gray from his apartment just off L.A.'s Miracle Mile. Among its features is a predictions game—not using real money—that stems from Gray's uncanny track record in informal box office pools in the late 1990s. A graduate of USC, Gray has always been a movie fan, but his particular gift came in sifting through the numbers. He began down the path toward box office punditry in Art Murphy–like fashion: while writing movie reviews and features for the Tribune Media Service he displayed an uncanny ability to project weekend box office. After using that knack to win betting pools, he started kicking around the idea of starting a Web site. Box Office Mojo was launched on August 7, 1998.

Gray's initiative is the next wave in Hollywood's data revolution. With input from studios, he began posting Friday numbers on Saturday: a quick, though not always reliable, index of the weekend horse race. Movie fans and executives log on and by lunchtime Saturday they have a pretty good idea if a movie is working or not. Incrementally, these early numbers could further distort the natural weekend, putting a public spotlight on opening day, which is already immensely pressure-packed on studios' back lots. Along with stirring the pot with numbers, Gray has also demonstrated the same scrappy ability as Exhibitor Relations to get quoted in the press. In the heat of box office battle, that qualifies him as an expert.

The open-wide system reached its zenith on May 3, 2002, the start of Hollywood's first $100 million opening weekend. Forty years had passed since Spider-Man, Stan Lee's web-slinging superhero, broke into print in the Marvel Comics anthology *Amazing Fantasy #15*. For years, the *Spider-Man* movie rights had been tangled in a copyright battle of Dickensian proportions. Three rights holders had gone bankrupt. More than ten screenwriters, including James Cameron, had tried without success to adapt it. In 1999 Sony paid close to $7 million for the movie rights, then committed close to $200 million to produce and market their movie. Executives had visions of a lucrative franchise spanning several sequels, DVDs and theme-park rides. Decades of grandiose ambitions, creative struggles and dashed expectations had funneled into one decisive, super-charged Friday night.

The cast and filmmakers rode around Los Angeles in a party van stocked with champagne. The first stop had been The Grove, a brand-new outdoor mall with a fourteen-screen theater complex that was already one of the top-grossing locations in the country. The showings were not only sold out; there was an undeniable electricity running through the crowds. Meanwhile, Jeff Blake, the leonine vice chairman and lead number-cruncher for Sony Pictures, was at home counting the grosses. Having witnessed firsthand the public's appetite for *Spider-Man*, the film's principals next gathered for dinner at a big table in the middle of Morton's, the venerable West Hollywood celebrity hangout that hosts *Vanity Fair*'s Oscar party every year. There was Tobey Maguire, the star of *Spider-Man*, the film's director, Sam Raimi, producer Laura Ziskin, Marvel Comics mogul Avi Arad, Sony film chief Amy Pascal and her marketing deputy, Geoffrey Ammer, and a half dozen executives and managers. Their mood was giddy. It was after 9 P.M., but the group didn't yet have a fix on the box office tally. The evening shows in New York had closed, but there wasn't a national projection for the night. At 10:15, Pascal got a call from Blake.

The silver-maned Blake is one of the industry's most canny interpreters of the distribution vernacular. His handwritten weekend faxes, which recap the performance of Sony films and wryly size up the overall box office race, are an institution that some producers and executives have taken to framing.

For Ziskin, May 3 was do-or-die day. Ziskin had been a producer with left-of-center tastes who had never produced a film of such scale. "I call myself the handmaiden of *Spider-Man*," she quipped. In an effort to temper expectations, Blake originally advised Ziskin the film could earn $60 million in ticket sales on opening weekend. She replied that "Amy Pascal will come to my house and string me up by my thumbs if we open in the sixties." *Harry Potter and the Sorcerer's Stone*, released six months earlier, held the record for an opening weekend: $90 million. That was their true goal.

Every studio has its opening night rituals. Tom Sherak, former head of distribution at Twentieth Century Fox, presided over an opening-day ritual known as "The Vigil." On one such occasion in 1994, Sherak invited Arnold Schwarzenegger and several of those involved with *True Lies* to come to the Fox lot, where he was throwing a special party on the set used to shoot New York street scenes. Speaker towers were set up to carry Sherak's conference calls with ebullient exhibitors. Lou Pitt, then Schwarzenegger's agent, recalled Sherak sounding like a talk-radio host. "Let's go to Phil in Buffalo—Phil, whaddya got?" Another time, at the start of Fourth of July weekend in 1996, Sherak's vigil again turned euphoric. *Independence Day* was piling up $17.4 million on the way to a record-breaking $85 million long weekend. When someone called News Corp. chairman Rupert Murdoch during a charity banquet to slip him the numbers, he left the event immediately with his wife and headed to the vigil. Still wearing a tux, his wife in a glittering gown, he looked for someone to celebrate with. "He gave me a kiss on the face," remembers Dean Devlin, the film's writer and producer.

At Morton's, when Pascal got the call from Blake, she looked stunned. "Can I tell them?" she asked. Conversation at the table stopped. They knew Blake had told her the number. Then, her announcement: Friday looked like $30 million. The table erupted in raucous applause.

The opening-day number would continue to rise. Half an hour later, Ammer got a call from a colleague who had moved the target to $35 million. Blake was convinced it would reach at least $37 million—many of the West Coast late shows were yet to be tabulated.

In the wee hours, by the time the celebrants straggled home, many of their lives had been transformed, to say nothing of the movie business. The final Friday number would be $39.4 million and the weekend would hit $114.8 million, shattering *Harry Potter*'s record by 27 percent.

As the members of the *Spider-Man* clan arrived at their homes, each had a fax waiting. Blake's exuberance leapt from the page. "How does the biggest day ever sound, on the way to the biggest opening ever, on the way to the biggest movie in Columbia's 78-year history?" he wrote. "I've always dreamed of a $30 million day (at times I've dreamed of a $3 million day)." He ended with thanks to everyone involved with the movie, "and most of all my attorney, Tom Hoberman, for getting me those two extra points in the bonus pool."

In the upper right-hand corner of the fax was a testament to the intoxicating but ephemeral sensation shared by those who break records in Hollywood. Blake marked the time of the fax as 11:59 p.m., conceding, "I don't want it to end."

MGM was not looking to prolong its weekend as *Legally Blonde 2* reached commercial audiences on July 2, 2003. Some of the early returns were favorable, but wild fluctuations and regional variations, not to mention the curveball of the Friday holiday, meant the ground still felt shaky underfoot.

Executives were bleary-eyed after attending premieres on both coasts and waking up early on opening day for the reviews, which were mixed. Elvis Mitchell of the *New York Times* called it a "frosted vanilla Pop-Tart" that is "all context and no subtext." The reshoots and relentless tweaking had never alleviated the movie's two chief problems: It was too repetitive of the first film and it dealt in an uninteresting way with the world of Washington.

MGM distribution chief Erik Lomis had not had more than ten hours of sleep in the past week. A former film buyer for United Artists Theatre Circuit, Lomis had been at

MGM for about a decade. He worked well with Kops and Adee, though he had an altogether different style. The stuffed and mounted head of a deer adorned one wall of his office. The fact that sporting equipment was strewn about was not surprising given Lomis's penchant for golf and fast-pitch softball. In weekly recreational softball games, he was a pitcher. Hitters would often get an intense stare when he was about to deliver, and the pitch was nearly always a fastball. "I do have a change, but I figure if they're going to beat me, it ought to be with the hard stuff." Along with this intensity and ability to intimidate—used to great effect in the trenches of exhibition—Lomis possesses a buoyantly sardonic sense of humor. At an MGM event at ShoWest featuring a live lion cub, he joked that the lion "took some exhibitor's finger right off." Callers who asked how he was doing would often get a booming response: "Never had a bad day in my life, kid!"

As *Legally Blonde 2* opened, Lomis sifted through East Coast numbers, which were strong. He quickly set the floor at $8 million.

"It is not for the faint of heart," Peter Adee said upon the arrival of initial grosses. "You have to have an iron stomach. From moment to moment it's either good or bad or great or terrible. You're *exhausted* over 'What could it be?' and you're dreading that the bottom could fall out at any time. That first day, we did $9.1 million. At one point it seemed really high. It seemed like we were going to do really well. The number was a great number. Eleven would have been godlike."

Earlier on Wednesday, Adee had spoken with his Warner

Brothers counterpart, Dawn Taubin, and wished her good luck. "She has a great elegance about her," he said. "She was like, 'Hey. It's gonna be what it's gonna be.'"

Lomis often hosted stars and filmmakers in his office on a film's opening day, ordering in cheesesteaks, hoisting glasses of scotch and smoking cigars. (The latter part of the ritual was easier to pull off at MGM's old Santa Monica headquarters, which had a balcony.) July 2, 2003, would be different. Reese Witherspoon was in London, Marc Platt was in New York and Charles Herman-Wurmfeld was in Vermont, so the crew in Lomis's office was a cluster of executives.

One of them was Kops, whose tenure at MGM was inextricably linked with the *Legally Blonde* films. He was the keeper of the flame, more than almost anyone else at the company. The reality was finally hitting that the tenor of his entire year and the direction of the months to come would be forged on this day. He remembered, "Lomis was going through theater by theater and he would read off our number, then *T3*, *Sinbad*, the next, the next, the next. He sounded like the MovieFone guy—'*T3*, Racine, Wisconsin, $10,000.' It was this constant neck-and-neck thing. *Sinbad* did look painful, too."

Yes, the rout was on. Jeffrey Katzenberg's variation on *Arabian Nights*, so carefully engineered for mass consumption, was scarcely being consumed at all. This film, whose combined production and marketing costs were estimated at $100 million, was struggling to reach just $1 million in ticket sales. And the weekend was just one day old.

The New Main Street

Charles Herman-Wurmfeld lined up on July 4 at the Plaza Movieplex 9 in Rutland, Vermont, and bought twenty tickets for *Legally Blonde 2*. It was a superstitious gesture, designed to stave off the intense anxiety of feeling every dip and climb in the weekend roller coaster from three thousand miles away. The director was spending the Fourth at his family's farmhouse in the Goshen–Four Corners area of Vermont, so he felt only intermittently connected to the flow of box office data that would shape his career.

"I was wise enough to get to Vermont but not wise enough to turn off the phones until Monday morning," he said. The weekend had already brought "all kinds of panicked phone calls, like 'It's a tremendous first night, we're doing terrifically' and then the next day, 'The audiences are rejecting the movie. They're not coming.' Then, 'We think it's getting better.' Then, 'Oh, it's a hit, we're sure.' And I am emotionally chained to it. No perspective whatsoever. One day I was like a pig in shit, the next day life was shit." He couldn't suppress a rueful smile. "I'll never do that again. I'll either be at the studio with the guys as the numbers roll in, drinking scotches and smoking cigars and really living that experience, or I'll be completely out of touch and get the number Monday morning."

Back in Los Angeles, Erik Lomis wished he had the luxury of tuning out until Monday. Except for the fact that he would not go into the office, he was spending the holiday as he had spent the previous two days: working the phones, sifting through real-time grosses. Sleep was still a scarce commodity. The only time Lomis left the house was to drop off some old clothes at the Salvation Army.

Kops, on the other hand, badly needed to detach. He had been running on fumes for the past month, since the junket in London. With the movie now open and little for him to do until the media was given the final weekend tally on Sunday, he was content to lounge around his apartment near the Miracle Mile district. His office calendar, usually covered with scribbled notes, had a completely blank square on July 4. It would be a day to zone out and, as he put it "sit at home and watch some bad TiVo." The consequences of the weekend could wait.

Adee, like Herman-Wurmfeld, was in New England. He was taking part in a family reunion on Cape Cod, where cell phone reception tended to be sketchy at best. The vacation had been planned for a while, but there was no ambivalence about how he would spend it. For periods of up to an hour at a time, he would excuse himself from the festivities, find a spot on the lawn where he could get a call to go through, and get a dollar-by-dollar update on the fate of Elle Woods.

Those connected with *Legally Blonde 2* had ample reason to be anxious. They had all expected soft holiday business on Friday the Fourth, but Thursday's results were surprisingly mediocre. Although it was the night before a holiday, meaning teenage girls would theoretically be out in force, Thursday receipts totaled only $7.1 million, a 22 percent downtick from the movie's solid opening day. Friday looked like it would end up even weaker. The gap was widening between Elle and the Terminator.

Sinbad, meanwhile, was floundering. Opening day had reaped just $1.5 million, substantially less than the day's grosses for *Finding Nemo,* which had already been open for thirty-five days. On Thursday, *Sinbad* had inched up to $1.6 million but would struggle to hit $10 million over the five-day weekend. DreamWorks would not need to offer the rain checks it promised to any ticket buyers unable to get a copy of the *Shrek* CD-ROM. Supplies would last.

T3 producers Andy Vajna and Mario Kassar were on a victory tour of Baghdad with their star. After the Tokyo premiere, they'd flown to Kuwait City, then crossed the border into Iraq to spend the holiday on a USO mission screening the film for U.S. servicemen. *Access Hollywood* picked up footage of the troika surrounded by troops as they toured one of Saddam Hussein's former palaces. "I play Terminator, but you guys are the real Terminators," Schwarzenegger said to the men and women in uniform.

With the film finally released to theaters Stateside,

Schwarzenegger was readjusting his script. He'd been coy for months about his plans to run for California governor, but his Independence Day *Top Gun*–style tour of Iraq had all the trappings of a campaign stop. "It is really wild driving around here," Schwarzenegger told the troops. "I mean the poverty, and you see there is no money, it is disastrous financially and there is the leadership vacuum, pretty much like in California right now." Back in Burbank, the money was rolling in. *T3* had earned $16.5 million by Wednesday night, and nearly $12 million more on Thursday. East Coast matinees on Friday put it on track to increase its business on the Fourth. The Terminator was poised to take the weekend.

Some of the nation's most robust box office grosses were piling up at the dueling megaplexes in Southern California's Ontario Mills mall. There, at the AMC Ontario Mills 30 and Edwards Palace 22, *Terminator 3, Legally Blonde 2* and *Sinbad* were playing on a combined twenty-five screens, at twenty-minute intervals. Ontario, home to the Technicolor depot that ships posters and trailers to every theater in the country, was one of the most consistently lucrative exhibition zones in the nation. Twenty-one million people a year visited the mall. Here a popular film could vacuum up $1 million in a few days and saturation booking could be executed to its full, dizzying potential. Here the gears and pistons of the open-wide system formed an unstoppable sales machine. Here was the man behind the curtain making the great Oz talk.

But while studios reaped prodigious benefits from the place, few film executives ever bothered to travel the yellow-brick road forty miles east of Los Angeles, to the region known as the Inland Empire. Its name a euphemism coined in the 1950s for an area encompassing San Bernadino and Riverside counties, the Inland Empire is an area that exists for Hollywood only as a pit stop en route to Las Vegas or Palm Springs. More recently, it has become a mark of denigration on Fox's hit drama *The O.C.,* in which spoiled Orange County teenagers routinely refer to their Inland Empire peers as "white trash." Despite the harsh desert climate and the smog, however, this jagged rectangle between Palm Springs and Pasadena is home to as many people as the entire state of Oregon, about 3.5 million. Ontario is a sprawling city of 165,000 studded with distribution warehouses that was incorporated in 1891 in what settlers billed as California's first planned community. Projected to double in population by 2020, it is one of a dozen people-magnets that have made the Inland Empire one of the nation's fastest-growing suburban regions.

The best seat in the house for a movie at the AMC 30 is the projection room of the theater. The only distraction is the soft, fluttering sound of reels of celluloid traveling at twenty-four frames per second, winding down dank industrial corridors, across giant metal platters, and through refrigerator-sized projectors, transmitting the latest studio attractions into dozens of auditoriums. The projection room is the cerebral cortex of the multiplex, where a ten thousand-foot thin strip of perforated plastic—the consummation of years of work and hundreds of millions in marketing and production dollars—is processed and fed through narrow glass windows to capacious auditoriums. It's the bottleneck between the studio and the marketplace, a secluded area where up-to-the-minute digital filmmaking technology collides with creaky, analog distribution technology: a projection system using light, shutters and sprockets that dates back to the Nickelodeon era.

The weekend releases arrive at the theater on Wednesday and Thursday, divided among fifty-pound film cans, each of which contains four seventeen-minute, two-thousand-foot reels. *The Sinbad* and *Terminator 3* reels, manufactured by the Technicolor plant forty-six miles away, come in shiny, new orange plastic containers. Other prints, among them *Legally Blonde 2,* travel in bruised metal cans decorated with twenty years of grime and shredded mailing labels. The projectionists spend hours toiling at buildup tables, outfitted with splicing machines and roles of Permacel tape, assembling the prints and attaching the trailers on platters the diameter of bicycle wheels.

The thirty screens and six thousand seats at the AMC are serviced by two long, L-shaped projection rooms. The projectionists use a technique called "interlocking." They run a single print through several projectors at once, sending the movie across a pulley system running the length of the room, and beaming it into separate auditoriums at thirty-second intervals.

Over the long July Fourth weekend, the Mills popped 1,800 pounds of popcorn kernels, used 635 gallons of soda fountain syrup to make 3,815 gallons of soft drinks, and sold 1,736 hot dogs. Bob Garcia is the general manager of a workforce that numbers 150 people on a busy summer weekend. They circulate in red-and-black uniforms beneath LED boards displaying movie times that resemble stock tickers or airport departure monitors. The ceilings are low but the theaters extend in all directions, protruding from both sides of the circular lobby and two long, narrow corridors connected by a purple, teal and black carpet. There are eighty-six poster cases inside and outside the theater, and a freestanding box office in front, a useful crowd-control device that helps distinguish the movie house from the GameWorks arcade next door. "We often get confused with the mall," Garcia said. Rising above the box office is a giant, tilted globe bisected by the AMC logo. A poster in the offices upstairs trumpets a company motto from the late 1990s: "Changing the way the world sees movies."

When the AMC opened on December 13, 1996, at a cost of nearly $30 million, advertisements in regional papers billed it as the world's largest theater. Three months later, a rival circuit, Edwards Theaters, spent $27 million erecting its own twenty-two-screen megaplex across the street. The Ontario Palace 22 was the biggest theater Edwards had ever built. Suddenly, there were fifty-two screens on one parking lot, more screens in one spot than anywhere else in the country.

The Ontario megaplexes—the fruit of a 1990s movie-theater building boom that industry boosters called the "re-screening of America"—are the theatrical equivalent of the

SUVs that clog the Ontario Mills parking lot. The two houses play many of the same movies and serve many of the same concessions. Both have floor-shaking Dolby, DTS digital and THX sound systems and stadium seating—steep rows of plush high-backed rocking chairs with unobstructed views, and liftable arm-rests inset with plastic cup holders. But architecturally, the AMC 30 and the Edwards 22 are distinctly different.

The AMC blends into the surrounding mall shops, but the Edwards Palace resembles the suburban theater in Walker Percy's *The Moviegoer*, "a pink stucco cube, sitting out in a field all by itself." The only difference is that the field in Ontario is a parking lot. If the lobby of the Mills most resembles an airport lounge, the lobby of the Palace gives its patrons the feeling of being trapped inside a giant pinball machine. The entryway is lavishly lit with fluorescent lights, mirrored columns and flashing, multicolored neon squiggles. Twin box offices are surrounded by noisy video games and $8,000 plasma screens showing trailers and ads. The harshly lit, high-ceilinged lobby is decorated with kitschy paintings of silent-era actors, and its four largest auditoriums are named after famous movie palaces: the Chinese, the Hollywood, the Egyptian and the Grand Palace. The complex has just 4,500 seats, but its biggest auditorium, the Grand Palace, with seventy-foot-long, floor-to-ceiling gold curtains and 780 seats, is the biggest in the Inland Empire.

The megaplex—officially defined as a movie theater with at least sixteen screens—is a concept attempted sporadically in Europe and Australia but thus far placed on the mass production line only in America. Since 2002, according to the MPAA, the number of total U.S. screens has hit a plateau between thirty-five and thirty-six thousand. The number of megaplex locations, however, increased 10 percent in 2002 and another three percent in 2003. AMC, long the pioneer of the concept, now builds nothing but megaplexes. Exhibitors began the drive toward supersized movie theaters in the late 1980s, shelling out more than $1 million per screen to update their traditional suburban theaters with new sloped floors and multiple screens. But nowhere has the megaplex building boom resulted in a showdown as grand and acrimonious as the rivalry between AMC's Ontario Mills and Edward's Ontario Palace. And without the rivalry and the high-volume weekend extreme megaplexes across the country produced, the films released over July Fourth 2003 would have faced a formidable battle just to break even.

Stanley H. Durwood, the eminence grise of AMC until his death in 1999 at the age of seventy-eight, is the man who let the multiplex genie out of the bottle in the 1960s. Durwood grew up in Kansas City, the son of a silver-haired tent-show actor-turned-entrepreneur who built a small chain of movie houses and drive-in theaters beginning in 1920. After graduating from Harvard and serving as a navigator in the Army Air Force during World War II, Durwood came home and joined the family business. The multiplex idea came to him in 1962, when he was managing a six-hundred-seat second-run theater called the Roxy that his family operated in downtown Kansas City. Saddled with a lackluster Abbot and

Costello movie, he decided to close off the balcony. "I thought, 'If I had another crummy picture upstairs, I could double the gross," he told *Variety* years later. "I don't need another manager or anything." A year later, Durwood built the nation's first shopping mall multiplex, the two-screen Parkway II, above a grocery store in the Ward Parkway Shopping Center. "It was like punching a hole in the floor of your living room and oil coming out," Durwood said. It became the cornerstone of the theater circuit started by his father and called American Multi-Cinema, or AMC.

When rivals built copycat multiplexes, they found that more screens usually translated to more popcorn sales. In 1967 concession revenue was 15 percent of a theater's total revenue, according to the U.S. Department of Commerce. In 1982 that figure had risen to 23 percent. Today it is 35 percent for major circuits. In 1978 only 10 percent of indoor theaters were multiplexes, with 80 percent of those being twin-screen houses. Today only a quarter of theaters have a single screen. Movie theaters average 6.1 screens and there are more than five hundred megaplexes with more than sixteen screens under one roof.

As with any large-scale industrial shift, the multiplex revolution was predicated, in part, on new technologies: the use of Xenon projector bulbs and the implementation of Dolby sound systems. Xenon, unlike the old carbon arc bulbs, did not require a trained projectionist to monitor and maintain them. Computers would simply notify a theater manager when bulbs were about to burn out. Dolby, meanwhile, appealed to exhibitors looking to enhance the experience for customers, and buying systems for four three-hundred-seat auditoriums instead of one twelve hundred-seater made better economic sense. That in turn gave a big boost to films like *Saturday Night Fever,* whose soundtrack sales exceeded their box office tally, and blockbusters of the nascent MTV era like *Flashdance* and *Dirty Dancing*.

One of Durwood's earliest imitators was an entertainment attorney named Garth Drabinsky, who founded the Canadian circuit Cineplex Odeon in 1979 when he was twenty-nine. Drabinsky was also a movie producer; his producing partner was Joel B. Michaels, who would later join Andy Vajna and Mario Kassar at C-2 and serve as a producer on *Terminator 3*. Drabinsky sensed where the tide of 1970s blockbusters was headed, and quickly built an array of venues designed to showcase them. Vice president Linda Friendly called them "film bazaars." In 1979 he built North America's first eighteen-screen theater, situated in Toronto's billion-dollar Eaton Centre. One box office served the tiny auditoria, ranging from 60 to 130 seats, and the projection equipment (mostly 16-millimeter) ran by remote control. The place was a hit, so Drabinsky replicated it with the Beverly Center, a fourteen-plex on the top floor of a mall that opened on the Westside of Los Angeles in 1982. Five years later, he ventured into the San Fernando Valley, teaming with Universal on a $16.5 million eighteen-plex in Universal City. The theater had marble floors and an Art Deco lobby. It opened on the Fourth of July.

The trend was welcome in Hollywood. Movies could now enjoy extra showtimes without extra negotiation, and a big hit could generate cash with unprecedented speed. In this era, *Billy Jack* would not just have flooded a particular neighborhood of screens; it would also have grabbed several screens under the same roof. As box office grosses increased, the circuits plowed their profits into building even bigger theaters. Cineplex got abundant credit for improving the viewing experience for audiences conditioned by two decades in a shoebox. Most people applauded the change, assuming that more screens would mean more options for moviegoers. George Lucas told Peter Biskind that more choice would be the result of the surge in capacity: "Of the billion and a half that *Star Wars* made, half of it, $700 million of it, went to theater owners. And what did the theater owners do with that? They built multiplexes." Those multiplexes, Lucas told Biskind, played art films alongside the blockbusters. "And once they started making money, you got Miramax and Fine Line."

In reality, however, the multiplex boom only led to greater concentration of movie theater ownership by a few big theater chains; sometimes these chains played art films; in the summer blockbuster season, they often didn't. After a respite during recessionary times, megaplex building exploded again in the mid-1990s. The year 1995 saw the entrance of giant venues like AMC's Grand 24 in Dallas and Edwards's Irvine Spectrum in Orange County. The Grand demonstrated that a twenty-four-screen, eighty-five-thousand-square-foot colossus with twelve box office windows, six layers of wall between each screen and thirteen acres of free parking was more than just a worthwhile experiment. It was a prototype to make the entire industry salivate. The Grand opened on May 19, 1995, at the start of a lackluster summer whose biggest performers were *Batman Forever, Jumanji* and *Casper*. The great strength of the complex was that it allowed AMC to wring considerable revenues from mediocre big studio movies. By the time bona fide holiday hits like *Toy Story* and *Goldeneye* arrived, the idea of movies playing on multiple screens every few minutes had rendered obsolete Lew Wasserman's treasured concept of a line around the block. All corners of the industry were captivated by the possibilities.

The fashion in the mid-1990s was not only megaplexes but a category dubbed "location-based entertainment" developed by theater circuits. Many of them sought to expand upon their century-old function as movie venues, adding full-service restaurants and other enticements. Cinemark USA drew up plans with Wal-Mart for a retail-meets-movies concept. There were press reports that McDonald's held discussions about acquiring AMC, though the exhibitor denied it.

Regal Entertainment, the nation's number one exhibitor, developed a brand called Funscape, which it rolled out in 1995 in Chesapeake, Virginia. The ninety-five-thousand-square-foot site had fourteen screens, but most of its space was devoted to a small-scale theme park. To hear CEO Michael Campbell's description of it at the time is to recall the dot-com-like excesses of the decade's rampant building boom. Regal was backed by the deep-pocketed leveraged buyout firms Hicks, Muse, Tate & Furst and Kohlberg, Kravitz and Roberts. Caution was not exactly its mantra.

"Yes, it's all under one roof," Campbell told *Film Journal* in 1995. "We're going to have motion-simulation theaters. We're going to have a very elaborate miniature golf course. We're going to have soft-play and gymnastic-play areas for children. We're going to have high-tech arcades, which will feature virtual-reality helmets and flight simulators, as well as more traditional arcade games. We will have a food court, and we're bringing brand-name food into the complex with Pizza Hut, Taco Bell, Arby's. And we'll have a series of family party rooms. And it's all done up in a Victorian motif."

Few of these schemes paid off. In fact, they worsened the companies' already worrisome debt loads. Part of the problem was heavy investment in the theater business by outsiders. A leveraged buyout subsidiary of Merrill Lynch paid $680 million for United Artists Theatre Circuit in 1992. Hicks, Muse and KKR each spent more than $500 million to control Regal, which they vowed to turn into a profit gusher as they had done before with Dr Pepper soft drinks and Vlasic pickles. Such gambles often backfired, however. They only fueled reckless building and staggering levels of debt— $1.8 billion in Regal's case—that would ultimately put nearly all of the nation's top ten circuits into bankruptcy as the total screen count mushroomed 39 percent between 1994 and 1999. Philip Anschutz, in a supremely opportunistic move, bought up distressed debt for pennies on the dollar, giving him the leverage to consolidate United Artists, Edwards and Regal into one megachain under the Regal banner. Regal, which acquired Edwards and its Ontario site in 2002, now owns nearly twenty percent of America's movie screens, by far the biggest market share in a fragmented industry.

Buyout firms "believed the theater business was just like the radio business," recalled Raymond Syufy, co-CEO of Century Theatres. KKR "wanted to buy us out. I remember them telling me that, saying, 'We've just done that in radio, consolidated it and gotten all of these benefits out of it. We're going to consolidate you and other circuits under one umbrella. You're a positive cash flow business.' The glaring thing to us that they didn't see is that there are barriers to entry in the radio station business. It's very difficult for me to say, 'You know, I want to start a radio station.' It's not so difficult in the movie theater business. As long as you have money, you can build."

For theater tycoons like Durwood and Drabinsky, the multiplex business was a war the battle lines of which spanned generations, stretching back to the vaudeville years. The modern era of film exhibition began in 1940, the year the Justice Department, working on behalf of independent movie theaters, brought an antitrust case against Paramount that paved the way for the 1948 Consent Decree and set in motion the gradual divestiture of theaters from studios. Once they left the exhibition business, studios for the most part never looked back, though many have taken small stakes in theaters in the decades since the decree. A "clearance system" that gave theaters the right to show certain films exclusively in certain territories was agreed upon by all exhibitors. Southern California's Westwood Village, for example, used to be able to "clear" every theater west of

Beverly Hills. Clearances were eroded by saturation releases like *Billy Jack* and *Jaws*. With megaplexing, they became all but extinct. Another formerly sacred institution that multiplex building helped kill off was blind bidding, in which exhibitors would have to commit to booking a particular movie before it had even been screened. A decision affecting what played on an entire region's screens would be based on the barest information, sometimes just the title. After theaters got burned on movies that underdelivered (*Exorcist II* was a famous example), states began banning the practice. There are still anti–blind bid laws on the books of twenty-six states, forcing studios to hold screenings of every release for all exhibitors in the state, usually in central, if low-grossing, territories like Paducah, Kentucky. But as the clearances system deteriorated, long-simmering battles between circuits boiled to the surface.

Durwood's most bitter lifelong rivalry was with a man known both to colleagues and to competitors as Old Man Edwards. Jim Edwards stood just 5 foot 6. He grew up in the working-class Los Angeles neighborhood of Boyle Heights, holding odd jobs like selling vacuum cleaners and running a chain of parking lots. In 1930 he borrowed $400 to buy the first theater in what would become the largest circuit in the Western United States. Edwards became known for his hard-driving, cash-scrimping style. In the 1990s, former managers of his theaters successfully sued Edwards for $10 million in allegedly withheld overtime wages. Their attorney charged, "He started in the 1920s and as the years went by he didn't realize that the world had changed. You're not allowed to work people without paying them." Edwards's tombstone, in Orange County, reads: "William James Edwards Jr. Born November 1906. Died March 1997. Showman."

When AMC leapfrogged Edwards in 1996 and swung a deal with the Mills to be the mall's tenant, Edwards decided he did not want to cede the valuable real estate, so he bought a patch of land across the street and built his company's largest house. Durwood recalled that Edwards told him at the time, "I had to teach you a lesson."

In the blockbuster era, the biggest anxiety about theaters going up right next to other theaters was about who would get access to prime product. In the highest-grossing zone in America, Times Square in New York City, two theaters have been slugging it out on Forty-Second Street since 2000. The twenty-four-screen AMC Empire followed the thirteen-screen Loews E-Walk by about a year and had a drastic shortage of must-see films during its initial months. But no theater-to-theater clash stirred industry passions like Ontario.

At ShoWest in March 1997, shortly before the opening of the Edwards 22, Bill Kartozian, former head of the National Association of Theater Owners, issued a commandment to the exhibitors gathered in Bally's hotel-casino. "Thou shalt not Ontario each other," he intoned. His attitude was widely shared. Years after the two megaplexes opened at the Mills, studios and exhibitors both were convinced it was a kamikaze mission. Universal, New Line and Miramax were the first to play the theaters "day-and-date"—industry parlance meaning their films would be booked simultaneously at both locations—a complete reversal of the old system of clearances. On Friday, March 21, 1997, searchlights strafed the sky and street performers circulated through the parking lot as the new Edwards megaplex opened opposite the AMC 30, both houses playing Universal's Jim Carrey comedy *Liar, Liar*. "I was the first to break that clearance," says Nikki Rocco, the studio's president of distribution. "I had to go to Lew [Wasserman] on that one." Some in Hollywood feared disaster was at hand. Others believed they had hit a gusher. New Line distribution head Mitch Goldman later enthused, "More money has been taken out of the city of Ontario than anybody even thought existed." Only Sony and Paramount have held out, opting to distribute their films in Ontario via an alternating "allotment" system. *Spider-Man* played only at the AMC in 2001. But the Mills theaters would drive smaller area multiplexes out of business. In 2000 alone, a dozen theater complexes in the Inland Empire would be forced to close.

The Ontario Mills mall, built for $200 million in 1996 on a high-volume lot where I-10 meets I-15, sits in the middle of a vast, asymmetrical parking lot that resembles an asphalt moat. Inside, there are 1.7 million square feet of retail space, with more than 250 stores and attractions. Outlet stores, formerly relegated to malls of their own on deserted stretches of the Interstate, adjoin regular retailers. Theme restaurants like the Rainforest Café and Dave and Buster's jockey for attention with kiosks selling cell phones and inflatable, oversized frisbees. There's an Osh Kosh B'Gosh, a Virgin Megastore, a Red Lobster, and a Vans skate park.

There's only one bookstore: a Foozles remainder shop, carrying nothing currently on the *New York Times* bestseller list. No store in the mall sells the *Inland Empire Daily Bulletin*, the only newspaper left to serve the city since the *Ontario Daily Report* shuttered a decade ago. The mall's official slogan is "There's Just More at the Mills. Shop. Save. Eat. Play." Shops are packed together along a 1.5 mile-long loop.

Mills Corp., the Virginia-based real estate investment trust that owns the mall, has developed more than a dozen "Mills" sites across the country. Together these malls house hundreds of movie screens that collectively gross millions of dollars every weekend. Along with Wal-Mart, the largest DVD and movie merchandise retail chain Mills Corp., is one of the few American companies whose role in the U.S. film industry is so pervasive and yet so invisible to most people working in Hollywood. Company brochures claim that Mills malls generate more revenue per square foot than any other shopping format. Mills Corp. CEO Laurence Siegel says his role model is retail impresario Mel Simon, who produced *Porky's*, then lost a fortune in Hollywood before building the Mall of America, in Minneapolis, in 1992. Mills Corp. has a formula for all of its malls: a mix of chain retail, food and amusements housed in some of the biggest shopping complexes ever built. Under Siegel, Mills Corp. has trademarked its own term for the formula: "shoppertainment." It's a variation on Regal's Funscape, built on an unprecedented scale. The Block, another Mills outpost in Orange County, is located on a street called Shoppertainment Way.

Initially envisioned as a multistate magnet supported by tourists en route to Las Vegas, the Mills now draws about 95 percent of its patrons from within a twenty-mile radius. Most spend at least four and a half hours there. How do mall managers know all of this? When the place first opened, they used video cameras to obtain shoppers' license plate numbers and DMV files in order to assemble a marketing database. With that practice now banned by antistalking laws, the management makes sure every sale at every store is accompanied by a request for the purchaser's ZIP code.

In 1988, seven years before ground was broken for the Mills on the former site of a racetrack, the *Daily Report* carried the initial headline, "First of its kind in the West: 'Super-regional value-oriented' shopping mall planned." The center would employ between two thousand and three thousand workers, the article said. It was exactly the kind of development sorely needed by the city a decade after the passage of Proposition 13, a landmark ballot amendment capping residential property taxes. Prop. 13 may have saved politically organized homeowners money, but it hastened suburban sprawl across the state by forcing cash-strapped governments to favor retail businesses capable of generating sales tax.

Through 2003, the mall has brought $20 million in total sales tax revenue into city coffers. That is not a staggering amount, but city leaders are more focused on using the Mills to establish Ontario as a destination. Ontario native and City Councilman Jerry DuBois, who lives near the city's mostly Latino downtown, said the rapid commercial development of the area around the Mills and the airport, including Technicolor's movie marketing depot, has created two distinct, local economic hemispheres: "the glass tower and the adobe." The Mills, he said, raising a pulsating fist to his chest, "is the heartbeat." Few residents would disagree. *The Riverside Press-Enterprise,* in a story about the joys of spending a night at the Mills, quoted Jon Monroe, twenty-three, of Ontario: "We can eat, go to the movies. It's like a zoo, but it's fun." A *Daily Bulletin* headline called Ontario Mills "the new downtown." The design of the mall drives the point home. Its ten zones are referred to as "neighborhoods." Trees, benches, landscaping and courtyards added to a few entryways "give customers a point of reference so they don't get lost," said Jerry Engen, VP and head of development for Mills Corp. "It gives the mall an outdoor feeling, a downtown Main Street setting." A 1997 editorial in a regional weekly, the *Business Press,* crowed: "The mall is bringing national attention to the Inland Empire—a spotlight it has rarely, if ever, enjoyed. There should be little doubt that the region will prosper from such positive national attention."

The region was indeed prospering, but progress was bypassing the community's real Main Street, which once united the region in a way that the Mills' potted-plant simulacrum never could. Ontario's first movie house was the downtown Granada Theatre at the corner of Euclid and C Street. Dr. C. L. Emmons, who owned the building, made a deal with Fox Theatres to turn the site into the chain's second theater on the West Coast. Locals immediately took to calling it the Little Fox, to distinguish it from the Big Fox in nearby Pomona. On the eve of its opening in 1926, the *Daily Report* published a paean to Emmons, who "has changed the complexion of C Street and Euclid Avenue from an insignificant corner to one of the fine business centers of the city. He has planned a fine three-story business block which would be a credit to any city." The newspaper's coverage of the June 3 opening suggested a new era had dawned in Ontario. "Father, mother and the kiddies hurried through dinner last evening and hastened to town," the *Daily Report* noted on its front page, "where the greatest crowd of Ontario's history choked the west driveway of Euclid Avenue."

A reported 1,426 people managed to get a ticket for the festivities, which included a fashion show, organ concert, newsreel and song-and-dance program. The feature that first night was *Tramp, Tramp, Tramp,* a six-reel comedy written by Frank Capra and starring Harry Langdon and Joan Crawford. In the film, Langdon falls in love with Crawford, whose father owns Burton Shoes, a conglomerate trying to put Langdon's father's shoe shop out of business.

With its Art Deco exterior, neo-Moorish interior and prominent concession stand, the Granada was the city's grandest public venue to date. The day after the premiere, Harry Sugarman, president and general manager of the West Coast Junior Circuit Inc., published an ad in the *Daily Report*. It read in part: "We have hoped to make that theatre a center of the community in which we now take a part—we want to grow with you; to share in your progress and in your success." By the 1970s, however, Ontario's downtown had been bypassed by newer commercial attractions linked by the burgeoning Interstate highway system, whose inception in the 1950s crippled thousands of other American Main Streets. General Electric closed its Ontario plant in 1982. Soon thereafter, the Kaiser Steel Mill shut down, serving as a cheap location for *Terminator 2* before being completely demolished. The factories that once churned out Hotpoint irons and Sunkist orange crates were gone, and thousands of jobs were sent overseas. Norton Air Force Base and Santa Fe Railroad facility laid off thousands more.

Dr. Emmons's old corner of Euclid and C still serves as the terminus for the city's July Fourth parade. In 1930 Ontario's population was less than 10 percent Latino. Today, it's nearly 60 percent Latino, and many of the signs in the downtown business district are in both English and Spanish. The Granada Theatre, which was segregated like most of the region's theaters in the 1930s and 1940s, for a few years clung to life as a second-run Spanish-language cinema, before closing for good in the 1980s. One entrepreneur after another tried and failed to revive it. In early 2003 the Granada was taken over by Christian City Church International, which reduced seating capacity to a few hundred to better serve its Pentecostal congregation of about 130.

Eight miles away, at the AMC and Edwards, the megaplex revolution did not manage to lift *T3* and *Legally Blonde 2* to record heights on July 4, but the movies were holding steady. *Sinbad* was playing to nearly empty houses. By the end of the evening, the day's grosses would total $13 million for *T3*, $6.1 million for *Legally Blonde 2* and $1.7 million for *Sinbad*.

July 4 brought scorching, smoggy weather and temperatures exceeding 100 degrees to downtown Ontario for the city's annual holiday parade. The parade wound its way down Euclid as it had since 1895, along the same grassy median strip where mule-drawn streetcars had whisked early settlers to and from the mountains. A few spectators waved flags. There was a silk-jacketed Uncle Sam on stilts. Some box office prognosticators had warned that patriotic sentiment after the war in Iraq might hamper grosses on the Fourth. In Ontario, lethargy seemed a more likely culprit.

Since 1939, the parade has been followed by a ritual known as the All-States Picnic. Along the Euclid median, residents and visitors unfold lunches and thermoses of cool drinks at wooden picnic tables with blue-and-yellow, state-shaped flags marking each of the fifty states. In its heyday after World War II, the event attracted up to one hundred and twenty thousand people from throughout the region, according to local accounts. Today, newspaper clippings commemorating the event are laminated onto the tops of tables at the Ontario Mills food court.

About an hour before the All-States Picnic, some four hundred Ontarians of all stripes—the police chief, a state senator, a tree trimmer, a steam cleaner—gathered for breakfast in the backyard of Mayor Gary Ovitt's house farther up Euclid, next door to Jerry Dubois. Flags, pinwheels and bits of bunting covered the front of the nouveau-Victorian and a sign in the front window proclaimed, "We support our president." The aim of the annual breakfast was to celebrate America's independence and the trappings of a small town. But something with more immediate consequences was afoot: Petition-gatherers circulated, collecting signatures for the nascent effort to recall Governor Gray Davis, a movement that would propel action star Arnold Schwartzenegger to the governor's mansion. They were also out in force at the Republican-leaning Inland Empire's big-box retail stores; many of the 1.7 million petitioners who eventually signed the recall petition did so at a Wal-Mart or Target. An official roster of candidates would not be determined until the petition was certified, but already a consensus was building around the Terminator.

Ovitt decided to ask the activists to leave in order to preserve the civility of the annual breakfast. But he and Dubois could not find fault with the recall drive. "To me, Gray Davis is just a suit," said Dubois, who runs a local advertising agency. "Arnold seems to know what he's doing."

Back in Burbank, it was dawning on Fellman and his team of numbers swamis that $100 million was out of the question for *T3*. Even $90 million now looked unattainable. *Legally Blonde 2* had collected $22 million and would need a huge Saturday night to reach $40 million for five days, a figure that many executives had used as a target. And what could be said of *Sinbad*? DreamWorks now knew it would be dealing with the most extreme worst-case scenario in its ten-year history. It had endured a few flops, to be sure. But never before had a four-year animated project, with so many employees and so much potential for ancillary revenue been completely squandered. In Disney's skyrocketing summer of *Finding Nemo* and *Pirates of the Caribbean*, DreamWorks had released the animated equivalent of *Gigli*.

Sunday Spin

At 10 A.M. on Sunday, July 6, Peter Adee was driving to get what he called "the finest clam chowder in New England" from Arnold's, in Eastham, on Cape Cod. He took back roads to try to avoid the traffic getting off the Cape after the Fourth of July weekend. He pulled over every few hundred feet to try to get a signal on his cell phone, which had been inconsistent throughout his vacation.

Adee had spent the weekend in nearby Chatham at a reunion of fifteen relatives. Compounding the signal difficulty, his cell phone was in bad shape. Having taken the red-eye from Los Angeles, Adee groggily left it on the side of the road after pulling over and another motorist had run over it. Like any of the weekend players thirsting for information, he would not be hindered by such technological limitations. "I couldn't see [numbers on the phone's broken display]," he said. "But I could still call."

He would frequently talk with, among others, Reese

Witherspoon's manager, Evelyn O'Neill, and MGM's Erik Lomis and Chris McGurk. "There are weekends where you spend a lot of time on the phone and you think, 'Ugh, God, I wish it were better.' This was a pleasure in the sense that we knew we were doing great. You *always . . . want . . . more.* That's the basis of the movie business."

Back in Los Angeles, at the same time Adee was navigating the Cape, Kops was walking from his apartment off Olympic Boulevard to Starbucks for a mocha. As he sat by the pool outside his apartment, he considered the whirlwind he had just survived.

"It was the flip side of the first movie because on that one we were like, 'Fourteen, fifteen, sixteen . . .' It progressively got bigger and bigger, and so when it hit $22 million. . . ." Kops paused, reliving the moment. "With this movie, the range of the projection from the low end to the high end was so big."

More than anything, Kops felt relief. In five days, *Legally Blonde 2* had collected $38.5 million to finish a solid No. 2 for the weekend. It was a much more modest total than the $50 million or more that had seemed within reach during the film's $9.1 million opening day, but it put the film on a profitable track. "When we first got into this, we said anything with a four in front of it [for five days] would be awesome, and we're only a few hundred thousand away," said Kops, irrepressible as always despite a grueling week in which he had slept only about four hours a night.

"I've just been trying to recover today. I know Reese

spoke to McGurk today and they both seemed OK [with the number]," he said.

If anyone had slept less than Kops, it was Erik Lomis. Like Fellman, he immediately put the best spin on the weekend. "We're going to make a lot of money, and the core demo loves the movie," he said, citing exit polls of women under twenty-one. Of that segment, 85 percent declared the film either "very good" or "excellent" and 72 percent said they would "definitely" recommend it to a friend. That was the audience they always knew they would get. Overall, the reaction was as tepid as it had been in Aliso Viejo. MGM had not surmounted the problems discerned by test audiences. *Legally Blonde 2* would not be one of the summer's surprise hits. It would not become a girl empowerment blueprint for a new generation of teen-agers, reverberating in the nation's malls and megaplexes. It was profitable product that the audience would soon forget.

Don Roos had an idea why the energy of the first film could not be reproduced. The screenwriter who rewrote *Legally Blonde 2* identified a fundamental flaw that he was powerless to change—a flaw in the design of the film set in stone by Platt and Witherspoon at the outset: Elle Woods spent the entire movie in a happy, committed relationship. "With that character, it was a whole Cinderella story," Roos said. "The end of the Cinderella story is she gets the guy, she gets the prince. So you can't do a Cinderella story again because she has the prince, and you can't tell the audience that relationship isn't the ideal relationship they believed in. We were cutting Elle off at the knees. We couldn't hurt her the way she needed to be hurt in order for the audience to sympathize with her. You always have to hurt them, these Cinderellas, in order for the audience to adhere to them. We couldn't hurt her enough."

By Sunday evening, Jonathan Mostow sounded drained. He was in the office of his home on Mulholland Drive, trying to come to terms with the opening weekend, now fading with the daylight. *Terminator 3* had dominated the weekend, as everyone had long predicted. But its tally of $72.5 million, counting Tuesday night previews, was a disappointment to Mostow and others who had invested so much in the film. "For whatever reason, not as many people are going as I wanted," he said.

He didn't point any fingers. He just felt an even stronger dose of what he had expressed over lunch a few days before the opening. "It's a myth that July Fourth is a powerful weekend," he said. "The decision to go on that date was about ego. I don't think it was the best thing for the movie. If I knew then what I know now I would have pushed for another date."

Mostow remembered getting the numbers while driving to the Japanese premiere, held July 4 in an indoor stadium before six thousand fans. Though the figures were certainly respectable, he felt a bit like he had at the *T3* junket weeks earlier while scrutinizing the Warner Brothers printout of grosses showing the unexpected softness of the marketplace. What was happening out there? What was in the air?

"My expectations were higher, based on what the studio

and all of the Web sites were saying. I had dreams of a number with a nine in front of it. I even thought we could get to 100. When the numbers came in below that, the part of me that had the unrealistic fantasy before that [had a] confirmation of the uneasy feeling that I had over the last two months, that something was not right and never would be." He continued: "This film was always about fighting expectations, meeting often unrealistic expectations. I was getting calls from people within a week of release, 'Don't worry, you're going to do $100 million.' I was suspicious of them. I didn't feel it. At a certain level, you feel it in your gut."

Having spent two years wrestling with Cyberdine, Mostow was grateful for the human feedback that came from sitting in a theater. Even for a perfectionist, it was far more satisfying watching the movie than watching the numbers. "What really surprised me was when I went to see it in front of a couple of paying audiences, and they laughed," he said. "They really loved it."

Moritz Borman, head of Intermedia and one of *T3*'s many producers, did not waste much time watching the movie again with an audience. On the way home from work on Thursday, he stopped by a multiplex in Malibu. "I saw half the industry out there, a lot of my friends and their families and I said, 'Forget it,' and drove off." He was more passionate about the record-setting numbers in Russia, one of the dozens of territories where Intermedia will realize most of its gains on *T3*.

"I have not been attached to a computer," Borman said as the weekend wound down. "There are so many variables.

It's good to know how it's doing, but at a certain point it just gets exhausting. Trying to figure out if the audience had burgers for dinner or if it's too hot out or too cold . . . how does that matter?

"The numbers are very solid. I would have been happy with sixty-five. Seventy-two is fine. Would I have been happier with eighty? Of course. But the most important thing is that people like the movie, so that could help us hang around. That would make us different from everything else out there."

It was a far-fetched hope—an action movie with legs in 2003—but it appealed to the *T3* crew. The last *Terminator* movie had a multiple of five, meaning the final gross was five times the opening weekend. For most summer movies, a multiple of three is above average. If this one could even get to three, meaning a domestic gross in the neighborhood of $135 million, it would be a notable achievement.

Dan Fellman shrugged off the fact that Warner Brothers had projected a five-day figure for *T3* in the range of $90 million to $100 million. "We were a little aggressive," he said—and then came the rationalizations every distribution chief trades in on Sunday. "We should have discounted it more for the R-rated factor and the Fourth of July falling on a Friday. Plus the weather back East didn't help us." On Sunday, before the lava flow of hot data had cooled into immovable rock, studios had ample opportunity for spin. Some companies were more brazen than others about exaggerating the numbers. Miramax famously got chastised in 1997 by parent company Disney after inflating the opening of

Scream 2 by $6 million. Fellman elicited similar howls after posting $93 million for the first *Harry Potter*. The next day, he reduced the figure to $90 million—taking care to keep it $100,000 ahead of Universal's then-record holder, *The Lost World*.

Fellman immediately rattled off some upbeat statistics generated by the Warner Brothers 4-Star computer system: This was the biggest opening weekend in Arnold Schwarzenegger's career; *Terminator 2* by comparison had done $52 million in its first five days; and *T3* was now the "fourth-biggest July Fourth opener ever." The last bit was dubious, perhaps, but box office trivia never sounded trivial coming from Fellman.

"I was looking for a jump on Saturday of at least 30 percent and we got 36 percent. As for how we fared against the competition"—here was the payoff pitch—"we terminated them."

Brandon Gray sat in his cramped apartment off of L.A.'s nondescript Miracle Mile, also the headquarters of the Web site Boxofficemojo.com. Up since 6:30 in the morning, he displayed none of the battle fatigue of the MGM and Warners contingents. He seemed to take a perverse delight in the pathetic showing by *Sinbad,* which managed a meager $10 million over five days, but praised DreamWorks distribution chief Jim Tharp for his honesty. Speaking to the number-gatherers Sunday morning, Tharp had conceded the fact that *Sinbad* was an anachronism that simply could not be sold in today's marketplace due to "a continued down-

turn in the popularity of noncomedy, traditionally animated movies." Gray said, "Usually, they don't want to talk
at all when they have a bad weekend like that." That was certainly the case for Katzenberg, who had taken his family to
Mexico for most of the long weekend, making almost no
contact with anyone back at DreamWorks.

Upon his return to work on Monday, July 7, Katzenberg
would convene a meeting of all animation employees, the
same ones who had been so dumbfounded at the *Sinbad*
screening a month earlier. "He said he knew how hard
everyone had worked, but market forces had been a lot different when the project started in 1999," said one person
who was there. "His main point seemed to be: This is pretty
bad but we just have to move on." Throwing the meeting
open to questions, he faced a lot of tough ones. He said 2-D
animation could still be done, but only with a great story.
And what about the way the movie had been marketed?
"That will be addressed," he promised.

Earlier in the weekend, Gray had offered a mid-contest
assessment via e-mail: "The only word that comes to mind
is 'ouch,'" he wrote. He picked up on that point on Sunday
morning. *T3* had not exceeded his inflation-adjusted figure
for *T2*. Neither had it lifted the industry out of its summer
malaise, he pointed out. Industrywide, grosses had fallen 15
percent from the July Fourth weekend in 2002. The slump
meant the summer was trailing the *Spider-Man*–fueled
2002 edition by almost five percent.

Surveying the wreckage strewn about the landscape,
Gray launched into a rant about *T3* that was equal parts

quantitative analysis and abject sci-fi geekery. "The story was finished in *T2*! The marketing for this movie never addressed that. They just assumed people would like the same story to be told again." One could say the same thing about the competition on July Fourth.

USE
THE FORCE

The Audience Strikes Back

Creatures from Middle Earth swept through the San Diego Convention Center, dressed in cloaks, flood pants, plastic elf ears, and capes with pointy hoods. It was Saturday, July 19, 2003, the third and busiest day of Comic-Con. The conventioneers, many in costume, had begun massing like wayward trick-or-treaters outside the building at 2:30 A.M. By midmorning the line wrapped around the building and stretched for a mile along the San Diego waterfront. By noon, an assortment of Anakin Skywalkers, Spider-Men, Daredevils and X-Men had collected inside the vast convention hall, mingling with the noncostumed masses. A band of hobbits chatted by walkie-talkie and posed for photographs. An African American teenager with a slender moustache wore a hand-stitched, brown leather Daredevil bodysuit, two leather D's sewn like varsity letters to his chest. There were no Terminators, Elle Woods or Sinbads.

One year earlier, Jonathan Mostow and Arnold Schwarzenegger had journeyed to Comic-Con to drum up support from this most vocal contingent of blockbuster movie fans. They had been greeted with raucous applause; the Comic-Con audience lionized Schwarzenegger, but they remained apathetic about the movie. They asked Mostow not to ruin it. Opening weekend was still a long way off, and its prospects appeared iffy.

One year later, the fans' apathy was even more pronounced. Here it was less than three weeks after opening weekend, and *T3* had been elbowed aside by a new crop of blockbusters. At Comic-Con, the focus was on next year's movies. At megaplexes, the weekend belonged to Jerry Bruckheimer, producer of both the number-one film in America, *Bad Boys II,* and number two, *Pirates of the Caribbean.* Schwarzenegger, who was traveling in Europe on the *T3* international junket, had yet to say whether he would join the race to unseat California Governor Gray Davis. The films of July Fourth were in rapid decay at the box office. Ticket sales of *T3* plummeted 56 percent in its second weekend, and another 52 percent on its third. *Legally Blonde 2* was falling almost as rapidly and now seemed certain not to reach the box office heights of the original *Legally Blonde,* $96 million. *Sinbad* was a certified disaster, eking out less than $2 million on its third weekend. Less than three weeks after opening weekend, it no longer rated a place in the weekend's top ten.

A smattering of *T3* merchandise was still scattered across the convention. Atari's *T3* game, scheduled for release in the fall of 2003, wasn't ready, but a trailer for the game screened in an endless loop on the TV monitors in the Atari booth. Like many action movie video-game spin-offs, it had a first-person shooter function, allowing players to step into Schwarzenegger's boots. Across from the Atari kiosk was Gabriel Benson, a former director of development at C-2 Pictures, who was hawking the official comic prequel, *Terminator 3: Before the Rise*, signed by the writer and cover artist. Elsewhere, a manufacturer of collectibles and Bobble-head toys from Saddlebrook, New Jersey, called Comic Images, was selling official *T3* trading cards. An official *T3* pinball game was parked in his booth. Snippets of dialogue spoken by Schwarzenegger emanated from the machine: "Shoot here and here," the machine said. "Use the gun grip."

Movie fans have influenced the making and marketing of movies since the era of the five-cent moving picture shows, or nickelodeons, that proliferated in small towns and big cities in the first decade of the twentieth century. Film studios in the early silent period concealed the identities of their actors, but even anonymous players like the Vitagraph Girl or the Biograph Girl were inundated with marriage proposals. As the star system took root in Hollywood, actors began endorsing cosmetics, clothing and cigarettes, and the first movie fanzines—*Motion Picture Story, Film Fun, Film Play, Photoplay, Screenland* and *Shadowland*—attracted a readership of hundreds of thousands of people.

In the 1920s, fans submitted scripts to the studios and wrote to the producers, advocating roles for their favorite stars. *Motion Picture Story*, the first full-blown fan magazine, featured a regular column by someone known as the Answer

Man who was portrayed in a pen-and-ink drawing as a spindly man with a bulbous head and a vast beard, a quill poised above tall stacks of letters. The Answer Man became a celebrity in his own right, receiving some twenty-five hundred letters a month. They asked about the personal lives of stars and weighed in on the relative merits of movies and actors. These missives were occasionally accompanied by cookies, poems and trinkets. In the 1930s Hollywood news became a staple of modern media. Magazines like *Life, Look* and *The Saturday Evening Post,* newspaper columns and radio reports percolated with dispatches from the fast-growing movie colony on the West coast. Gossips like Hedda Hopper, Louella Parsons and Walter Winchell reached a huge audience.

Robert Altman's *Come Back to the Five and Dime, Jimmy Dean, Jimmy Dean* compares small-town movie fans' idolatry of celebrities to a religious ritual. Altman's story, adapted from a play by Ed Graczyk, depicts a James Dean fan club reunion held at a Texas Woolworth in 1975, two decades after the star's death. The film opens as the drugstore proprietor, Juanita, listens to an evangelical radio broadcast and illuminates the neon Jesus that hangs in her shop. When Altman's film came out in 1982, the world of *Motion Picture Story*'s Answer Man was long gone. The studios and the mass media were controlled by a few giant corporations, and NRG was laying the foundations of a market research business allowing studios to promote their movies across a shifting sea of carefully targeted demographic groups. Altman's small-town women were just one of those groups. Blockbuster films were a wedge for the studios' ancillary businesses; they were commercials for merchandise and media spin-offs. They were engineered to appeal to audiences across every age group, gender, class and race.

But even as blockbuster films became a big corporate business, a sea change swept over the fans. They began to organize. The first Comic-Con, held in 1969, was a comic-book swap-meet in the basement of a San Diego hotel. Comic-Con and the World Scifi Convention were the first of the Cons— huge carnivalesque fan rallies, packed with comic books and toy dealers hawking collectibles. The first *Star Trek* convention was sponsored by two teenagers from Queens who called themselves the Creation Group, and was held at a New York hotel in 1972. The scifi subculture that bloomed around *Star Trek* and, eventually, *Star Wars* gave rise to a new breed of fanzines and fan fiction, fan filmmaking and highly specialized fan conventions.

These events were camp meetings for America's ascendant religion—Hollywood celebrity—and its new Creationists: fans of movie and TV franchises, which follow their own sets of rules and references. As Jack Sorenson, the president of LucasArts, told the *New Yorker*: "*Star Wars* is the mythology of a nonsectarian world. It describes how people want to live."

The Cons showcased the corporate by-product of that mythology. They were sprawling flea markets for the movie tchotchkes that spilled from studios' ever widening licensing deals: comic books, role-playing games, novelizations, trading cards, T-shirts, action figures and bobble-head dolls. And they provided a rare occasion for fans to mingle with the stars, who came to the Cons to promote their new projects. By the 1980s, fan conventions became prolific enough to provide gainful employment to even the most marginal TV and film actors. Jeff Walker, a marketing consultant who now serves as the chief liaison between the studios and Comic-Con, said "A person could appear on one episode of *Star Trek* and make a career out of doing the convention circuit." Today there are hundreds of Cons: Dragon Con, Wizard World, Wonder-Con, and smaller events like the X-Files Con, Fangoria Con and Muppetfest! The TV show *Xena: Warrior Princess* has given rise to several different conventions by itself. In April 2001 two hundred *Xena* fans in Miami boarded a cruise ship called the *Norwegian Dawn* for a seven-day jaunt through the Caribbean, the first Annual Creation Salute to Strong Women of Scifi Cruise featuring Xena.

It didn't take Hollywood long to recognize the potential here. In 1972 the World Scifi Con was held in Los Angeles, generating extensive coverage in the city's alternative press. In 1974 director Frank Capra spoke at Comic-Con in San Diego as a special guest of the convention, along with Majel Barrett, wife of *Star Trek* creator Gene Roddenberry. Animation studios began recruiting employees at Comic-Con, and even genre movie stars like Chuck Norris and George Pal began descending on the event in increasing numbers.

In 1976 George Lucas came to Comic-Con to present a *Star Wars* promotional slide show. It was a year yet before the movie would premiere at Mann's Chinese Theater, and

Lucas's fledgling effects company, Industrial Light & Magic, was still shooting cardboard cutouts and plastic models in a Van Nuys warehouse. But thanks to events like Comic-Con, the *Star Wars* phenomenon was slowly building at the grass roots. In Hollywood, Lucas had endured the taunts of his peers Brian De Palma, Martin Scorsese and Paul Schrader, who dismissed *Star Wars* as an insipid kids' movie. Twentieth Century Fox had so little faith in *Star Wars*, it would pull all but 100 trailers from theaters in the months before the movie opened. The studio didn't understand the audience for the movie, but at Comic-Con, Lucas addressed fans who got it. Lucas's marketing guru, Charlie Lippincott, was already fielding questions from members of the scifi community deeply interested in Lucas's gestating space opera. "It was adults against the fans," Lippincott later told *Variety*. "Fans loved it, adults hated it."

And at no time were so many fans concentrated in one place as at Comic-Con. By 2002, when Schwarzenegger visited Comic-Con, the event was expanding at warp speed. That year saw sixty-three thousand visitors to the convention. One year later the number of visitors climbed north of seventy thousand. Though sales of comic books had cratered in the 1990s as a wave of new leisure activities and a booming video game market competed for teenage boys' attention, the event continued to grow. Comic-Con was by then a fixture of the marketing terrain for Hollywood genre movies, a bellwether of the tastes and preoccupations of the most powerful market demographic: teenage boys. *Star Wars* appealed to all segments of the market, cutting across gender, race, sexual orientation and age. But no quadrant of the population was as profoundly affected by the movie as teenage boys. In 1977, a decade before the VCR was a fixture in American homes, there was only one place to see *Star Wars*: in movie theaters. And boys returned to the theater to see *Star Wars* again and again and again.

The novelist Jonathan Lethem, who was thirteen in the summer of 1977, recalls traveling twenty-one times from his home in Brooklyn to Times Square to see *Star Wars* at the Loews Astor Plaza on Forty-fourth Street. Sir Alec Guinness—Obi-Wan Kenobi to *Star Wars* fans—wrote in his autobiography, *A Positively Final Appearance,* of meeting a twelve-year-old who had seen the movie more than one hundred times. The child burst into tears when Sir Alec asked that he never see it again.

Will Brooker, who teaches modern media and culture at the American International University in London, spent two years poring over *Star Wars* fan Web sites, fan fiction and fan films like *The Phantom Edit*—a version of the *Star Wars, Episode I—The Phantom Menace* edited to exclude all references to widely derided character Jar Jar Binks—in an effort to assess why the movie continues to hold so large an audience in its thrall. He talked to a police officer in Indiana obsessed with Boba Fett and the Web mistress of starwarschicks.com, and read long volumes of "slash" fiction— graphic stories of forbidden love between Luke and Leia, Luke and Han, Jedi Master Qui-Gon Jinn and his apprentice, Obi-Wan Kenobi. "*Star Wars* is not just a film, or a trilogy, or a trilogy and two prequels," Brooker writes. "For many people, myself included, it is the single most important cultural text of their lives; it has meshed with their memories of childhood, with their homemade tributes, from the amateurish childhood comics to the professional product of an adult fan, with their choice of career or education, with their everyday experiences."

Hollywood films are woven deeply into the lives of people who gather at Comic-Con. Rebecca Rockwell, a twenty-two-year-old veterinarian's assistant, came to Comic-Con from Santa Barbara. She wore elbow-length black gloves and long blonde bangs in the style of Rogue, a character in the *X-Men* comics and movies. Rockwell had seen *X-Men 2* five times and *Lord of the Rings: The Two Towers* eleven times—all in movie theaters. At midafternoon during Comic-Con, Rockwell was to be found standing with friends near the autograph area of the convention center. As she spoke about the objects of her affection, the sun streamed through the building's glass ceiling, raising the temperature in the crowded corridors below. The air was heavy with the smells of fried food, tortilla chips, melted cheese and body odor, and Rockwell was debating whether or not to attempt to get inside a huge ballroom where Elijah Wood and other cast members from *Lord of the Rings* were holding a press conference.

Nearby meeting rooms housed hundreds of panels featuring comic-book artists, scifi writers and creators of hit TV shows and movies, scheduled at hour-long intervals. The panels had titles like "'Oh, I've Wasted My Life': Collecting *Simpsons* Merchandise," "*Archie*: Still Relevant after

All These Years," and "Do You Have What It Takes to Pitch and Write for *Star Trek*?" At one talk, "Starship Smackdown II," a "panel of spaceshipologists" evaluated "who would win in a battle between the Starship Enterprise and an Imperial Star Destroyer."

Downstairs, the convention floor bulged with multimedia exhibits and sales booths. Some booths touted the industry's latest fads—graphic novels on DVD; Japanese animation imports like Manga and Anime; Yu-Gi-Oh, a new franchise from 4Kids, the licensing company that made Pokemon a household word in the United States. Some booths featured long-established franchises like *Elfquest, Wolverine* and *Batman*. Comic books and comic-book art were everywhere. But alongside the printed matter was a crazy-quilt of toys, trinkets and curios.

At one booth, fans stood in line to pay $60 for a miniature chrome statue of Colossus, one of the X-Men, signed by renowned action-figure sculptor Randy Bowen. They would later sell on eBay for as much as $500. Elsewhere, bodybuilder and one-time Canadian pro football player Lou Ferrigno, who starred in the original CBS series *The Incredible Hulk* from 1978–82 (and squared off against Schwarzenegger in the bodybuilding documentary *Pumping Iron*), sold autographed weightlifting photos for $20. Nearby, Daniel Logan, the thirteen-year-old actor from New Zealand who played Boba Fett in *Star Wars, Episode II—Attack of the Clones,* signed movie stills that he sold for $15 apiece. In the adjoining booth, an adult-film actress named Jewell Marceau, dressed in a latex catsuit, signed erotic cartoons.

These characters provided an interesting sideshow. But they operated in the margins of the corporate machinery driving the Con: the mass merchandising of blockbuster films and the explosion of studio licensing revenue from new businesses like DVDs and video games that were fast becoming more lucrative than the movies from which they'd sprung. Box office might provide a road map for the success of these licensing deals, but it was also a diminishing portion of the financial pot. Judging from the floor of the convention, these merchandise trends have had a paradoxical effect on the industry. Even as the movie business has become a worldwide, bottom-line driven behemoth, run by corporate accountants with little access to the fans, the licensing of toys, video games and comic books have had an empowering effect on the fans. These items provided fans with a mechanism with which to step into the alternate worlds the studios purveyed. They allowed the fans to bridge the gap between themselves and the movies.

Hence the pageant of costumes at fan conventions, and at opening-night campouts. At Comic-Con, the fans who weren't in costume thronged around those who were, snapping photos of the men and women in spandex superhero uniforms: the glowering, muscle-bound Wolverine with long, tin-foil-wrapped blades protruding from his knuckles; the pirates, space cowboys and hobbits; and the storm troopers from the Garrison of the 501st Legion, an organization that calls itself the premier *Star Wars* costuming group in the world, with some eighteen hundred members in twenty-one countries.

The staunchest movie fans at Comic-Con on July 19 didn't

waste time on the movie memorabilia. They were massed in the airplane-hangar-sized ballroom on the convention's second floor, where for eight hours on Saturday, the studios screened footage and trotted out movie stars from as yet unreleased (but presumptive) blockbusters like *Spider-Man 2, Gothika, Van Helsing* and *Lord of the Rings: Return of the King.*

Here, in a well-staged production, *Spider-Man 2* producers Laura Ziskin and Avi Arad presented the first public screening of footage from the July Fourth 2004 release that was certain to erase any memory of *T3, Legally Blonde 2* and *Sinbad,* to the extent that they had not already been forgotten. As the *Spider-Man* score boomed from a speaker system, the producers unveiled a marketing banner showing Doc Ock, the villain of *Spider-Man 2.* They rolled a sequence from the film showing Doc Ock wreaking havoc in an operating room full of doctors. Then Doc Ock himself, Alfred Molina, strode onstage to answer questions from the fans.

The crowd reserved its heartiest applause for a parade of movie stars—Hugh Jackman, who sang a number from *Grease* in falsetto; Halle Berry, who urged the fans to write letters to the producers of *X-Men* demanding a bigger role for her character, Storm; and Angelina Jolie, touting the next *Tomb Raider* installment, set to hit theaters the next weekend. The film would stumble at the box office, but Jolie was a hit at the Con. Her fans took turns approaching microphones positioned a safe distance from the stage, peppering her with questions. Did she like shooting guns? Did she dig Asian guys? Would she blow a kiss to the crowd? One woman openly wept, announcing that she was HIV-positive and had taken great comfort in Jolie's performance as supermodel Gia in the movie of the same name. Another asked her to autograph a piece of paper she could use to trace a tattoo of Jolie's signature onto her bicep.

This wasn't a passive audience, easily manipulated by the studio spin cycle. These fans spoke out at press conferences and spread their opinions across the Web. In the process, they helped shape the kinds of movies that studios greenlit, and the way those movies were marketed.

"Ten years ago, that didn't exist," says director Kevin Smith, who makes regular appearances at Comic-Con and in 2003 taped a *Tonight Show* segment from the floor of the convention. "People made their movies in a vacuum and put them out in a vacuum. Now people who have nothing to do with your movie are actively involved in your movie from the first announcement forward."

One fan with considerable influence is Harry Knowles, a college dropout who started the Web site Ain't It Cool News in 1996. Knowles lives in Austin, Texas, not Hollywood. But the persona that bubbles forth from his autobiography, *Ain't It Cool*, and his Web site (both named for a John Travolta line in John Woo's action movie *Broken Arrow*), is supremely plugged in. It's an expression of the fan culture that's blossomed around movie blockbusters since the early 1970s.

As Knowles tells it, he spent years traveling with his father selling movie memorabilia at flea markets and movie conventions before his first foray onto the Web. He began to explore the Web after injuring his back at an Austin memorabilia convention—a thousand-pound cart of movie posters fell on him. Bedridden for months, Knowles recalls, his weight ballooned to five hundred pounds, and he began to spend all his time online, frequenting movie bulletin boards, befriending movie industry sources around the world, and laying the foundation for a free Web site providing advance information—some reliable, some not—about big Hollywood movies in quantities that few mainstream media outlets can rival. Studios frequently fly Knowles or his "spies" to advance screenings; publicists have been known to impersonate fans and post fawning reviews of scripts or films on the site. Like Matt Drudge, Knowles was on the front lines of the Internet revolution that began to reshape the news business in the late 1990s. In the eyes of its detractors, Ain't It Cool News has been co-opted by the very system it sought to subvert and now is just another arm of the studio publicity machine. Those criticisms gained traction after Comic-Con 2003, when Knowles became a producer on film projects at Revolution Studios and Paramount Pictures.

Kevin Smith communicates regularly with his fans via a web site called Movie Poop Shoot and personal appearances across the country. Internet fans, he says, participate in the opening of some movies more than others. "The online audience is not actively involved in *The Human Stain*. But they're actively fucking involved in *Terminator 3*. They're actively fucking involved in the *Batman* movie Chris Nolan is directing. That's their movie, man. They're as much a part of it as the filmmakers. Whether it's because they've read a lot of press that says these people can sway an opening, or whether by writing something in cyberspace, they have a sense of authorship, these people are actively involved."

One of those people in 2003 was Robert Sanchez, who runs a fan site in Ontario, California, called the Inland Empire Strikes Back. Sanchez, who used the online moniker Jedibob, had rented a trailer to take his family from Ontario to San Diego for the weekend, and he spent most of the day Saturday careening from one studio presentation to another. Members of "IESB," as they call it, met while camping out in a megaplex parking lot before the opening of *The Phantom Menace*. Many of them were at the convention, capturing footage of movie stars and publicity stunts for films that wouldn't appear on Ontario's fifty-two screens for almost a year.

The intense enthusiasm at Comic-Con was deceptive, however. It was a tough crowd. Studio marketing departments might try to reduce these fans to a set of herd-like demographic impulses that could be targeted, tabulated and factored into box office models. But they ultimately defied prediction. They didn't show up en masse over July Fourth weekend to support *Terminator 3*, *Legally Blonde 2* and *Sinbad*. Three weeks later, those films were ancient history. If hardcore moviegoers didn't care for the movies opening on a particular weekend, there were always a thousand other DVDs, videogames and comic books to occupy their time.

Open Wide

Jonathan Mostow stepped gingerly through his chaotic bungalow on the Universal Pictures lot. It looked like a tiny Terminator had swept through his office, knocking over everything in its way. Mostow's five- and six-year-old sons had come in over the weekend to play the *Terminator* pinball game. It was late September. Mostow was expecting another child in November. There were open cardboard boxes and toys scattered everywhere. A model train positioned on a long, looping track covered most of a coffee table. There was a coating of dust on the leather furniture. Standing next to a desk that was a mountain of papers, *T3* trinkets and assorted gewgaws, dressed in a T-shirt, gym shorts and black, Teva-style sandals, the director surveyed the chaos around him. He had defied the critics and delivered the most popular film of his career. Yet he had barely had time to bask in its success.

T3 had been spectacularly expensive, but it would also

prove soundly profitable. It opened at the top of the U.S. box office and became one of the year's highest grossing films with $150 million in domestic ticket sales and $282 million overseas. The film had also become part of a bigger story, a political groundswell that by late September was rattling California's electoral system. One month earlier, Arnold Schwarzenegger had gone on the *Tonight Show* to announce his run for the state house as part of a historic recall campaign to oust Governor Gray Davis. Schwarzenegger's run for office was forcing people throughout the state—and especially in Hollywood—to re-examine the relationship between politics and entertainment. Sitting in his office surrounded by unopened boxes of *T3* merchandise, Mostow was still putting the finishing touches on the *T3* DVD, scheduled for release in late October. Warners was anticipating sales of five million *T3* DVDs in the first six months, but the studio was running different projections based on the possible outcomes of the gubernatorial election. The studio estimated it would sell the most DVD's if Schwarzenegger was elected; second most if the recall passed and Schwarzenegger was defeated by Gray Davis; least if the recall didn't pass at all.

Mostow was proud of the movie. Working at arm's length from the studio system, under the protective watch of old-fashioned, pugnacious producers who nurtured the film and financed it on their own terms, Mostow had delivered the summer blockbuster that he was hired to make. "This film was always about fighting expectations and meeting often unrealistic expectations," he said. "I had so many people telling me, 'Don't do it. It will never get made, and if it gets made, it will never succeed.' Against those expectations, I feel very victorious." But Mostow was a perfectionist, and he couldn't shake the feeling that the film hadn't achieved its full commercial potential. "In my opinion, this film was never 'event-ized,'" he said. "When we started, we thought, 'Oh, we have July Fourth weekend.' I thought it was going to make a statement: This is the big summer film to see. That never happened."

In one respect, Mostow was right. *T3* never became a box office colossus like *Independence Day* or *Terminator 2,* which shared its release date. By generating close to a billion dollars in combined box office, DVD and merchandise revenue around the world, not to mention a generous profit for its principal players, *T3* qualified as an event. But even that didn't feel like enough.

Mostow's disappointment in his film's box office performance was perfectly in keeping with the queasy feeling that descended across Hollywood like a heavy layer of smog as the studios emerged from the summer of 2003. The same executives who arrived at ShoWest six months earlier with high hopes for the summer now felt like tourists who had barely survived a casino bender. Box office for the summer was flat compared to the summer of 2002; full-year box office would dip in 2003 for the first time in twelve years. Ticket sales would fall 4 percent from the previous year.

But studios had spent a nightmarish amount of money to achieve those results. The combined cost of producing and marketing a studio film in 2003 rose 15 percent to $102.8

million, according to the MPAA. Driving those costs were marketing expenditures, which climbed to $39 million in 2003, thanks largely to the furious TV advertising campaigns that were now the cornerstones of studio release campaigns.

The opening-weekend system that had delivered instant profits for films like *Spider-Man* and *X-Men 2* had brought severe repercussions for the film industry as a whole. Studios were spending money at a perilous rate in an effort to package their blockbusters for a restive mass audience that increasingly spent their disposable income on other things. In retrospect, the summer of 2003 looked like a suicide mission, in which several of the most expensive gambles— among them *Sinbad, Tomb Raider 2, Gigli, Charlie's Angels 2* and *The League of Extraordinary Gentlemen*—fell flat. As *T3* producer Moritz Borman put it, "There is a certain point when the industry is leaving a huge chunk of the audience on the beach."

The previous summer had "run out of gas in the last seven weeks," Paul Dergarabedian, president of Exhibitor Relations, told us. "But it also had much better movies. You had *Minority Report, My Big Fat Greek Wedding, Bourne Identity,* and all of the headlines about *Spider-Man* having the biggest opening of all time. This summer just didn't have that kind of feeling. Every summer has its own pathology. This summer everyone had a negative feeling about it." Dergarabedian was right. The summer did have a pathology. But it wasn't just a reflection of the movies the studios released or their box office performance. It was a function of the market they swam in, with its frenzied cycle of opening-weekend hype and quick obsolescence. "When you live and breathe something for two years, you want that moment to be as gloriously spectacular as possible," Mostow said. "And it all comes down to one moment."

That moment was a high point for Vajna and Kassar. The producers were back in business, their partnership restored after a painful, decade-long rift. They, too, complained that the film wasn't enough of an "event" in the United States, and they, arguably, had more to lose. With the Terminator on his way to the state house in Sacramento, C-2 would have to look elsewhere for its next action franchise. But by late fall, the indefatigable duo was hatching new plans: straight to video *Terminator* films and *Terminator* TV spinoffs. The *Terminator* was a brand, Vajna said, the way Gucci was a brand. There were no limits to how it might be exploited.

It was a low point for the Glendale campus of Dream-Works, which went into a collective depression after *Sinbad* slunk out of theaters with a gross of $26.5 million, less than a third of what it cost to make and market. Sources within the company have confirmed that losses associated with the film totaled roughly $100 million—a nasty blow to Jeffrey Katzenberg and his partners, David Geffen and Steven Spielberg, whose personal fortunes were tied up in DreamWorks' slate of films.

The most tangible effect of *Sinbad* was that it sounded the death knell, at least for a while, of big-budget traditional feature animation. Disney would continue to put together low-budget movies based on Winnie the Pooh characters and Paramount, blessed with an ideal farm system in Nickelodeon, would continue down that path. But no studio appeared likely again to green-light a big-budget, hand-drawn project like *Sinbad*. DreamWorks worked to divert attention from its floundering summer title, the nadir in the most disappointing year in its ten-year history. It turned up the flame under the promotional effort for the fully computer-animated *Shrek 2* and *Shark Tale*. And on the live-action side it was eagerly anticipating a promising slate in 2004 and anticipating an initial offering of shares in its animation division. But 2003 had been the year that Hollywood's maverick dream team ate crow. Shortly after *Sinbad* retreated from theaters, Katzenberg had to cope with another animation crisis. Las Vegas performer Roy Horn, one half of the duo Siegfried and Roy, was attacked by one of his white tigers, putting the Vegas show in limbo and jeopardizing DreamWorks Television's series *Father of the Pride*. The show, which was slated to debut on NBC in the fall of 2004, revolves around one of Siegfried and Roy's famous cats.

The story at MGM was more complicated. *Legally Blonde 2* did not match the $96 million gross of its predecessor, finishing just shy of $90 million at the domestic box office. MGM took heart in its overall economics, which would allow significant profits to be realized once DVDs and other ancillaries were factored in. Profits from *Legally Blonde 2* would not approach the level of the charmed first film, but the sequel was the studio's top-grossing film of the year. An Oscar campaign was mounted for Lee Ann Rimes's song "We Can" and she performed the song in MGM vice-chairman Chris McGurk's backyard, during the company's holiday party in

December. But a rival marketing executive considered the movie "a sniper bullet through the heart of a franchise." That was indeed the measure of many sequels; they could not be viewed on their own terms, but rather had to be judged on whether they kept the ball rolling. *Hulk* and *Charlie's Angels 2* fell into the same category. In that sense, *Legally Blonde 2*, which was fraught from the beginning with disputes about who it was being made for and what it was trying to say, fumbled the ball. Marc Platt said he would not discuss a third installment "in any detail until an idea comes into my head that takes that character in an interesting direction." Nonetheless, he added, "I was very pleased that our movie made a lot of money, and at the end of the day, although it wasn't for me a perfect movie in any way and exactly what I had in my head, it was nonetheless a movie I was proud of."

Whether or not it was a result of the punishing logistics of delivering a franchise movie on an accelerated schedule, Charles Herman-Wurmfeld appeared haggard when interviewed December 5 at Madame Matisse, a small café on Sunset Boulevard on L.A.'s Eastside. His head was tucked inside the hood of a stained gray sweatshirt. He wore olive cargo pants and black leather clogs and two silver rings on his right index finger, one with a peace insignia. He arrived listening to a French-language instructional program on his I-Pod. He was polishing his language skills for a trip to France, where he would start work on commercials for friend and fellow director Doug Liman's production company.

It was difficult to tell for sure, but the hooded sweatshirt looked like the one he'd worn in an effort to blend in with the mall rats during that terrifying test screening at the Edwards theater in Aliso Viejo. When it became clear he had to reshoot the first scene in his movie. "I could hear that it was dead, and I don't know that we fixed it," he said. He looked away, across Sunset, collecting his thoughts.

"I don't know that taking her to Washington was necessarily the most sensitive choice in terms of the desires of the audience. For the whole team, it was an interesting way to go. But kids are notoriously apolitical these days, unfortunately. I thought that maybe it could inspire them to think, 'If Elle Woods can go, she's cool, maybe I can go.' "To this day, I'm only halfway satisfied with where we ended up. According to the *Mr. Smith Goes to Washington* model, the action, the great exposé, is supposed to peak during the speech. One thing that we never addressed is that it happened earlier, so then during the speech there wasn't anything personally going on. The larger arc of the character is complete." Originally in the script, he continued, "it was the Dalai Lama and she had earlier run into him and taken him for spa treatments and it had somehow profoundly affected him. So he turned the floor over to her as a woman of the earth and compassion. As I tell it, it sounds better because it was so crazy."

Whatever the problem, Herman-Wurmfeld did not seem surprised by the end result. "I get from everyone that I'm supposed to feel burned by MGM," he said. "My own assistant gives it to me, like, what are you still talking to them for? I just feel like they're a studio and I never expected them to not act like a business. . . . I feel like everyone was themselves. I never felt disrespected personally." The most powerful validation he received was an impassioned column by Arianna Huffington, contending that Elle Woods "reminds the rest of us how important our involvement is to the well-being of our democracy." Huffington, a political commentator and former wife of a senatorial candidate, would end up running against Arnold Schwarzenegger in the recall election—a real-life Elle Woods entering politics, some might say. "Arianna's essay made my life," the director said. "I sent her an e-mail to say, 'I feel so seen and acknowledged.'"

For studio filmmakers like Herman-Wurmfeld and Mostow, box office grosses are a double-edged sword. They have no bearing on a director's gut instinct that a movie is good or bad. But they're the lingua franca of an opening weekend business, in which jobs are scarce, and in which studios are loath to green-light a movie they can't open wide. In the wide-release era, it will always be easier to get hired to direct a trashy film that seems like an instant hit than to direct a film whose merits may take weeks to establish at the box office. "It's been bad for movies in that it makes filmmakers edit their choices of the movies they would do," Mostow says. "It scares filmmakers away from movies that have more creative risks. Filmmakers have families and mortgages, too."

One director hoping to buck the trend is Gary Ross, the director of *Seabiscuit*, one of the few 2003 summer blockbusters with legs. *Seabiscuit* opened wide on July 25 to $21 million, fell off just 15 percent its second weekend, and stayed in theaters for weeks en route to an Oscar nomination for best picture. Ross, the son of screenwriter Arthur A. Ross, who wrote *The Creature from the Black Lagoon,* says film-makers of his father's generation didn't talk about the box office gross of their films; it was considered coarse. Ross has an encyclopedic interest in the arcana of studio marketing and distribution, and he follows opening-weekend box office closely. But in the fall of 2003 he told us there was hope for films that weren't one-weekend wonders. "The movie business thinks people want Big Macs," Ross says. "We were a horse drama. If anything should have failed this summer, it was our movie. But people don't just want shit that blows up. They want a real story."

As studios pressed on with their major campaigns for the fall, nobody seemed to be listening to him. Arnold Schwarzenegger, an actor who owed his superstardom to fancy pyrotechnics, not to realistic stories, certainly wasn't. On October 7, the Independence Day battle for box office supremacy was no longer a Hollywood event. It had become the springboard for an inauguration. Early in the evening, polls were projecting that the gubernatorial recall of Gray Davis had passed, with Schwarzenegger winning a landslide election by the California electorate. In news reports, coast to coast, scenes from *T3* were being interspliced with coverage of the scene at the Century Plaza ballroom, where Schwarzenegger made his victory speech. Who better to introduce him than his frequent late-night Boswell, Jay Leno? Not one of Schwarzenegger's movie premieres had attracted as big a media swarm as the one that descended on this victory celebration. What made the citizens of California decide to vote for him? Was it the things he said on the political stump, or was it the image he'd cultivated in his film career? The distinction between box office and ballot box never seemed fuzzier. Sheryl Main, the former film unit publicist in "Arnold's Army" who had shepherded Schwarzenegger around *T3*'s Westwood premiere, now worked in the governor's communications office, fielding reporters' calls on the state budget deficit.

That blurring of lines between show business and politics was certainly one of the legacies of Schwarzenegger's long acting career, and of the Hollywood showmen before him who created the wide-release movie derby that he thrived in. The pundits who sniffed that any Hollywood star would never be able to withstand the bloodsport of politics had obviously never been invited to a studio press junket. Hundreds of interviews at a shot, reciting talking points and sound bites with a camera-ready smile—what better way to learn the art of political stagecraft? "Watching him on the campaign trail, I sensed he had a great advantage," Mostow said. "It's not all that dissimilar from campaigning—staying on message, having an unflagging enthusiasm, making sure not to make any missteps, and having a lot of stamina." And when it came to publicity, Schwarzenegger had a level of stamina that would have impressed even the indefatigable B movie titans who smashed the road-show system in the 1950s and flooded the nations with prints of their movies, drumming up an endless parade of outlandish stunts to capitalize on the fleeting trends of fast-shifting consumer culture.

Like most American cities, Los Angeles was changed by

those trends. Its suburban population exploded after World War II, and its movie theaters followed, proliferating in outlying areas, popping up at regional shopping centers and other suburban destinations, which siphoned traffic and retail dollars away from traditional urban centers. The new shopping malls were standardized and homogenous, with movies to match. The old urban centers were left to decay.

Today, a secret Hollywood graveyard sits in a trench of rundown office buildings less than a mile away from the soundstages in which *T3* and *Legally Blonde 2* were filmed. It's the theater district on South Broadway in Downtown Los Angeles, home to a row of the most spectacular movie palaces ever built. Proclaimed by boosters decades ago as the "Best Lighted Street in the World," South Broadway is now dark. The street still bustles with pedestrian shoppers, though it doesn't have the amenities of a suburban mall. There's no Baby Gap, Rainforest Café or GameWorks. You won't find a megaplex here playing *T3*. But pirated DVDs of the latest Hollywood movies are everywhere. Street vendors sell them for $5 a pop. Boiled ears of corn and mangoes are sold from plastic tubs on the curb. Mariachi music blares from jewelry stores and pawn shops.

The grand, arched glass façade of the Broadway Arcade Building, built in 1910 to resemble the opulent nineteenth-century shopping emporia of Paris and Rome, hides a grid of retail stalls selling fashion knockoffs and communion dresses, Zippo lighters, plastic bongs and glass crack pipes. Downtown, with its generic cityscapes and easy access, has long been a lure for filmmakers. At times, several film sets operate simultaneously around its three-square-mile area, undeterred by the gritty environment. Ben Affleck shot a scene from *Daredevil* in an alley just off Broadway. The film crew wore hard hats and built a net across the set to protect themselves from bottles and hypodermic needles flung at the actors from windows on the floors above them.

South Broadway at the outset of the twentieth century was an upscale residential corridor. Nickelodeons and vaudeville houses sprouted up, rapidly transforming the street into a West Coast version of Times Square. In 1918, at the corner of Third Street and Broadway, Sid Grauman built the city's first movie palace, the Million Dollar Theater. It was a wildly eclectic, twenty-three-hundred-seat pleasure dome, with a baroque terra-cotta facade, piles of Spanish ornamentation, sculpted bison heads and Texas longhorn skulls. A series of picture cathedrals soon rose from the surrounding blocks; the Rialto, the Pantages, the Morosco, the Mayan, the Belasco, the State, the Palace, the Orpheum, the Tower and the Los Angeles. The Los Angeles Theater, the last to be built, was the grandest of them all. It opened its doors on January 30, 1931, for the world premiere of Charlie Chaplin's *City Lights*.

In the weeks before opening night, developer H. L. Gumbiner ran a series of ads in the *L.A. Times* touting his venue as "The Theater Unusual," a rococo hall of mirrors built in five months for more than $1.2 million. The 115-foot-long foyer was hung with French chandeliers. A marble staircase led to a crystal fountain with ornamental marble dolphins and an oil painting meant to look like a Fragonard.

An iridescent curtain showing Louis XIV riding a white Arabian horse, returning victorious from battle, was pulled up for each show to reveal a 60-foot-tall screen. There was a children's play room with circus tent ceiling, filled with stuffed animals. There were electric cigarette lighters built into the walls and a smoking lounge with a miniature screen connected to the main auditorium by a series of prisms and glass tubing. The theater was air-conditioned by one of the largest ventilating systems on the West Coast. Today, like most of the South Broadway theaters, it's closed to the public, the mirrors are tarnished and the furniture is gone. At night, the vertical neon sign on the Los Angeles Theater is still illuminated. But the message on the marquee doesn't announce the coming attractions. Most days, it reads, "Now Available for Location Filming." Paramount exploited the location as part of its ShoWest 2004 clip reel, dressing the lobby and lighting the auditorium to evoke Gumbiner's opulent vision. But Paramount films like *The Stepford Wives* and *Spongebob SquarePants* will never be projected there.

For most of Hollywood, South Broadway is just a location of no intrinsic interest. Therein lies one of the greatest risks of the opening-weekend system that now holds the movie industry in its grip. This increasingly trivial indoor sport is a vast and all-consuming distraction. In their headlong rush toward their next film's opening weekend, film executives rarely pause to consider why the great theaters of the past closed down. Few stop to ask whether these relics of recent film history might hold clues to the shape of its not-so-distant future. The fixation on box office has become part of the bubble that insulates Hollywood from the world beyond the red carpet. That disconnect is arguably as old as Hollywood itself. The *City Lights* premiere at the Los Angeles snarled traffic for blocks. A well-heeled crowd, including Chaplin, Albert Einstein and Universal Pictures founder Carl Laemmle struggled to reach their seats as people standing in bread lines across the street surged toward the theater. They booed the arrival of premiere guests and smashed the window of a shop next door. James Cameron chose to shoot the first *Terminator* in downtown L.A. to show a side of the city far removed from the studios, according to producer Gale Anne Hurd. Its trash-strewn streets, industrial corridors and spider-webbing freeway overpasses were the perfect backdrop for his apocalyptic nightmare. Two decades later, downtown L.A. was the perfect backdrop for a *Terminator* press junket.

Hollywood's apathy toward its own recent history was strikingly evident as we researched this book. Nobody seemed to remember which films were the first to open wide, which were the first ones to advertise on TV and radio, which, if any, were the first blockbusters. Conversations in Hollywood revolve around last weekend's box office grosses and this week's tracking, but distribution records are spotty; many are permanently lost. People like Dan Fellman, Nikki Rocco and Marcie Polier are the last oral historians of the business that existed before opening weekend became an American institution, keeping the whole equation of pictures in their heads. This history isn't available elsewhere, and few people seem to care. For the studio executives who plan movie releases, opening movies is an all-consuming vocation that leaves little time for anything else. The appetite for more is insatiable. Trailers are created with faster and flashier cuts, the volume pushed to the 85-decibel limit. If one show is sold out, there's usually another one about to start with good seats available. The blockbuster business revolves around gushers. It drills deepest where the payoff is the richest; tapped-out theaters are condemned. Today it's South Broadway; tomorrow, it could be the megaplexes at Ontario Mills.

Warner Brothers, pioneer of the saturation release campaign, has maintained a singular focus on high-volume business since its 1927 release *The Jazz Singer* introduced the world to talking pictures. And on November 5, 2003, it set a new standard for opening wide. At 1400 Greenwich Mean Time, the earth became planet *Matrix*.

Warner Brothers dubbed it "zero hour": a tightly synchronized, simultaneous global event, engineered by film distributors in more than one hundred countries, heralding the opening of *The Matrix Revolutions,* the final installment of Larry and Andy Wachowski's groundbreaking, megahyped, science fiction trilogy. At 6 A.M. in Los Angeles, 8 A.M. in Mexico City, 9 A.M. in New York, 3 P.M. in Berlin, 4 P.M. in Durban, 5 P.M. in Moscow, 7:30 P.M. in Mumbai and 10 P.M. in Singapore, in gleaming multiscreen entertainment supercenters and moldering single-screen, inner-city houses, more than eighteen thousand *Matrix Revolutions* prints twirled from projector to projector. All at once, the film's dazzling pyrotechnics were beamed into the collective consciousness of the largest opening day audience in movie history.

It was a revolutionary new distribution model for Hollywood, tailor-made for a franchise once thought to be Hollywood's most groundbreaking blockbuster. Time Warner touted the maneuver as a forceful salvo in the war against copyright theft, delivering the film to theater audiences in far-flung piracy-wracked nations before bootleg DVDs could be offered for sale on the streets. But there was another, more insidious strategy at work. In the fall of 2003 the *Matrix* franchise no longer seemed quite so groundbreaking. Six months earlier, the second installment, *The Matrix Reloaded,* had enjoyed a robust opening weekend, then quickly capsized in a sea of bad publicity. Critics called it at best anticlimactic, at worst an empty spectacle betraying the spellbinding promise of the original *Matrix.* It was a sentiment repeated among reviewers of *The Matrix Revolutions* from New York to Bangkok. "At the risk of understatement," wrote *Rolling Stone* film critic Peter Travers, "*The Matrix Revolutions* sucks."

The Matrix Revolutions release campaign was carefully designed to eclipse that fact. The production budget of *The Matrix Revolutions* was an estimated $200 million; the worldwide marketing budget was estimated at $140 million—enough to focus the world's attention on the spectacle of opening weekend and away from the quality of the film itself. And what a spectacle it was. Tokyo's sprawling Shinjuku Milano-za movie theater was bathed in green floodlights for a premiere attended by Keanu Reeves and the Wachowskis, part of a global, traveling contingent of talent dispatched by Warner Brothers, including gala openings at Frank Gehry's new Walt Disney Concert Hall in Los

Angeles, and the harborfront Opera House in Sydney, Australia—the first film premieres ever held in those venues.

With clockwork precision, the film opened everywhere. At 6 A.M., at the SuperMall of the Great Southwest in Auburn, Washington, more than three hundred *Matrix* fans poured into the seventeen-screen Regal Cinema for the day's first show. Beijing's Oriental Plaza moviehouse screened the film simultaneously in six auditoriums. Overall, tens of thousands of Chinese citizens attended opening night screenings—the first film ever to open on the same day in the United States and on the Chinese Mainland. At the Pushkinsky Entertainment Centre in Moscow's Pushkin Square, dozens of Communist Party loyalists wearing Red Army helmets and trademark *Matrix* sunglasses picketed the theater, toting signs that read "DESTROY THE MATRIX."

Dan Fellman proclaimed it the widest opening in the history of the movie business. Even the screens were bigger. The Toronto-based IMAX company was screening *The Matrix Revolutions* in sixty auditoriums with trademark eight-story IMAX screens and twelve thousand watts of digital surround sound, the widest IMAX release of a studio event film since the advent of the company in 1969.

Before *The Matrix Revolutions,* the only synchronized global media events had been television broadcasts: the Olympics, the World Cup, Princess Diana's funeral, the events of September 11. There had been synchronized global peace meditations and political actions. And to be sure, other films had opened around the world on the same weekend. The previous May, Fox had released *X-2* in eighty countries on the same day. But never had a studio marshaled the resources that Warner Brothers put behind *The Matrix Revolutions,* setting in place an interconnected release mechanism to open a single film worldwide at a fixed moment in time.

The first *Matrix* was hailed as a clever, *Brave New World*-esque satire of a global population plugged into a computer-generated illusion, trapped like a multiplex audience in a rapt state of mass distraction. It was an inside joke—a commercial blockbuster that was also an indictment of the blockbuster culture that sustained it—tricked out with gravity-defying martial arts battles, dimension-bending slow-motion gunplay, black leather fetish gear and references to postmodern theorist Jean Baudrillard. But the sequel was a crushing letdown; another generic special-effects vehicle from the mindless blockbuster factory. And *Revolutions,* with its muddled cacophony of unending computerized battles, was even worse. "There are still a few loose ends that might be spun into future sequels," wrote A. O. Scott in the *New York Times.* "'The Matrix Recycled,' perhaps, or 'The Matrix Recall Election.'"

Even *Good Morning America*'s perky, blockbuster-friendly film critic, Joel Siegel, standing in the dark in front of the historic Mann's Chinese Theater seventy-five minutes before zero hour, labeled it a "disappointment." The negative reviews came too late to stop the stampede. The fans weren't listening.

The line at the historic Mann's Chinese had begun forming at 7:30 P.M. the previous evening. Thirty members of the Web community Liningup.net, a fansite dedicated to the obsolete practices of waiting in line at theaters, were the first to arrive, led by Alyse Pozzo, a twenty-seven-year old production manager from Culver City. Another group of eleven friends left San Diego in a rented van shortly before midnight. By 5 A.M., the line coiled around the block, reaching the corner of Orange and Franklin nearly a quarter mile away. Some wore long black trenchcoats and dark sunglasses. Felli Fel, a DJ from local radio station Power 106 stood nearby, wearing a baseball cap and a knee-length football jersey, rallying the crowd from a red-carpeted platform and periodically tossing *Matrix* merchandise to the fans. Six news vans with satellite dishes were parked in a row on Hollywood Boulevard.

Sid Grauman, one of Hollywood's great showmen, built this temple to blockbuster movies in 1927. The theater's cement courtyard bears the hand- and footprints of legendary Hollywood stars. Here at the *Star Wars* premiere in 1977, Darth Vader, R2D2 and C-3PO had left their tread and boot marks in the cement. Next door is the Kodak Theatre, the new site of the Academy Awards. The building's red interior is decorated with kitsch oriental motifs, its jade green and bronze roof rises sixty-nine feet in the air. The morning of November 5, a digital *Matrix* clock dangled from the roof, counting down the minutes to 6:00. For the crowd that slept on the sidewalk, the Chinese Theater was the center of the universe; ground zero of *The Matrix Revolutions*. But things had changed since Sid Grauman's day. An audience hungry for blockbuster entertainment now had its own show palaces in thousands of neighborhoods around the world. Just 40 miles away at the Ontario Mills mall, *The Matrix Revolutions* unspooled every three hours at a Chinese Theater knockoff with six hundred seats, a seventy-foot screen, a shiny new concession stand and video games in the lobby.

Sid Grauman would have appreciated the *Matrix* launch. It was a heady PR stunt, after all, a new global spin on the old take-the-money-and-run release strategy of 1950s B-movie distributors. Racking up $84 million in ticket sales by Monday morning, *The Matrix Revolutions* would soon be the number one movie in America. It perfectly demonstrated the old Joseph E. Levine motto: "You can fool all the people all the time if the advertising is right and the budget is big enough."

Epilogue

Not long after the "zero hour" opening of *Matrix Revolutions*, the cycle began again.

CBS' Super Bowl broadcast in 2004 featured more than $20 million in movie ads, including the first TV spots for summer spectacles *Van Helsing* and *Troy*. Two months later, the same Paris Las Vegas Casino theater in which Robert Goulet sang a tribute to *Finding Nemo* in 2003 was the backdrop to a publicity stunt for *Spider-Man 2*. This time, the theater was bathed in red lights. Female acrobats in black leotards dropped from the ceiling and twirled in mid-air. A smoke machine emitted the dank, waxy smell of a spider-infested basement, as conventioneers trundled to their seats, carrying goodie bags bursting with ShoWest promotional curios—souvenirs of the raft of summer blockbusters splashed across the casino ballrooms and restaurants. There were *SpongeBob* backpacks, *Manchurian Candidate* sweatshirts, a slipcase of *Lemony Snicket* hardcovers.

The sequel to the skyline-vaulting *Spider-Man*, which in 2002 achieved the unthinkable—Hollywood's first $100 million opening weekend—would plow the same pastures that *Terminator 3*, *Legally Blonde 2* and *Sinbad* had one year earlier. It would open in thousands of theaters over Independence Day weekend 2004. But it would have the field to itself. Or so it seemed until a few weeks before opening weekend.

Enter Michael Moore. In May, the guerilla filmmaker from Flint, Michigan initiated a late end run on the summer competition. When the Walt Disney Company dumped his incendiary, low-budget documentary, *Fahrenheit 9/11*, Moore took his cause to the one place where a maverick showman in the Joseph E. Levine mold could generate more media coverage than a studio blockbuster with a $100 million worldwide marketing budget—the Cannes Film Festival.

Moore was as big a star on the Croisette as Arnold Schwarzenegger. Photographers and gawking tourists shadowed him everywhere. *Fahrenheit 9/11* received a 20-minute standing ovation and won the Palme d'Or. Even before he had signed a deal with a new U.S. distributor, Moore declared that he wanted the film to be playing in American theaters on the summer's most patriotic weekend—July Fourth.

Spider-Man vs. Michael Moore wasn't a showdown for the ages, to be sure. Nobody imagined that *Fahrenheit 9/11* would stanch the geyser of box office dollars expected to spew forth from *Spider-Man 2* on opening weekend. But something decidedly new was in the air. Months earlier, the overwhelming and unorthodox success of *The Passion of the*

Christ subverted the studio mantra that box office could be bought by conventional means. Mel Gibson and Michael Moore—the latest in a line of mavericks whose guile and showmanship had ushered the movie business into the wide-release era—had a different message for Hollywood. They showed the audience something new, finding alternative routes to the inner sanctum. They proved that showmanship was very much alive.

Fahrenheit 9/11 had no A-list stars. It hadn't made any of the glossy magazines' summer preview issues, folded alongside the seductively framed computer effects. It would eventually be released on June 25—five days before *Spider-Man 2*—by a coalition of independent companies. Nevertheless, it would prove irresistible to the companies controlling the nation's 35,000 movie screens. Studios might rail against Moore's bombastic style, but they would salute the bonfire of publicity he had so artfully incited, creating a level of unaided awareness for *Fahrenheit 9/11* that was the envy of every marketing chief in town.

Most of those executives found themselves in the summer of 2004 saddled with recycled goods. Even films that didn't appear to be sequels or remakes borrowed liberally from the past. In May, Jeffrey Katzenberg came to Cannes to promote his animated sequel, *Shrek 2*, and a new project, *Shark Tale*. Borrowing a tactic that had proven effective for Andy Vajna and Mario Kassar the previous year, Katzenberg staged a publicity stunt in front of the Carlton Hotel. In the Bay of Cannes, a few yards from the Carlton Pier, the stars of *Shark Tale*, Angelina Jolie, Will Smith and Jack Black, straddled an inflatable banana boat in the shape of a shark. Dozens of photographers snapped pictures as Jack Black dove into the sea and dog-paddled to shore. *Shark Tale*, which would arrive in U.S. theaters October 1, was oceans apart from the earnest, squeaky-clean *Sinbad*. It was a cheeky undersea "hip-hopera," with musical tracks from Missy Elliott, Mary J. Blige and Chingy. *Shark Tale* riffed on the seminal summer blockbuster *Jaws*. And unlike *Finding Nemo*, it had Steven Spielberg's imprimatur. A promotional reel screened for the press at Cannes showed Spielberg inspecting *Shark Tale* storyboards. "No sharks were harmed during the making of this picture," he said.

At ShoWest, Twentieth Century Fox screened footage from Roland Emmerich's disaster thriller, *The Day After Tomorrow*. It opened with a familiar scene of scientists in parkas scurrying across the Antarctic tundra. Suddenly, a vast ice shelf rumbles, crashing into the ocean. The camera pans across choppy seas, revealing a tidal wave rushing toward Manhattan. It was a note-for-note ripoff of *The Beast From 20,000 Fathoms*, though few people at ShoWest seemed to notice. Instead of Herman the rhedosaurus marauding through the streets of Manhattan, smashing buildings and flipping cars, Emmerich's beast was Mother Nature in the guise of global climate shift, unleashed by greenhouse gases, rippling down from the Arctic, leveling cities with eye-popping digital verisimilitude. "Nobody wrecks the planet like Roland Emmerich!" Fox chairman James Gianopulos crowed.

The same could be said about the summer movie season,

as studios unleashed their blockbusters with awesome force around the globe. Unbowed by the weak results of the previous year, studios had increased their production and market budgets to hair-raising levels. *Troy* reportedly cost $180 million to produce; *Spider-Man 2* more than $200 million.

These films were opening wider and wider. And box office records continued to fall in their wake. DreamWorks opened *Shrek 2* wider than any movie ever had played in the U.S., beginning with 3,737 theaters its first day, expanding to 4,223 in its second weekend. According to the National Association of Theater Owners, that meant that the film played in three out of four American movie houses. *Shrek 2* became the second movie after *Spider-Man* to sell $100 million worth of tickets in a single weekend at the American box office. *The Day After Tomorrow* went worldwide in one weekend, opening in 100 countries outside the U.S. and Canada—the widest day-and-date opening ever. Memorial Day weekend overall wound up as the highest-grossing four days in movie history—to that point, anyway.

Reading the box office scorecard week after week, people in Hollywood felt a measure of relief. The results proved the system might be able sustain itself after all. In a way, that is largely what box office had always been—a palliative on a Monday morning offering some pretense of rationality in an inherently irrational business. That's how it filled a media vacuum and insinuated itself into the culture, fitting neatly with Americans' obsession with lottery numbers, batting averages and the Fortune 500. That's also how studios got hooked on box office. What was the alternative? Gut instinct?

Joe Farrell of the National Research Group said his data "got them off the hook." To ignore the numbers, *Variety*'s Art Murphy had warned, "is to risk business failure."

Jeff Blake, vice chairman of Sony Pictures, took those principles to heart. He also knew how to work the crowd at ShoWest. Standing onstage at the Paris Las Vegas Casino theater, Blake announced *Spider-Man 3* already had a release date—the first weekend of May 2007. Grateful applause rolled through the audience. The American public was tough to predict. But the studios would keep trying at all cost. They might be barreling down a perilous path, but the blockbuster machine could not be stopped.

Afterword

Open Wide was not intended as a warning, exactly. When we set out to chronicle one weekend of the 2003 summer blockbuster season, we merely wanted to tell the story of three films duking it out for Hollywood's box office crown. We knew from the outset that our contenders—*Terminator 3*, *Legally Blonde 2*, and *Sinbad*—weren't likely to become enduring classics. But we hoped the drama of opening weekend would yield a fresh look at the unhealthy system that holds American movie-goers in its grip from May to August: the big-budget Hollywood sequel factory, its full-tilt marketing campaigns, the mania for focus groups and rewrites, the creaky infrastructure of the nation's movie theaters.

We had no idea as we wrote *Open Wide* that 2005 would be the apotheosis of all these self-destructive instincts and one of the worst moments for Hollywood in the blockbuster era. In April of 2005, Hollywood embarked on a record-setting slump of nineteen consecutive weeks in which opening weekend box office dropped below the previous year's level, a period in which the studios pumped out an especially woeful assortment of motion pictures that Joe Levine might have called "super-colossals."

Open Wide revealed glaring signs of a system in need of repair, but these problems reached their apogee in 2005, as the studios turned out one blockbuster flop after another: *XXX: State of the Union*, *Kingdom of Heaven*, *Herbie: Fully Loaded*, *Stealth*. When DreamWorks' 2005 sci-fi action blowout *The Island* tanked, actress Scarlett Johannsen and producers Walter Parkes and Laurie MacDonald exchanged fire in the press. They blamed her lack of star power for the film's feeble opening; her camp retorted that the producers had made "calculated mistakes throughout the film's marketing." Director Michael Bay, creator of bombastic opening-weekend spectacles like *Armageddon* and *Bad Boys II*, complained about DreamWorks' TV spots and said that most of the studio's posters made Johannsen "look like a porn star." Terry Press, the DreamWorks marketing chief who had presided over *Sinbad*'s wipeout in the summer of 2003, blamed the studio's headlong rush to opening weekend. "The biggest mistake this company made was we made a date, not a movie," she told *Variety*.

The full-year 2005 box office total of $8.8 billion was off 5 percent from 2004. Factoring in ticket-price inflation, the picture darkened. Admissions fell 7 percent in 2005—the biggest drop in twenty years. As they dissected these numbers, media outlets openly speculated that moviegoing as an American institution might be doomed. Studio executives jeered at the idea, but privately, they also conceded that it wasn't getting any cheaper to open wide. When Disney CEO Robert Iger expressed interest in the idea of releasing movies simultaneously in theaters and on DVD, exhibitors rained down their disapproval. John Fithian, president of the National Association of Theater Owners, called it a death threat to the theatrical movie business. As of this writing, no wide-release movie has attempted that gambit, but distrust between exhibitors and the studios was deepening to a point that no amount of ShoWest glad-handing could possibly repair.

At least Press could look forward to greener pastures. Like many of the protagonists in *Open Wide*, she changed addresses in 2005, joining Jeffrey Katzenberg at DreamWorks Animation, a publicly traded company releasing just two animated films a year. Sinbad was long forgotten, but then again so were the Terminator and Elle Woods, all three characters consigned to that dusty studio vault in the sky that houses Hollywood franchises unlikely ever again to grace the nation's multiplexes. Arnold Schwarzenegger would vanish from the movie world altogether to take up residence at the California State House, while Reese Witherspoon would win her first Oscar for her role as June Carter Cash in *Walk the Line*, making an encore performance of *Legally Blonde* as unlikely as a real-life run for the White House.

DreamWorks proper ended its eleven-year life as an independent company when Paramount Pictures paid $1.6 billion to acquire the company. MGM, too, reached the end of its historic Hollywood run when it was bought by Sony

Pictures, scattering the people who had only recently toiled for months to sear the story of Elle Woods and her gay Chihuahua into the cerebral cortex of every teenage girl in America. MGM publicist Eric Kops moved over to Paramount and marketing executive Peter Adee resurfaced as a consultant.

Some of the personalities from our story seemed stuck in time. Andy Vajna and Mario Kassar collaborated again with Intermedia Films, their partner on *Terminator 3*, to produce *Basic Instinct 2*. The film's release followed years of litigation with star Sharon Stone. After Stone settled her lawsuit, which alleged that Vajna and Kassar had reneged on a verbal guarantee of $14 million against 15 percent of the film's gross, the producers shrugged and decided it would be better to pay her to reprise her role as sociopath Catherine Tramell than to pay her to walk away. Conceived during one of Carolco Pictures' epic trips to Cannes in the early 1990s, when Stone was one of the hottest stars in Hollywood, the sequel took fourteen years to reach the screen, longer than *T3*. In an eleventh-hour bid for attention, a soft-core promotional reel surfaced online featuring a startling array of scenes with Stone naked and cavorting with male and female co-stars. Vajna and Kassar, in an unusual arrangement, were even paying for the film's marketing. As its March 2006 release neared, they engineered a bold announcement that the Motion Picture Assn. of America had threatened the movie with an NC-17 rating due to explicit sex. It was just the kind of unabashed showboating you'd expect from a pair who had once shut down the Cannes waterfront for a photo-op with the soon-to-be-elected governor of California.

T3 director Jonathan Mostow, although still haunted by the experience of opening weekend, retained a fascination for the Terminator character. He co-wrote a script for *Terminator 4*, a storyline that would involve none of the original principals, and told us that Vajna and Kassar loved it. The only trouble would be getting a studio or financier to back it without the draw of Schwarzenegger. "To do it right, it'd be $150 million," he said. As he waited to see if another Terminator would happen on the big screen (Fox was simultaneously developing a TV show based on James Cameron's creation), Mostow planned to direct a Will Smith thriller and a big-budget remake of *Swiss Family Robinson*.

In the fall of 2005, Mostow saw Schwarzenegger for the first time in nearly a year, when he filmed an anti-piracy public-service commercial. They palled around a bit, the same odd couple from Comic-Con and the blowout *T3* event on the Warner Bros. lot. But something fundamental had changed. In leaving the blockbuster world behind, Schwarzenegger had seemingly leveraged all the power of opening weekend to further his political career. His first few months in office had been a honeymoon of typically Olympian proportions. But as a series of state initiatives failed and Schwarzenegger approval ratings began to drop, the former bodybuilder found, for the first time in his Horatio Alger life, that his audience—the California electorate—was unmoved. Mostow wasn't surprised to hear Schwarzenegger's response when the subject of another Terminator movie came up. The governor looked forward to at least a cameo, and wouldn't rule out something more.

Revisiting the summer of 2003, it's easy to spot the cracks in the system that have sent Hollywood's opening weekend juggernaut skidding toward an uncertain crossroad. But it's easier to critique the system in hindsight than to predict the future. Studios are massive battleships trying to plow through rough seas rather than change course. Theater owners are finally beginning to grasp their vulnerability after dominating American pop culture for a century, but they may be powerless to reverse the box office declines of the last few years. And yet the summer of 2006 will see a new batch of studio blockbusters competing for the shrinking attention spans of American consumers. This time, the movies might just work. It's now or never.

Dade Hayes
Jonathan Bing
March 2006

Endnotes

The workings of Hollywood movie campaigns are shrouded in secrecy. The weeks before opening weekend are a nail-biting ordeal for the studio executives and filmmakers laboring around the clock to perfect the movies they've labored for years to bring to the screen. Most are extremely reluctant to talk to journalists outside the tightly controlled environment of a studio press junket.

Numerous people involved in the releases of *T3, LB2* and *Sinbad* nevertheless did invite us into the process. In Los Angeles, New York, Las Vegas, Cannes and London, we conducted interviews and attended events critical to the opening of each film, all of which are documented and, in some cases, supplemented with reflective comments of the principal figures. This book draws upon hundreds of interviews. Many of the participants found time to meet with us in the sensitive weeks leading up to opening weekend. A number of others talked to us in subsequent months, sharing documents, transcripts and diaries. Most of the people named in the book were either interviewed or offered an opportunity to comment.

Some of the information found in this book is readily available to anyone who follows Hollywood's weekly box office derby. The way the media covered the contest is as much a part of our story as the contest itself, and we've drawn material from the full range of media outlets covering the business of box office. Our chapters source the *Wall Street Journal* and the *New York Times* alongside tabloid TV programs like *Access Hollywood* and Internet sites like Ain't It Cool News, theArnoldFans.com and Chud.com, whose reports are unreliable and sometimes hard to verify. But our goal throughout has been to recreate the echo chamber of a movie campaign, whose participants are buffeted daily by a bewildering range of news stories, some reliable and some not, as opening weekend approaches.

Box office statistics, unless otherwise noted, are from Nielsen EDI. Interviews were conducted by the authors between January 2003 and May 2004. As mentioned in the text, reliable written source material pertaining specifically to marketing and distribution is remarkably limited. The authors benefited from the Warner Brothers Archives at the University of Southern California, the S. Charles Lee Archives at the University of California, Los Angeles, and the Margaret Herrick Library of the Academy of Motion Picture Arts and Sciences. *Variety* records often served as substitutes for original studio documentation of release patterns and ticket sales. The authors' understanding of Ontario, California, and the Inland Empire was enriched by multiple visits to the Ontario Museum of History and Art and the public library's Model Colony Local History Room.

This book is the fruit of a long-standing collaboration that began a few years ago in the pages of *Variety* on a wide range of jointly written news stories. The idea of writing a book on opening weekend was conceived by Hayes, who covered the box office beat as a *Variety* reporter from 1999 to 2000. Bing and Hayes together developed the architecture of the book, choosing to focus on one weekend, three competing studio release campaigns, and the dueling megaplex theaters of a single shopping mall. The writing of the book was an intensely collaborative process.

AUTHORS' NOTE

Tom Hanks is quoted in *Entertainment Weekly,* Dec. 15, 2000; quotation from John Logan is from a fax to the authors dated March 3, 2004. Logan declined a request for an interview. S. Charles Lee is quoted in Maggie Valentine's *The Show Starts on the Sidewalk: An Architectural History of the Movie Theatre, Starring S. Charles Lee* (New Haven: Yale University Press, 1996).

INTRODUCTION

Interviews with MGM president of marketing Peter Adee, senior vice president of publicity Eric Kops; producer Marc Platt, Sony Pictures vice chairman Jeff Blake and Taylor Research general manager Patsy Trice were conducted by the authors.

The description of Taylor Research is based on a visit to the facility as well as summaries and tape recordings of the *Legally Blonde 2* focus groups.

Background on the construction and scope of Ontario Mills is derived from sources such as "Arundel Mills a Textbook Case of Development," *Washington Post,* Sept. 14, 2000, "Ontario Mills: A Different Kind of Mall," *Riverside Press-Enterprise,* Nov. 10, 1996; and Mills Corp. literature. Inland Empire population figures are from the *Inland Empire Quarterly Economic Report* and

United States Bureau of the Census. Regional economist John Husing's research on regional demographics and business development proved especially useful.

Terry Press's fax to the authors was dated Jan. 3, 2002.

Information on L. Frank Baum comes from *The Annotated Wizard of Oz: A Centennial Edition,* edited by Michael Patrick Hearn (New York: W.W. Norton, 2000) and Jack Zipes's comprehensive introduction to the Penguin Twentieth-Century Classics edition of *The Wizard of Oz* (New York: Penguin, 1998). See also Stuart Culver, "What Manikins Want: The Wonderful World of Oz and The Art of Decorating Dry Goods Windows, *Representations* 21 (Winter 1988): 97–116; and Katharine M. Rogers, *L. Frank Baum, Creator of Oz: A Biography* (New York: St. Martin's Press, 2002).

FIRST AND GOAL

Interviews with director Jonathan Mostow, Warner Brothers marketing president Dawn Taubin, producer Hal Lieberman and Revolution Studios marketing president Terry Curtin were conducted by the authors. On pages 22 and 23, Adam Fogelson quoted in the Aug. 17, 2003 *Los Angeles Times.*

Select details about Super Bowl television viewership, consumer consumption patterns, parties and advertising stem from Bernice Kanner's *The Super Bowl of Advertising* (New York: Bloomberg Press, 2003). To place movie ads in Super Bowl XXXVII in the appropriate context, the authors relied on regular coverage of Super Bowl advertising in *The New York Times* and *The Wall Street Journal.* The chapter also incorporates information from the *Super Bowl Viewer's Guide* prepared in 2004 by the media and advertising firm Carat. Ratings data is from AC Nielsen. Descriptions and quotations from ABC broadcast material are based on transcriptions and analysis by the authors.

LEGALLY BLAND

Interviews with Peter Adee, Eric Kops, Marc Platt, director Charles Herman-Wurmfeld, screenwriter Don Roos, MGM vice chairman and chief operating officer Chris McGurk were conducted by the authors.

Information about the production of *Lethal Weapon IV* appeared in Peter Bart's *The Gross: The Hits, the Flops—The Summer That Ate Hollywood* (New York: St. Martin's Press, 1999). Information about *American Pie 2* came from documentary material on the film's 2003 "Beneath the Crust" DVD release.

Cited review of *Legally Blonde* is "Who Let the Underdogs Out?" by Jessica Winter, *Village Voice,* July 11–17, 2001.

Variety has provided extensive coverage of the corporate mandate of MGM under Chris McGurk and chairman Alex Yemenidjian, including Marc Graser's "Laid-back Lion Seeks Friendlier Lairs" (March 16, 2003).

Legally Blonde author Amanda Brown quoted in "Blonde Ambition," by Sam Whiting, *San Francisco Chronicle,* July 13, 2003. DVD sales for *Sweet Home Alabama* were estimated from industry sources by trade publication *Video Business.* Billy Wilder quote is from Cameron Crowe's *Conversations with Wilder* (New York: Knopf, 1999). Reese Witherspoon and Jennifer Coolidge quotes came in response to the authors' direct questions during the *Legally Blonde 2* press junket in London, June 8, 2003.

GET ME SINBAD

Details about DreamWorks' founding and early animation efforts are drawn from the authors' own reporting for *Variety,* as well as conversations with current and former employees. Published sources include "Cash Me Out if You Can," Peter Kafka and Peter Newcomb, *Forbes,* March 3, 2003; "It's Taken More than One Leap of Faith," by Amy Wallace, *Los Angeles Times,* November 22, 1998; "Dream Team in Pricey Scheme," by Dan Cox, *Variety,* September 15–21, 1997; and Thomas R. King's *The Operator: David Geffen Builds, Buys, and Sells the New Hollywood* (New York: Random House, 2000). The account of the Michael Eisner–Jeffrey Katzenberg legal battle draws on sources including *Keys to the Kingdom: The Rise of Michael Eisner and the Fall of Everybody Else* by Kim Masters (New York: HarperBusiness, 2001) and *Work in Progress* by Michael Eisner (New York: Random House, 1998).

Quotations from Mireille Soria, Tim Johnson and John Logan are from a commentary track on the DVD release of *Sinbad.* Logan's comments also come from Mark Wheaton's "*Sinbad*: High Adventure, High Seas, and High Expectations," from Issue 2 of British fanzine *Movie Insider.* Katzenberg's praise for Frank Thomas and Ollie Johnston was quoted on the Web site of Michael Barrier, animation expert and author of *Hollywood Cartoons: American Animation in Its Golden Age* (New York: Oxford University Press, 2003).

Budget estimates for animated movies are notoriously slippery because the technology implemented in a production can be reused on future films and its costs therefore amortized over a longer period. *Sinbad,* for example, benefited from DreamWorks' long-term deal with Hewlett-Packard, whose software was used to create ocean effects. The $60 million figure for *Sinbad* is an official company estimate of production costs that appeared in several publications. Some reports, however, put the number at $70 million. *Treasure Planet*'s costs were often reported to be $140 million, but sources within Disney suggested $200 million was a more accurate figure. Budget disparities like this are becoming more common, especially for summer movies.

Discussion of early blockbusters was informed by clippings and studio press books in the collection of the Cinema-Television Library at the University of Southern California. The authors' descriptions of road-show distribution methods benefited from articles such as Justin Wyatt's "From Roadshowing to Saturation Release: Majors, Independents, and Marketing/Distribution Innovations" in *The New American Cinema,* edited by Jon Lewis (Durham, N.C.: Duke University Press, 1998); and *Kings of the Bs: Working Within the Hollywood System: An Anthology of Film History and Criticism,* edited by Todd McCarthy (New York: Dutton, 1975). Steve Neale's essay, "Hollywood Blockbusters: Historical Dimensions" from *Movie Blockbusters,* edited by Julian Stringer (New York: Routledge, 2003) directed us to the history of *Quo Vadis?* and was essential to our understanding of the distinctions between 1950s colossals and wide-release blockbusters.

BIRTH OF A BLOCKBUSTER

Accounts of the 2002 edition of Comic-Con are based on the authors' visit to the 2003 edition as well as interviews with Jonathan Mostow and numerous people who attended.

The intertwined histories of the *Terminator* movies and Carolco Pictures is as complicated a saga as any in Hollywood. Interviews with producers Andy Vajna, Mario Kassar, Gale Anne Hurd and Roger Corman, along with other principals involved in the three *Terminator* films, helped us tease out the strands in this chapter. The authors also benefited from the many *Variety* stories tracking the Carolco bankruptcy and the packaging of *T3*; as well as the following books and articles: *How I Made a Hundred Movies in Hollywood and Never Lost a Dime* by Roger Corman and Jim Jerome (Chicago: Da Capo Press, 1998); *You're Only as Good as Your Next One: 100 Great Films, 100 Good Films, and 100 for Which I Should Be Shot* by Mike Medavoy and Josh Young (New York: Atria Books, 2002); and an authoritative March 8, 2002, *Wall Street Journal* story on the financing of *T3* by John Lippman, "The Producers: The Terminator Is Back—After Millions Spent to Get It Started."

Cameron declined numerous interview requests. His comments on the *Terminator* films are taken from a January 20, 2004 appearance at a *T2* screening at Pacific's ArcLight Hollywood, and from interviews from MGM's 2003 special edition DVD release of *The Terminator* and Artisan's 2003 "Extreme" DVD release of *Terminator 2: Judgment Day.*

CASINO ROYALE

Most of the information in this chapter is based on events witnessed firsthand at ShoWest, March 3–7, 2003. Interviews with Lion's Gate distribution president Steve Rothenberg, EDI cofounder Marcie Polier, New Line president of distribution David Tuckerman, Dawn Taubin, Peter Adee and producer Dean Devlin were conducted by the authors.

Media analyst Hal Vogel outlines the financial relationship between movie distributors and exhibitors in *Entertainment Industry Economics*, fifth edition (New York: Cambridge University Press, 2001). It's also covered extensively in Lee Beaupre's unpublished 1975 dissertation *American Film Distribution: A Survey*, in the collection of the Margaret Herrick library. Another useful volume is *America Goes to the Movies: One Hundred Years of Motion Picture Exhibition* edited by Barbara Stones and Jim Kozak (Los Angeles: National Association of Theatre Owners, 1993).

Details on early history of ShoWest and Show-a-Rama are derived from "Exhibs Mull Up-front Bank Loans," *Variety*, March 26, 1975, "Justice Dept. Letter to NATO Clouds Issue of Blind-Bidding," *Daily Variety*, February 25, 1975, and "Venerable Movie House to Shut Down," by Jennifer Mann, *Kansas City Star*, March 20, 1999. Ad in *Variety* ("biggest national TV spot campaign") was dated February 26, 1975.

Details of Regal Cinema's showdown with New Line over firm terms are drawn from interviews with New Line and Regal and secondary sources, including "Firm Terms Jamming Circuits," by Carl DiOrio, *Daily Variety*, June 28, 2001, and "Screen Savers" by Dan Gilgoff, *U.S. News and World Report*, January 21, 2002. Similarly, accounts of *Casino*'s screening at ShowEast stem from interviews with attendees of the screening conducted by the authors as well as a *Hollywood Reporter* article by Monica Roman, dated October 23, 1995. Additional background on ShoWest and its participants comes from a profile of Terry Press in *Advertising Age*, March 26, 2001; "The World According to Arnold" by David Shaw, *Cigar Aficionado*, Summer 1996; and Kenneth Turan's *Sundance to Sarajevo: Film Festivals and the World They Made* (Berkeley: University of California Press, 2002). Hunting trip detail comes from Jill Goldsmith's "H'wd Vexed by Plex Success," *Variety*, May 16–22, 2004.

FRANKENSTEIN LIVES

Details of MGM's trailer and advertising campaign for *Legally Blonde 2* are based on interviews conducted by the authors with Peter Adee, Eric Kops, Charles Herman-Wurmfeld, and Marc Platt. Summaries and tape recordings of the focus group provided additional data on how market research shaped the advertising materials.

The authors also visited Technicolor's Ontario Depot as trailers were attached to release prints and shipped "in the can" to theaters; and they toured the projection rooms of the Ontario multiplexes, interviewing the projectionists who unpacked the cans and assembled the reels.

The descriptions of Aspect Ratio are drawn from a visit to the facility and an interview with CEO Mark Trugman. Details of the *Tomb Raider 2* trailer campaign are from conversations with trailer house executives who worked on it.

An account of the trailer for *The Adventures of Kathlyn* and the quotation from Jack Atlas are from Kenneth Turan, "The Lure of Trailers," *American Film,* October 1982.

Background on the *Star Wars, Episode II* trailer is from "Trailer Hitch" by Dade Hayes and Marc Graser, *Variety,* October 29, 2001.

Interviews with screenwriter Don Roos, director Cameron Crowe and Dream-Works' head of creative advertising David Sameth, were conducted by the authors.

Oren Aviv citation is from "The 150-Second Sell, Take 34" by Marshall Sella, *New York Times Magazine,* July 28, 2002.

Detail about *Charlie's Angels* screenplay is from "A Devil of a Time for 'Angels' Scribes," by Patrick Goldstein, *Los Angeles Times,* October 31, 2000. Details of the postproduction tweaking of *Kangaroo Jack* are based on an interview the authors conducted with producer Jerry Bruckheimer.

Data on the MGM offices in Century City are based on multiple visits by the authors and company literature.

Other sources for this chapter included "A Brief History of Trailers," by Peter Debruge, MovieTrailerTrash.com; "Trailer Trove," by Dade Hayes, *Daily Variety,* March 7, 2002; Marc Graser's "Frankenstein Effect," and "Big Six Hitching Hopes to Trailers," by Jonathan Bing, both in *Daily Variety,* July 9, 2003.

THE BEAST OF BURBANK

William Paul's "The Kmart Audience at the Mall Movies," *Film History,* Vol. 6, pp. 487–501, 1994, provided several key insights expanded upon in this chapter.

Discussion of *The Beast From 20,000 Fathoms* and *Them!* was aided by news clippings, advertisements, press books and studio memos at the Warner Brothers Archives at USC and the Marty Weiser Archive at the Margaret Herrick Library. The authors also interviewed Ray Harryhausen and referred to materials on Warner Brothers' 2003 DVD release of *The Beast.*

Details about Joseph E. Levine's work on *Duel in the Sun* came from *Those Great Movie Ads* by Joe Morella, Edward Z. Epstein and Eleanor Clark (New York: Galahad, 1972).

Descriptions of the production and release of *Jaws* are based in part on the authors' interviews with producers Richard D. Zanuck and David Brown, former MCA Universal executive Sid Sheinberg and current Universal distribution president Nikki Rocco. Other sources include Lee Beaupre's dissertation *American Film Distribution: A Survey,* which the authors reviewed at the Margaret Herrick Library; and David A. Cook, *Lost Illusions: American Cinema in the Shadow of Watergate and Vietnam 1970–1979* (New York: Charles Scribners Sons, 2000); Suzanne Mary Donahue, *American Film Distribution: The Changing Marketplace* (Ann Arbor: University of Michigan, 1987); and *Variety History of Showbiz* (New York: Ramboro Books, 1997).

Text from *Airport* ads came from official studio scripts.

WHO'S BAD?

Details of the production of *Sinbad* come from studio production notes and interviews with DreamWorks executives who spoke on condition of anonymity. Details were also drawn from interviews in a documentary on the making of *Sinbad* included as part of the DreamWorks 2003 DVD and the DreamWorks "2003 Summer Preview Reel," a videotape mailed to journalists in the spring of 2003.

Other sources are "Hey, Does This Sound Familiar?," by Lynn Smith, *Los Angeles Times,* May 4, 2003, and "Shrek Promo Catches a Ride with *Sinbad,*" by Susan Wloszczyna, *USA Today,* June 24, 2003.

Reports on Web sites like Aint It Cool News, Chud and Dark Horizons were also a useful reference point. Quotation from Tim Johnson comes from Chud.com ("Tales From the Junket Circuit," July 2, 2003).

Information on "tradigital" animation is drawn from numerous sources, including "Katzenberg's Spiritedly Behind *Spirit,*" by Desson Howe, *Washington Post,* May 24, 2002, and "Animation Producer Is Betting on the Horses," by Michael H. Kleinschrodt, *Times Picayune,* May 24, 2003.

Details on DreamWorks' negotiations of release dates with Miramax and Paramount are based on interviews with studio executives at the three studios.

The description of Technicolor's Ontario Depot is based on the authors' visit to the facility. Additional information about Technicolor and National Screen Service provided by Stuart Snyder, president of Technicolor cinema distribution, and Marcie Polier. The details of the "distribution economy" of Ontario, California, are drawn from conversations with regional economist John Husing and select issues of the *Inland Empire Quarterly Economic Report.* The book *Ontario: Gem of the Foothills* (Carlsbad: Heritage Media Corp., 1999) is a useful overview of recent economic developments in the area.

THE RUNNING MAN

Interview with Schwarzenegger was part of a two-hour session in his Santa Monica office for a cover story, "The Candid Candidate," in *V-Life,* May 2003. Quotations from Jonathan Mostow, manager Lou Pitt and Mandalay Pictures chairman Peter Guber came from interviews conducted by the authors.

Details of *Terminator 3* publicity campaign were taken from internal Warner Brothers publicity memos and conversations the authors conducted with studio executives.

Schwarzenegger's publicity antics for *Pumping Iron* are explored on the film's 2003 DVD release and were also described during the authors' interview.

Quotations from Schwarzenegger ("Everybody would like to be the Terminator") and James Cameron ("He's never gonna play a character" and "The ultimate

rude guy") are from Bill Zehme's "The Importance of Being Arnold," *Rolling Stone,*
August 1991. The piece is reprinted in *Intimate Strangers: Comic Profiles and Indis-
cretions of the Very Famous* (New York: Delta, 2002).

The authors drew from two *Esquire* pieces on Schwarzenegger that appeared
under the headline "The Amazing Arnold!" in the July 2003 issue, by Jeanne
Marie Laskas and Robert Kurson.

Discussions of Schwarzenegger's Hollywood career phases were aided by stories in *Variety* and the *Los Angeles Times,* including: "CAA Will Rep Arnold in All
Areas" by Cathy Dunkley and Dana Harris, *Variety,* August 6, 2002; "Mobilizing
the Machine" by Claudia Eller, *Los Angeles Times,* August 20, 2003; and "Agents of
Misfortune?" by Claudia Eller, *Los Angeles Times,* February 14, 1997.

WASH. RINSE. REPEAT.

Much of the material in this chapter is based on original firsthand reporting and
interviews with principal figures involved in the junkets for *Legally Blonde 2* and
Terminator 3.

Mark Ramsey's quote is taken from "Where a Nose for News May Be Out of
Joint," by Dana Kennedy, the *New York Times,* May 13, 2001. *Aladdin* junket de-
scription and Jean-Pierre Jeunet quote taken from "Tales of the Junket," by Gary
Susman, *The Guardian,* October 5, 2001. Earl Dittman blurb taken from "Earl
Dittman Exposed—Film Criticism's Greatest Shame," by Chris Parry and Erik
Childress, eFilmCritic.com.

Production data for *T3,* including the budget, the shift from Vancouver to
Los Angeles, the fire on the set and the number of people employed by the crew is
based primarily on interviews with Jonathan Mostow and producers Hal Lieberman, Moritz Borman, Andy Vajna and Mario Kassar, as well as L.A. Center Studios co-owner Chris Ursitti.

Other useful reference points were: "*Terminator 3* Was Almost the Big Movie
That Couldn't Get Made" by Terry Lawson, *Detroit Free Press,* July 1, 2003; Bill
Higgins's November 17, 2002, *Variety* story on the production, "*T3* Goes Home to
Pump Up Local Economy"; and "Filming Is a Crowd Scene; Soundstages a Hot
Commodity As a July Actors Strike Looms," *San Diego Union-Tribune,* January 28,
2001.

Statistics on runaway production are from the Entertainment Industry Development Corp.

When Schwarzenegger appeared on *The Tonight Show* on June 27, 2003, he
asserted that he personally covered the cost of a special effects sequence from *T3.*
Several sources involved in the production corroborated this fact. But the sources
said that on *The Tonight Show,* Schwarzenegger misidentified the scene he paid
for. It wasn't the segment in which the Terminator, dangling from the hook of a
Champion crane, hurtles through a building; it was the scene in which the Termi-

nator grapples with the T-X in an office bathroom, smashing her head through wall panels and toilets.

ROBOTS ON THE RIVIERA

Events surrounding the 2003 Cannes film festival and the *T3* merchandising efforts are based on the authors' original reporting and interviews with Arnold Schwarzenegger, Andy Vajna, Mario Kassar, Paula Hoppe and Jonathan Mostow.

Joseph E. Levine remains a poorly represented figure in Hollywood's historical records. The producer comes to life most vividly in Calvin Tomkins's "The Very Rich Hours of Joe Levine," *The New Yorker*, September 16, 1967; "The Supercolossal—Well, Pretty Good—World of Joe Levine," by Katharine Hamill, *Fortune*, March 1964; Donna Rosenthal's "A Mogul Till the End," *Boston Globe*, August 5, 1987; and *Variety*'s obituary, by Todd McCarthy, August 5, 1987. Also, as noted in the main text, the Maysles Brothers' Levine documentary *Showman* is indispensable. It screens at film festivals and has aired on cable television, but at this writing is not commercially available on video or DVD.

Among the notable accounts of the launch of *Hercules* are Louella Parsons's "Movie Man with the Midas Touch," *Pictorial View*, September 20, 1959; "Hercules Reveals a Ballyhoo Strongman," *Film Bulletin*, March 30, 1959; "Hard Sell 'Explodation' Party Gives Hercules a Rousing Sendoff," *Motion Picture Herald*, March 28, 1959; and "Showmanship: It Still Pays Off!" *Film Bulletin*, July 20, 1959. The authors also relied on studio records, memos and press clippings about *Hercules* in the Warner Brothers Archives at USC.

FINDING DEMO

Quotations from NRG founders Joe Farrell and Catherine Paura are from an interview conducted by the authors at the offices of their production company, FP Productions. NRG is now run by Howard Ballon and Kevin Yoder. The two executives did not respond to repeated requests for interviews. NRG's industry-wide tracking program is confidential. But studio executives who asked not to be named agreed to discuss the tracking results for *T3*, *Legally Blonde 2* and *Sinbad*. Interviews with Peter Guber and Peter Adee were conducted by the authors.

The story of NRG's domination of the Hollywood market research business has been widely reported. The most controversial account was a *Wall Street Journal* front-page story, "Flim Flam? Movie-Research Czar Is Said by Some to Sell Manipulated Findings," from December 17, 1993. The exposé by Richard Turner and John R. Emshwiller, alleged that Farrell and Paura falsified NRG data at the behest of filmmakers and studio officials. Farrell and Paura have denounced the report. The story of Farrell's background and the rise of NRG is drawn from multiple sources, including: "The Man Who Makes You King," by Elaine Dutka, *Los Angeles Times,* July 12, 1992; "L.A. Confidential," by Preston Lerner, *Los Angeles Times Magazine,* November 7, 1999; "The Science of Who Sits in the Movie Seats," by Mark Caro, *Chicago Tribune,* October 15, 2000; *Making Movies,* by Sydney Lumet (New York: Vintage, 1996) and *Francis Ford Coppola: A Filmmaker's Life* (New York: Crown, 1999).

The shadowy field of Hollywood market research prior to NRG is not well documented. Leo A. Handel's *Hollywood Looks At Its Audience: A Report of Film Audience Research* (Urbana: University of Illinois Press, 1950) was an invaluable resource. "Scientific B.O. the Nuts," an unsigned *Variety* article from May 2, 1933, provided an early overview of primitive efforts by the Motion Picture Research Council to influence box office. Details of the test screenings for *Jaws* are based on interviews with producer David Brown.

Quotation by Joel Silver is from a panel discussion with Peter Bart at the Cannes Film Festival, May 16, 2003, attended by the authors.

The effect of Daniel Yankelovich's study of Hollywood publicity and advertising was interpreted by Suzanne Mary Donahue in *American Film Distribution: The Changing Marketplace.* For context, the authors also consulted Kurt W. Marek's *The Archaeology of the Cinema* (New York: Harcourt, Brace & World, 1965).

The transformation of Columbia Pictures after its merger with the Coca-Cola Company in 1982 is based on interviews with former executives, including Guy McElwaine, who oversaw production during the transition.

Additional details of the market for Hollywood market research are drawn from a complaint filed October 10, 2003 in the U.S. District Court in Central District of California against Nielsen National Research Group by Reed Elsevier, parent company of *Variety* and MarketCast, and "Audience Tests: Plot Thickens" by Elaine Dutka, *Los Angeles Times,* August 31, 2003.

A STAR IS REBORN

Accounts of the Los Angeles premieres are based on the authors' original reporting. Some details and quotations from the New York premiere of *Legally Blonde 2* are from "Legally Fashionable," *Daily Variety,* July 3, 2003.

Descriptions of Technicolor's print operations in North Hollywood are based on the authors' visit and interviews with numerous Technicolor executives, as well as company literature.

FEELING THE NUMBERS

The overview of box office projections at Warner Brothers is based on two interviews with president of distribution Dan Fellman conducted by the authors in his office on consecutive days. The second interview also included vice president and general sales manager Jeff Goldstein, vice president of sales operations Richard Shiff and senior vice president of systems and sales operations Don Tannenbaum.

Fellman's comments on *The Green Mile* and *The Perfect Storm* are from *Daily Variety* in 1999 and 2000.

Discussion of the release campaigns for *Billy Jack* and *The Trial of Billy Jack* was shaped by two *Variety* articles: "*Billy Jack* Hits Reissue Jackpot," by Richard Albarino, November 7, 1973, and "*Billy* Sequel's Grand $11-mil Preem," by Albarino, November 20, 1974. It also draws upon news clippings at the Margaret Herrick Library. Interviews with *Billy Jack* director, writer, producer and star Tom Laughlin were conducted by the authors.

Quotation by Andrew J. Kuehn comes from film critic Peter Debruge's Web site MovieTrailerTrash.com.

Information about release campaigns for *Poor White Trash*, *Breakout* and *Earthquake* is based on Lee Beaupre's *American Film Distribution: A Survey*; "Movie Not Doing Boffo Box Office? Reissue It Under a New Title," by John Hartl, *Seattle Times*, September 9, 1994; and an ad that appeared in *Variety* on November 20, 1974.

Other sources for this chapter include *The Movie Business Book, 3rd edition*, edited by Jason Squires (New York: Fireside, 2004) and *The Amazing Story Behind the Legend of Billy Jack* by Jorge Casuso, a 1999 book published and distributed by Tom Laughlin.

DOLLARS IN REAL TIME

Interviews with Nat Fellman, Erik Kops, Erik Lomis, Marcie Polier, Universal Pictures president of distribution Nikki Rocco and former Universal Pictures chairman Tom Pollock were conducted by the authors.

Material on Nielsen EDI is based on visits to the company headquarters and interviews with EDI founder Marcie Polier and current executive vice president Dan Marks. Andrew Hindes, who at the time was vice president of Nielsen EDI, provided an overview of Nielsen EDI's data collection methodology and a tour of its phone room.

Description of Rentrak operations are based on the authors' visit to its Sherman Oaks headquarters and conversations with Rentrak senior vice president Ron Giambra.

Background on A. D. Murphy is based largely on his extensive writings in *Variety*, conversations with Murphy's former colleagues at *Variety* and his former students at the Peter Stark Motion Pictures Producing Program at USC.

The history of Exhibitor Relations stems from a visit to the company's Encino headquarters and interviews with current president, Paul Dergarabedian.

Details on Brandon Gray are based on interviews with Gray conducted by the authors.

Connie Bruck's *When Hollywood Had a King: The Reign of Lew Wasserman, Who Leveraged Talent Into Power and Influence* (New York: Random House, 2003) was a good guide to the box office culture at MCA/Universal in the Wasserman era.

In discussing the news media's growing appetite for box office data, the authors also drew upon Neil Postman's *Amusing Ourselves to Death: Public Discourse in the Age of Show Business* (New York: Viking, 1986) and Todd Gitlin's *Media Unlimited: How the Torrent of Images and Sounds Overwhelms Our Lives* (New York: Owl, 2003).

Details of Tom Sherak's box office "vigils" are drawn from interviews with Sherak, Lou Pitt and Dean Devlin.

The story of the opening of *Spider-Man* is based on interviews conducted by the authors with producers Laura Ziskin and Avi Arad and other sources. Sony Pictures Entertainment vice chairman Jeff Blake provided copies of his May 3 box office report.

Elvis Mitchell's review of *Legally Blonde 2*, "There's Nothing That a Little Cream Rinse Can't Fix," appeared in the *New York Times* on July 2, 2003.

Descriptions of Erik Lomis are based on numerous author interviews and a visit to his office.

THE NEW MAIN STREET

U.S. screen counts and theater data, unless otherwise noted, are from the National Association of Theater Owners and the Motion Picture Association of America.

The authors interviewed Erik Kops, Eric Lomis, Peter Adee, Charles Herman-Wurmfeld, Raymond Syufy, and Rick King, AMC's senior vice president of corporate communications. Regal Entertainment Group, which controls Edwards Theatres, would not assent to an interview specific to the Ontario Palace 22. The authors nevertheless toured the facility and had regular contact with theater employees who, citing corporate protocol, asked not to be identified.

Arnold Schwarzenegger's comments in Iraq were widely reported. A full transcript is available on CNN.com.

Inland Empire population statistics and projections are from John Husing's research (see Introduction notes).

Contemporary descriptions of the Ontario megaplexes are from the authors' original reporting, which took place over multiple visits.

Many details of Ontario's history, from its founding through the opening of the Ontario Mills mall, came from the Model Colony Room. Some historical specifics are from *Ontario: Gem of the Foothills* (Carlsbad: Heritage Media Corp., 1999). The authors also interviewed City Councilman and longtime resident Jerry DuBois as well as several people involved with the operation of the AMC Ontario Mills 30 and the Edwards Ontario Palace 22, not all of whom wished to be identified.

Stanley Durwood biographical background is from an official AMC bio, in addition to articles such as "AMC Theater Empire Playing Real-Life Drama," by Kathryn Harris, *Los Angeles Times,* March 27, 1988. Durwood quoted in a *Variety* special issue dedicated to AMC, March 5, 1996. Other company material was taken from the articles in that issue.

Jim Edwards' background stems from articles including "The Last Picture Show Mogul," by Laura Bleiberg, *Orange County Register,* September 25, 1990. The authors also interviewed former Edwards employee Phil Barlow about Edwards.

Discussion of multiplex and megaplex building in the latter half of the twentieth century draws on Douglas Gomery's *Shared Pleasures: A History of Movie Presentation in the United States* (Madison: University of Wisconsin Press, 1992). The authors also relied on Gomery's "Thinking About Motion Picture Exhibition," *The Velvet Light Trap,* Spring 1990; "The Shape of Theaters to Come," Karen Stabiner, *American Film,* September 1982; and "Tyrannosaurus Plex," by Degen Pener, *Entertainment Weekly,* June 6, 1997.

Concessions data came from AMC. Construction cost figures for the two Ontario megaplexes are from multiple press accounts, including "On with the Show," by Elliot Blair Smith, *Orange County Register,* August 22, 1997.

Details about the AMC Grand in Dallas taken from "AMC Opens Largest Theater Complex in U.S.," *Film Journal,* June 1995; Details about Regal Cinemas' Funscape concept and Mike Campbell quote from "Regal Cinemas' Domain Continues to Expand," *Film Journal,* June 1995.

Descriptions of the 1997 opening of the Ontario megaplexes are based in part on "San Berdoo Scrum," by Andrew Hindes, *Daily Variety,* March 21, 1997, and "Ontario Auds Ample for Multiplex Mania," by Ted Johnson, *Daily Variety,* March 24, 1997.

Having searched in vain for credible written sources on the subject, the authors came to understand the clearance system after interviews with more than a dozen current and former distributors and exhibitors who were working in the 1970s, when it started to erode.

Details about Inland Empire theater closings from "Movie Theaters Take Lumps," by Adam Eventov, *The Press Enterprise,* May 27, 2001.

Laurence Siegel's praise for Mel Simon came from "Shop Talk," an interview with Siegel by John Greenya, *Washington Flyer Magazine,* January/February 2001.

Ontario Mills information came from author interviews with John Husing, who has analyzed the Inland Empire economy for a living since the 1970s.

Other sources for this chapter include Richard W. Haines, *The Moviegoing Experience 1968–2001* (Jefferson, N.C.: McFarland & Co., 2003); Anthony Slide, *The American Film Industry: A Historical Dictionary* (New York: Limelight Editions reprint, 1990); Bill Daniels, David Leedy, and Steven D. Sills, *Movie Money: Understanding Hollywood's (Creative) Accounting Practices* (Los Angeles: Silman-James Press, 1998); Dolores Hayden's *Building Suburbia: Green Fields and Urban Growth 1820–2000* (New York: Pantheon, 2003); Mike Davis's *City of Quartz* (New York:

Verso, 1990); William Fulton's *The Reluctant Metropolis* (Baltimore: Johns Hopkins University Press, 1997); and select writings of Joan Didion, in particular her *Saturday Evening Post* article "Some Dreamers of the Golden Dream," reprinted in *Slouching Toward Bethlehem* (New York: Farrar, Straus & Giroux, 1968).

SUNDAY SPIN

Interviews with Peter Adee, Eric Kops, Eric Lomis, Dan Fellman, Don Roos, Jonathan Mostow, Moritz Borman and Brandon Gray were conducted by the authors.

Details of the July 7 DreamWorks meeting are based on interviews with employees in the animation division, who spoke on the condition that they not be identified.

THE AUDIENCE STRIKES BACK

Descriptions of Comic-Con 2003 are based on the authors' original reporting. Robert Sanchez and Rebecca Rockwell were interviewed by the authors. The history of Comic-Con is drawn from the authors' conversations with Jeff Walker and Kevin Smith, and numerous articles, including "Comic Book Convention Has Starring Role in Films," by Scott Bowles, *USA Today,* July 17, 2003; "When Trekkies Met Buffy," by Marli Guzzetta, *Miami New Times,* December 25, 2003; and "Pain and Ink," by Robert Wilonsky, *Dallas Observer,* August 10, 2000.

The George Lucas quote is taken from John Seabrook's *Nobrow: The Culture of Marketing, the Marketing of Culture* (New York: Vintage, 2001).

Details of the Strong Women of Scifi Cruise are chronicled on numerous Web sites catering to *Xena* fans, including Creationent.com.

Sources on Harry Knowles's background include his memoir, *Ain't It Cool? Hollywood's Red-Headed Step-Child Steps Out* (New York: Warner Books, 2002); "Seducing Harry" by David Weddle, *Washington Post,* September 17, 2000; and "Attack of the Fans" by Stephen Metcalf, Slate.com, April 15, 2002.

The authors also relied on Kathryn H. Fuller's *At the Picture Show: Small-Town Audiences and the Creation of Movie Fan Culture* (Washington: Smithsonian Institution Press, 1996). *Star Wars* fan accounts in *A Galaxy Not So Far Away: Writers and Artists on Twenty-five Years of Star Wars,* edited by Glenn Kenny (New York: Owl Books, 2002) and *Using the Force: Creativity, Community and Star Wars Fans* by Will Brooker (New York: Continuum, 2003) were also consulted.

OPEN WIDE

Interviews with Jonathan Mostow, Moritz Borman, Paul Dergarabedian, Marc Platt, Charles Herman-Wurmfeld and Gary Ross were conducted by the authors.

DVD sales projections for *T3* in advance of the DVD release were supplied to the authors by several sources connected with the film.

Descriptions of the South Broadway theater district were informed by the authors' visits to the street and a tour of the theaters hosted by the Los Angeles Conservancy, as well as the conservancy's historical records. Another useful resource was author Brent C. Dickerson's Web site "A Visit to Old Los Angeles and Environs," which is illustrated with vintage postcards of Broadway.

The global day-and-date release of *The Matrix Revolutions* was chronicled in newspaper, wire and Web reports around the world. The authors also visited Mann's Chinese Theater for the opening of the film. Most of the *Matrix* material in this chapter is based on the authors' interviews with Warner Brothers executives and a selection of international sources, including "*Matrix Revolutions* in China a Triumph in Fighting Piracy" by Fu Shangqi, the Xinhua New Agency, November 13, 2003; "*The Matrix* v. the Pirates" by Christopher Goodwin, *Evening Telegraph*, November 6, 2003; and "*Matrix Revolutions* Sets Record for Five Day Ticket Sales Worldwide," *Agence France Presse*, November 10, 2003.

Index

Acknowledgments

This book would not have been published without the enthusiasm of Jonathan Burnham and the wise and cogent criticism of Peter Borland. Jonathan grasped the premise, green-lit the project without reservation, and gently prodded us toward the finish line. Peter viewed the roughest of rough cuts, helped us place it in a structural framework, massaged the plot twists and polished the storyline. He was our one-man focus group—in the best sense of the phrase.

We'll always be indebted to Peter Bart, our friend and editor at *Variety*, for his role in helping *Open Wide* grow from a concept into a book. He offered encouragement and complete autonomy during the reporting and writing. Most important, he believed this was a trip worth taking—even when it involved long hours in the Inland Empire.

We're fortunate to have worked with JillEllyn Riley and Kristin Powers at Miramax Books, who patiently handled numerous revisions and rookie questions as they gracefully assembled *Open Wide* and launched it into the world. We're also grateful to our agent, Dan Strone, a loyal supporter of this book long before it was a book.

Many of the people we interviewed gave us hours of their time when they had few hours to give, and when the pressure of opening weekend was weighing heavily upon them. Peter Adee, Moritz Borman, Dan Fellman, Mario Kassar, Eric Kops, Erik Lomis, Jonathan Mostow, Andy Vajna and Dawn Taubin all graciously opened the door and invited us to understand their release campaigns from the inside out, sanguine in the knowledge that they couldn't expect to benefit from it.

We're indebted to all who helped us navigate the marketing and distribution thicket of July Fourth weekend, including Chris Aronson, Andrew Bernstein, Nadia Bronson, Marc Cohen, Peter Graves, John Gumpert, Dennis Higgins, Paula Hoppe, Seana Hore, Basil Iwanyk, Kate Kondell, Chris McGurk, Stephanie Palmer, Don Roos, Nigel Sinclair and Rex Weiner.

The interlocking components of an opening weekend are, by nature, difficult to capture on paper. They exist as an evolving oral tradition of anecdotes, opinions and strategies uniting distributors, marketers, filmmakers and exhibitors. Thanks to all who shared their insights and helped illuminate the path, especially Marc Abraham, Geoffrey Ammer, Phil Barlow, Ron Bernstein, Michael Besman, Jeff Blake, David Brown, Cameron Crowe, Terry Curtin, Paul Dergarabedian, Dean Devlin, David Dinerstein, Joe Farrell, Jack Foley, Steve Elzer, Steven Friedlander, Bob Garcia, Ron Giambra,

Josh Goldstine, Brandon Gray, Peter Guber, Andrew Hindes, Bob Hoffman, Gale Anne Hurd, Amy Israel, Kathy Jones, Bob Kaplowitz, Rick King, Nancy Klasky, Eric Kranzler, Tom Laughlin, Wayne Lewellen, Ryan Markowitz, Mace Neufeld, Sallie Olmstead, Catherine Paura, Eric Pleskow, Marcie Polier, Nikki Rocco, Gary Ross, Steve Rothenberg, Mike Rudnitsky, Robert Sanchez and other members of The Inland Empire Strikes Back, Sid Sheinberg, Tom Sherak, Marc Shmuger, Buffy Shutt, Bruce Snyder, Stuart Snyder, Ray Syufy, Patsy Trice, David Tuckerman, Chuck Viane, Barbra Wade, Bumble Ward, Doug Wick, Howard Welinksky, Jennifer Westfall, and Richard Zanuck.

Jason Blum, Bill Higgins and Hilary Liftin read early versions of the book and gave us many helpful suggestions. Other friends, including Lorin Stein, Geoff Kloske and Ira Silverberg, offered valuable publishing advice at key junctures.

Thanks to all of our colleagues at *Variety*, notably Tim Gray, Bruce Brosnan, and Jennifer Blatz; to our comrades at Comic-Con and Cannes, respectively, Marc Graser and Cathy Dunkley; and to Tom Tapp and Anna Lisa Raya at *VLife*.

For research assistance, we thank Leith Adams, Ned Comstock, Barbara Hall and Jennifer Prindiville, Boston Globe librarian Richard Pennington, and the staff of the Museum of History and Art in Ontario, including Faye Dastrup and Carolyn Holke.

Jonathan extends his deepest thanks and love to his mother, Claudine Bing, and his growing family: Danielle, Serafin, Debbie and Jon. Words aren't adequate to thank Andrea. This book could not have been written without her.

Dade extends his deepest gratitude and love to his parents, Carol and Philip Hayes, and his sister, Emily. And a toast goes to the staff, past and present, of *The Oberlin Review*.

Dade Hayes and Jonathan Bing
June 21, 2004